ICAP (H.D.)
...t for Race
" "

...t last season
... ion Good Battle
...kes soft.
... for up on age of
... had to be firm
... hot be ready
... ot ready
...ason last one

...oft seemed
... good battle
...oft may not be got slapy.
... a summer performer
... may get ...
...e soft
...ady
...y dee
" "
...y be got
...Time
...eason.

If I had a Donkey and he wouldn'
Do you think I'd whip him? Oh dea
no!
I'd buy him a carrot
And say "Look at this! Now here's
a nice treat
You must not miss."
Then off I would run And keep
running until He would just
catch me up At

LAMBOURN 438

FROM F. T. WINTER. UPLANDS. LAMBOURN. BERKS.

Don't really know whether to
congratulate or commiserate. Suppose
just bad luck on all concerned to
be born same century as L. PIGGOTT
Anyway, well done you.
Off to the sunshine, I hope!
Fred

Frankincense and More

To Emi

Best wishes always

Chris

To Eric

Frankincense and More

The Biography of

Barry Hills

Hope you find some winners in 2011

Best wishes

Robin Oakley

Robin Oakley

RACING POST

This edition first published in Great Britain in 2010 by
Racing Post Books
High Street, Compton, Newbury, Berkshire, RG20 6NL

1 3 5 7 9 10 8 6 4 2

A catalogue record for this book is available from the British Library.

ISBN 978-1-905156-79-5

Cover designed by Jay Vincent
Interiors designed by Fiona Pike

Printed in the UK by CPI William Clowes Ltd Beccles NR34 7TL

www.racingpost.com/shop

CONTENTS

Acknowledgments

My thanks are due first and foremost to Barry and Penny Hills for their warm and generous hospitality throughout the writing of this book, for their trouble in searching the attics of Wetherdown House for scrapbooks, pictures and memorabilia and for their patience during the many times I have interrupted the hectic business of running a supremely efficient racing yard. And, no, I never did get one of those famous bollockings!

Thanks too to all the Hills clan, especially Barry's five busy and successful sons, John, Richard, Michael, Charlie and George, for the time they have given me in interviews and follow-ups. Thanks also to Maureen Hills for giving generously of her time in Newmarket.

I am grateful to the many owners, jockeys, friends and former assistants who have been closely involved with the phenomenon that is Barry Hills and who have helped me to put this picture together. It has been a real joy to talk to the likes of Willie Carson, Steve Cauthen, Brent Thomson, Darryll Holland, Ray Cochrane, Jimmy Lindley, Neville Callaghan, Peter Chapple-Hyam, Tony Shead, Bobby McAlpine and John Francome about the experiences they have shared with Barry but dozens of others have been a huge help too. When they heard the subject, nobody refused me help. Any mistakes are mine, but I could not have managed without them.

I am grateful also for the friendly assistance of Tim Cox: there is no question in racing to which you cannot find an answer somewhere in his amazing racing library. But the biggest thank you of all goes to my wife Carolyn, whose forbearance passes all understanding. Most of the time while I was writing this book I was still working as European Political Editor for CNN and she has been wonderfully understanding about the long and unsociable hours required to pull everything together.

INTRODUCTION

Frankincense takes the Lincoln –
the gamble that launched a racing
dynasty

In 1968 the Soviet Union invaded Czechoslovakia and Martin Luther King was assassinated. It was the year Dick Fosbury, at the Mexico Olympics, revolutionised high-jumping with his 'Fosbury Flop'. In racing it was the year the late David 'The Duke' Nicholson rode Mill House to victory in the Whitbread Gold Cup, Sir Ivor won the Derby and the Australian wizard Scobie Breasley retired from the saddle. It was in 1968, too, that a brilliant gambling coup launched one of the most remarkable training careers British racing has ever seen, that of Barrington William Hills.

Barry Hills, the gritty little man who is the epitome of well-dressed traditionalism on the racecourse, is always as immaculately turned out as his racehorses. But he is the son of a head lad, not, as the well-cut suits and impeccable trilby might suggest, an indulged second son of the minor aristocracy or the stable-inheriting beneficiary of an indulgent aunt.

There has rarely been a better example of the self-made man. Brought up in a hard school and determined never to over-indulge his own children, the apprentice who started on five shillings a week plus £25 a year for clothes has planned, grafted and achieved to the extent that he now has his own £3 million self-designed, state-of-the-art training establishment, Faringdon Place, on the fringes of Lambourn. He also has the results-induced respect of the entire racing world. Not only has Barry figured among the top ten trainers for nearly forty years, he has founded a racing dynasty.

Barry Hills has won virtually every race worth winning (bar the Derby, in which he has saddled the runner-up on no less than four occasions). He has also sired five sons. John, the eldest, is, like his father, a successful Lambourn trainer. The twins Richard and Michael, the next in line, have been in the top twenty British jockeys for as long as most racing folk can remember. Charlie, the fourth son, is his father's assistant trainer at Faringdon Place and George, the youngest, is involved in studs and horse insurance in the USA. And it was all launched by a stunningly brave bet in the 1968 Lincoln Handicap.

Until 1964 the Lincolnshire Handicap was run at the now defunct Lincoln racecourse, the Carholme. Following the closure of that course, the race moved to Doncaster from 1965 onwards and was renamed the Lincoln Handicap. The 1968 race was won by the four-year-old Frankincense, a 100-8 shot, who was owned by Lady Halifax, trained at Newmarket by John Oxley and ridden by Greville Starkey. For Barry Hills, who was Oxley's travelling head lad and who had backed Frankincense to the hilt, it was a life-changing experience. He won enough on the race to be able to buy himself a yard and set up in his own right as a trainer, and he has never looked back.

Working for Oxley and before that for his predecessor at Hurworth House, George Colling, Barry had for some time been accumulating a significant pot of betting money. 'George Colling told me it was the best job in racing and he was absolutely right. If you couldn't get some money doing that you couldn't get money doing anything. These days you are supposed to tell your travelling head lad what the instructions are for the jockey. If we had known that when we were travelling head lads, we'd have made a bloody fortune.

'We were fairly familiar with one another. We used to have board meetings between us. The travelling head lads for Harry Wragg, Cecil Boyd-Rochfort, Jack Watts and myself would have a rest after we'd finished in the mornings, sorting out the cards. It was such fun.' Profitable fun? 'Of course it was profitable. Those boys, those travelling head lads for the big yards, did pretty well in those days.'

When travelling the horses further afield, the fearsome four would share rooms and they did not waste their time when they sat down to work out the time of day. Barry reckons he was earning around £20 or £25 a week but they would have a few hundred on their selection when they thought the time was right.

In a sense it all started with a bet he didn't have. 'I was big friends with Dick Westbrook (head lad to Jack Watts), Arthur Simmonds (head lad to Cecil Boyd-Rochfort) and Bob Middleton (head lad to Harry Wragg). One day we had a discussion about four races there were ante-post prices for at the time and we sorted out the winners of the William Hill Gold Cup, Cambridgeshire, Cesarewitch and November Handicap. Obviously we didn't do it or we would all have retired, but if we'd had a £5 yankee on them we'd have cleaned out the bookies.'

There were, however, some significantly successful bets. 'I'd made good money in 1967. A friend of mine who knew a few things told me that Sky Diver would win the Stewards' Cup. I got 50-1 and he did, ridden by Terry Sturrock.' Incidentally, Sturrock, whose mount started at 100-6, was until a few years ago one of Barry's work riders at his Faringdon Place estate.

More went into the Hills pot from Jack Watts's Ovaltine, who won York's Ebor Handicap in 1967 at 100-8, and from the Harry Wragg-trained Lacquer's victory in the Cambridgeshire at 20-1. Frankincense himself won the 1967 William Hill Gold Cup at Redcar. Barry and his betting partners had also swelled their betting pot with good touches on Little Buskins, who won several races, and when Violetta III dead-heated for the Cambridgeshire in 1961. 'We didn't bet big but we had some yankees and cross doubles. We more or less cleaned up in our own small way.'

So the stake for a significant gamble had been assembled. Then the opportunity presented itself. Syd Mercer was a canny ex-trainer who had made the business pay, owning or part-owning most of the horses he handled, who included the top-class stayer Trelawny. (Mercer was later to give Barry some help in preparing his own top horse Rheingold for the Prix de l'Arc de Triomphe).

Barry says: 'Syd learned a lot in the First World War. He was in the veterinary corps and all these animals got injured. They did a lot of post mortems and he got to know an awful lot about horses. He had these powders, old-fashioned remedies. He could look at a horse's eye and say if it had a liver problem.'

Mercer sent John Oxley a horse of his called Copper's Evidence, who had won five races in a year, to be trained for the Lincoln. 'It soon became obvious that Frankincense was superior. One day he gave Copper's Evidence two stone and beat him out of sight. I remember ringing Syd Mercer and telling him about it. But Syd wouldn't have any of it. His words were: "Lad, the Lincoln Handicap is on my sideboard."

'Copper's Evidence was a pretty good horse – he eventually finished fifth in the race – but I went out and started backing Frankincense at 66-1. We backed him from 66-1 to 5-1 favourite, though he drifted back on the day. He was a certainty. He worked on Side Hill in Newmarket one day and beat the others out of sight. You didn't need to see any more. We toured round bookmakers' shops putting small bets on everywhere.' Barry and his friends got good prices partly because Syd Mercer continued to back his own horse, Copper's Evidence.

The gamblers included Barry's friend Eddie Mills, one of those who was to help him set up his first establishment at South Bank in Lambourn. One of John Hills's earliest memories is of Eddie Mills, who was in the carpet and TV sets fitting business, rolling up, always in the latest model Mercedes, with his wife Dot. 'They were the first people I knew connected with racing coming down and being part of the family and having lunch. Eddie Mills loved punting.'

Another participant in the Frankincense gamble was Harold Dixon, a professional punter who lived in Harrogate. Barry still has the handwritten schedule Dixon drew up in the winter of 1967-68 as soon as the Lincoln Handicap weights were published, before Dixon took his usual winter cruise on the SS Vaal to Cape Town, South Africa. Barry says approvingly: 'He always backed his own opinion, watched the horses going down to the start. He wouldn't back a horse because somebody had told him to. He wouldn't back a horse unless he believed in it.' Interestingly Dixon's scrawled comment on Frankincense reads: 'May not be ready for race.' Of the runner-up on the day, Harry Thomson Jones's Waterloo Place, he wrote, 'Fine, big sort if got ready' and of the third, Norton Priory, he opined: 'Goes well in soft. May get a mile.'

On the day, 27 March, the going was described as 'good on top' and Frankincense was drawn on the wide outside of the 31 runners. Bluerullah, ridden by Lester Piggott for Irish trainer Seamus McGrath, was made favourite despite being drawn in the unfavoured number one starting stall, but he burned himself out early in the race getting across to a better position.

Greville Starkey on Frankincense let Joe Sime on Sunderton give him a tow along the stand rails while Ashford Lea and the grey Naymag disputed it in the centre with Private Imp, Norton Priory and Copper's Evidence also prominent. Waterloo Place, who had had a hard race winning over hurdles shortly before and who took a bump soon after the start, was right at the back before being switched to make up a lot of ground in the last quarter of a mile.

One-time champion jockey Doug Smith, says Barry, had told Greville Starkey that all Princely Gift horses needed to be held up and come with a late run. 'We basically knew how to ride Frankincense from then on.' But on the day Starkey opted to send his mount ahead a full furlong out. Despite his 9st 5lb burden Frankincense ran on strongly up the centre of the course and held the late challenge of Waterloo

Place to win by half a length, with Norton Priory two lengths further back. It was, said Timeform, 'a magnificent performance'. On his share of the bets alone, Barry had won over £60,000. Based on average earnings levels, that would be £1,520,000 today.

Two key factors had aided his bold plunge. One was that when the weights for the race came out, the 9st 5lb allotted to Frankincense was widely considered to have ruined his chances. Len Thomas's report on Frankincense's victory in *The Sporting Life* the day after the race was headlined 'The weight-humping feat of the century'. Two previous Lincoln winners had carried 9st 0lb and Dorigen, the winner in 1933, had carried 9st 1lb. But no horse had ever won the Lincoln with any weight heavier than that. No horse was to carry 9st 5lb or more to victory again until Cataldi, also ridden by Greville Starkey, in 1985. In fact those who joined Barry Hills in the gamble had evidence to support their hopes. Frankincense had demonstrated in the 1967 season that he was a high-class miler with a turn of foot and he had also shown that he could cope with carrying a big weight. He had won the Ouse Bridge Handicap at York carrying 9st 2lb and Timeform afterwards noted: 'He was cantering over them throughout and shot to the front close home to win back on the bridle.'

The other factor helping to keep Frankincense at a good price was that Syd Mercer had continued to back Copper's Evidence. Owner Lady Halifax, widely reputed to have been in on the gamble but whom Barry suggests actually had in mind the Tote Spring Handicap at the Newmarket Guineas meeting, said after the Lincoln: 'I feared that he had taken the lead a little too early with all his weight. But Starkey (no first-name terms in those days) told me that he was still on the bit and he had no choice but to send him clear.'

Watching from the County Stand just beyond the winning post, she was not certain at first her horse had won. But his jockey declared: 'I had the race won from the break and my mount was always travelling well. I never had the slightest doubt I would win.' He was confident that had Waterloo Place got any closer he could have pulled out a bit more. Just to demonstrate the threads which bind racing, Waterloo Place's trainer Tom Jones, who was later to buy Hurworth House, where John Oxley trained, also later became the employer of two of Barry's sons.

Greville Starkey's fortunes, too, remained intertwined with those of the Hills family. He was godfather to Barry's jockey sons Michael and Richard. But it was Starkey who was on Shirley Heights when in the 1978 Derby he came with a late run to snatch the race on the line from Hawaiian Sound, the Hills runner whom Barry was convinced had won. That's racing.

Surprisingly, Barry cannot remember where he stood as he watched Frankincense's victory in the 1968 Lincoln or who was with him. So how soon was he certain that he would be collecting on his hefty bet? 'Not until the last furlong – because the horse was never going to take up the running until then. He was always travelling well but in those days there were no big screens to watch on. You watched it with your own eyes through the glasses. I can't even remember if there was a commentary – I can remember the days when there was no commentary – but anyway he took it up and won, coming right down the middle of the course.'

Barry is not famous for displaying his emotions and his response when I asked if it felt like a life-transforming moment was typical. 'We'd done a good job backing the horse all through the winter. Obviously we'd had a good touch. I was expecting the horse to win and he did. It was mapped out. It happened.' Job done, as they say. 'After that it was simply a mater of looking for a stable to buy.'

But his then wife Maureen does say: 'It was so important that it should all come off. Syd Mercer was so convinced that his horse would win. Barry kept begging Syd Mercer to have some money on Frankincense and I think in the end he did have a saver. Barry had to keep reassuring Greville Starkey that he was on the right horse.'

Frankincense, at one stage the favourite in ante-post lists, drifted in price on the day but that never worried Barry. 'Short-priced horses in big handicaps normally get bigger on the day.'

Did Frankincense's rider Greville Starkey know there was a big bet at stake? 'He did, but he wasn't aware how much we had on. He didn't say anything afterwards other than the usual. We didn't have a celebration. I just went home and got on with the work, though we did have a few drinks on the Sunday.'

Maureen, too, has no memories of any glass of champagne that night. 'We just didn't do that sort of thing then.' But both have rather better memories of collecting the money and counting it a few days later at Eddie Mills's place. Maureen says: 'Dorothy Mills was there with a huge pile of notes saying "All my life I've wanted to be able to take a bath in fivers! Now I can." '

Barry says of the winnings: 'We collected them from all over the place, betting shops where we'd backed it, especially near Eddie's home in north London, cheques and cash.' Those involved included Harold Dixon and professional 'putters-on' like Len Brook, Arthur French and Bill Carter, who regularly acted for owners and trainers.

Did the rest of the Oxley yard back Frankincense? 'I'm sure they did,' says Barry. 'But you were looking after yourself. It's not something we discussed. The fewer you tell the better. If you're backing a horse you don't go shouting round the yard about it. If you are having a bet it's best kept quiet.'

Later that season Frankincense ran fourth behind Royal Palace, Taj Dewan and Sir Ivor in a thrilling Eclipse Stakes at Sandown Park. But he didn't do much in his racing career after that. You cannot say the same of the man who travelled him to the races on Lincoln Handicap day.

CHAPTER ONE

Early Days

The reluctant schoolboy bunking
off to learn from Fred Rimell

*'If George Colling gave you a ride on a two-year-old
and told you to "sit nice and quiet and try to beat a couple"
he meant beat a couple and not seven or eight. He got pretty angry
if you finished fourth or fifth.'*

BARRY HILLS.

There was a very special moment at the Horserace Writers and Photographers Association Awards – racing's Oscars – at London's Lancaster Hotel in December 2009. As the winner of the George Ennor Trophy for Outstanding Achievement was announced, the entire assembly rose instinctively to their feet to register the racing world's respect and affection for the recipient: Barry Hills. They were recognising the extraordinary skill, consistency and courage Lambourn's senior trainer has demonstrated in a training career that has already brought him well over 3,000 winners and that shows no sign of flagging.

But Barry Hills has given more to racing than a formidable list of winners. The Hills story is one, too, of the founding of a five-son racing dynasty. On that emotional occasion, marking Barry's recovery after months of battling the ravages of septicaemia, which nearly killed him, he was joined on stage by his wife Penny, one of the most popular figures in racing. With them were trainer John Hills and his wife Fiona, jockey twins Michael and Richard Hills with their wives Chrissie and Jaci, plus Barry's assistant trainer Charlie Hills and his wife Pippa and USA-based son George (since then engaged to Rebecca), who is a well-known figure in the stud and horse insurance worlds.

Barry is a modest man, sometimes a gruff one. He is not a flamboyant self-advertiser, more a man who likes to let his achievements speak for themselves. It took nearly two years to get him even to look at the manuscript of this book. But he does take a quiet pride in the races he has won and in his children's success and that day at the Lancaster it showed. He told the audience: 'I'm not finished yet,' and he has proved it since in emphatic terms with a brace of Royal Ascot winners and by purchasing two hacks to resume riding out at the age of 73 as he superintends his 140 horses.

A man as determined and as focussed as Barry Hills would have succeeded in almost any field he had chosen. Talk to the entrepreneurs and businessmen who have had horses in his yards and that is one of the first things they tell you. They have valued his advice on more than horseracing. But there was little doubt from the start that Barry's career would be one in racing. And it is to the credit of the sport that a man who entered his working life without any obvious advantages of birth, wealth or connections could have achieved the pre-eminence he has.

Barrington William Hills was born on 2 April 1937, the son of William George 'Bill' Hills, head lad to Worcestershire trainer Tom Rimell, and of Phyllis Biddle, whose family ran the hay and coal merchants Biddle Brothers of Upton upon Severn. Never a big child, Barry was the only one of five children his mother bore who was not stillborn. By a quirk of fate his birthplace in Worcester was South Bank nursing home, the same name as the stables he later bought from Keith Piggott to found his training career.

Early years were spent in the semi-detached Tintern House at

Quedgeley, a village some five miles from Gloucester on the A38, and father Bill was at that stage driving 'Queen Marys', the sixty-feet-long articulated vehicle in regular use at the time.

School during the war, initially at Ribston Hall in Gloucester, was not young Barrington's favourite way of spending time. Indeed the only exam he has ever taken in his life was the one he was forced to sit at the end of his basic training during National Service.

Even in rural Gloucestershire, Barry remembers the wartime air raids and the fires they started. He also remembers the treat of travelling by bus twice a year to Upton upon Severn, changing at Gloucester onto one known as the 'Midland Red Express'. He still recalls the odour of the Brown Windsor soup cooked by Ma Wilson at Upton upon Severn's King's Head pub.

Mercy Rimell, trainer Fred Rimell's widow, recalls one occasion when they were called to the local pony club because their son Guy and young Barry were considered uncontrollable and had been chasing the girls around the dormitory all night.

The first real love of young Barry life's, he confesses, was his first pony Polly, a Welsh Mountain bay standing 12.2 hands whose show name was Outlaw. Barry used to ride Polly down the quiet Gloucestershire lanes, with his father on a bicycle. The only problem with young Barrington's conveyance was that she was terrified of pigs. Polly's bolting when scared by local porkers, he says, 'steadied up my riding no end'.

Barry's father had served his apprenticeship with Sam Pickering at Kennett, near Newmarket. With Pickering, Bill Hills was paid sixpence a week and got his money only once every quarter. The last lad to arrive at Pickering's yard in the morning used to be made to ride out without a saddle.

Bill Hills, who rode winners over jumps, had enjoyed two six-year spells with Tom Rimell and in between trained ponies at Fareham, including the Northolt Derby winner Mountain Cloud. After the war he returned to his first love. He went back into racing as head lad to George Colling at Hurworth House in Newmarket, in the yard later occupied by Harry Thomson Jones.

Barry's pony Polly was fast enough at full tilt to keep up with the canter of the racehorse string and he was allowed to ride out with first lot before school. 'This meant that with a bit of luck I could miss the first hour at the Convent of St Mary opposite Tom Jones's place in Fordham Road.'

A leading owner at Hurworth House was the comedian Vic Oliver, owner of Voluntary, and Colling's regular riders included Charlie Elliott and Billy Nevitt.

After a couple of years, sadly, father Bill Hills developed tuberculosis and spent the winter in the White Lodge Hospital, mostly outside on a verandah, the common treatment at that time however bleak the weather. (It does not come much bleaker than it did in the blizzards of the winter of 1946-47). Hills senior had to give up his job and in the spring the homeless family moved to stay with his brother in Redmile, Nottinghamshire. In Nottingham grandfather Hills had a general supplies shop in Rupert Street and another selling vegetables in Arkwright Street, while up in the attic he manufactured carrier bags with an antiquated machine. Fortunately for Barry, Polly came too. Hunting was to be one of the passions of his life and soon he was going cubbing with the Belvoir Hunt.

Together Barry and his pony covered thousands of miles, he says. 'We were very successful since it wasn't easy for her to lose you unless you were very stupid or had no sense of balance at all. The only time she would ditch you was in the show ring. She could not stand coloured obstacles at any price and she would duck out at the last possible moment, leaving you going on without her.'

Later in 1947 the family moved to Barry's mother's home town of Upton upon Severn ('Our roots were there') and his father had the terrible thoracoplastic operation that entailed removing a lung and all of his ribs down one side. After six months' convalescence he took a job as head lad to Charlie Pratt in Lambourn, beginning Barry's association with the Valley of the Racehorse.

Pratt was based at the famous Uplands stables, which was later Fred Winter's base. It was next door to Fulke Walwyn's Saxon House yard, where Barry recalls seeing the great five-time Cheltenham Gold Cup winner Golden Miller in his retirement. Many of the Walwyn horses were owned by the famously eccentric Dorothy Paget, who stayed awake at night, slept in the day, and who was allowed by her bookmakers to bet long after the events had ended.

The Hills family lived in a cottage in Goose Green and at the age of ten Barry was getting his first few rides on some of the quieter racehorses. Just by the Malt Shovel pub, Bryan Marshall and Dave Dick, the stable jockeys at the time, shared a cottage.

Before long, however, Hills senior developed TB in his remaining lung and had to give up his Lambourn job. The family, and Polly, who was Barry's only means of transport to see his friends and play cricket, returned to the Upton upon Severn area.

School for Barry at this stage was the Arboretum Training Centre in Worcester, unofficially known as 'Mr Whittaker's Academy for Backward Young Gentlemen'. Barry and his friend Alan Spiers did little work and watched plenty of cricket. Once 'Witty' had been paid (he liked to get his cheque on the first day of term – not too easy for Barry's jobless father) he did not exactly keep an eagle eye on their attendance records.

'This gave me plenty of scope. The Midland Red bus left Upton at eight in the morning for school but it then passed through Severn Stoke, at which point I disembarked. I would then make my way down the hill to Fred Rimell's stables at Kinnersley, spend the day there and return in time to catch the same bus home at 4.20 as if I had been at school all day. I did this trick many times with great success.

'Obviously Fred and Mercy Rimell and my parents all knew what

I was up to. But they probably took the view I was learning far more at Kinnersley than I ever would at school.' When I asked him one day how much he had learned from the Rimells, Barry's answer was succinct: 'Everything.'

Polly was now stabled at the King's Head in Upton. Blacksmith Jack Dudding, who only worked when he needed the money, had no electricity in the yard. When Polly needed shoeing, says Barry: 'I remember hitching up my bicycle to a sort of dynamo and pedalling hard to make enough light for him to shoe her ready for the next day's hunting.

'Opposite was the hay and coal merchants belonging to my mother's family. Her brother Charlie used to sell all his hay to the mines in the Black Country, where it fed the pit ponies.'

Haymaking in the summer, by an army of men well refreshed with local cider, was a tremendous undertaking. Starting in early June, the banks of Fish Meadow were cut first so that people could use them on Sundays. The meadows were regularly flooded and in the Hills house there were nails in the beams so that the furniture could be hoisted and hung when the waters rose.

Barry's main pleasure was hunting with the Croome and the Ledbury. He scored considerable success all round Gloucester, Worcester and Hereford and as far afield as the Southport Flower Show jumping on a pony called Misty Morning, owned by his friend Mary Hughes, who had become too old to qualify as a rider in pony classes.

Soon he was riding out at Kinnersley, the yard from which Tom Rimell had sent out Forbra to win the 1932 Grand National and where Fred Rimell was to train four Grand National winners: E.S.B. (1956), Nicolaus Silver (1961), Gay Trip (1970) and Rag Trade (1976). Eventually Barry, who used to bicycle the four miles from Upton every morning, became apprenticed there, his first jockey's licence being granted by the Jockey Club stewards on 5 June 1952.

One day head lad Ron Peachey was driving the horsebox to Hurst

Park races and told Barry, who was travelling in the back with the horse, that when they were well out of sight of Fred Rimell and the yard he would stop and Barry could come round and sit up in the front with him. Unfortunately, Ron halted the lorry briefly on a hill at one stage to speak to a friend. Thinking this was his cue, Barry climbed down and was making his way to the front when the horsebox started up again and drove off. Ron Peachey only discovered the error some miles later.

Barry's first public ride was on 3 June 1952 in the Erdington Selling Handicap Plate for three-year-olds at the now long defunct Birmingham racecourse on a 20-1 shot called Golden Chance II, who did not live up to his name, being a chestnut of little ability. The race was won by Freddie Hunter, with Gordon Richards second and Stan Clayton in third. 'I remember being drawn in the very best company between Gordon Richards and Michael Beary, with them shouting at me "Keep straight". That was my introduction to a pretty modest riding career. Mind you, two things didn't help – my increasing weight and National Service.'

In the summer when Rimell's jumpers were turned out Barry was sent to Fred's father Tom, who was then training Flat horses at Windsor House in Lambourn, a yard later occupied by Syd Mercer and later still by Nicky Henderson, Peter Walwyn, Ralph Beckett and now Harry Dunlop.

'Tom Rimell always wore a bowler hat and certainly enjoyed a cocktail or two. You didn't work any set hours. You just did what you had to do. You got up whenever, finished the job and went home. If your heart was in it, you did what was needed. I used to be very interested in the horses when I was at home and I did a lot of extra fiddling around myself.'

Fred Rimell had few Flat horses and, feeling that he was missing something essential in his racing education, Barry wanted to move on. Fred wanted him to go to Ron Smyth in Epsom but Barry's father pushed successfully for him to go instead to Newmarket to his own old boss, George Colling (whose grandson James has had horses in training with Barry in Lambourn).

As a jockey Barry rode nine winners for Colling, four of them on a horse called Peter Pan. There were good role models available in the yard: 'Doug Smith was first jockey to trainer Colling and Manny Mercer was first jockey to his leading owner Lord Derby. (Although Colling was a public trainer he also trained all Lord Derby's horses). 'Manny was a perfect stylist. He was a wonderful jockey – he could make a bad horse run well. He was like a bit of electricity on a horse. Doug Smith wasn't the bravest jockey ever but he was the best jockey over two miles I ever saw ride.' In those days orders were orders. 'If George Colling gave you a ride on a two-year-old and told you to "sit nice and quiet and try to beat a couple" he meant beat a couple and not seven or eight. He got pretty angry if you finished fourth or fifth.'

Barry's first winner, Sudden Light, came on 14 July 1954 at Newmarket and there were other days to remember. One of the races the young apprentice won on Peter Pan, owned by Lord Derby, was the Christopher Wren Plate, worth £306, at Hurst Park on 20 May 1955. The 11-2 shot came home one and a half lengths ahead of a horse of the Queen's ridden by a certain Lester Piggott and the other distinguished jockeys to finish in the first five behind B.W. Hills that day were Charlie Smirke, Harry Carr and Bill Rickaby.

Barry's riding career was soon interrupted by a call-up in 1957 to do his National Service, to the frustration of his employer, who urged him to appeal. Once enlisted, Barry was lucky to secure an appropriate position, that of horse holder to the Regimental Sergeant Major in the King's Troop, the Royal Horse Artillery, based in St John's Wood, London, a job which earned him 28s 6d per week. Fellow soldiers there included future trainer Jack Berry and top hurdles jockey Jimmy Uttley.

But it was not a long period in Barry's life. Thanks to his father's serious state of health, Gunner Hills was released after only eight months on compassionate grounds. Getting too heavy to be a jockey, he rejoined Colling as travelling head lad, a position he still occupied at the trainer's death in 1959.

'It was the year Manny Mercer was killed at Ascot. We were good friends. He was brilliant, one of the best jockeys I've ever seen. Manny was part and parcel of a horse. They all ran for him.

'George Colling was a very good trainer. He never did anything with a horse without a reason. I learned a lot from him. I learned common sense. You can't go far without it. Take it as it comes. Don't jump your fences until you get to them. If you drive a pony and trap down the centre of the road you have the option of going left or right, or you can speed up a bit.

'He was very methodical, very quiet. He understood his horses. When I knew him he wasn't very well. He spent most of the winter in bed and died quite young.'

How much has stable life and discipline changed since then?

'People are more punctual about work these days than they used to be but there's no continuity now with people in the game. There's no-one you can carry through. You can't get apprentices. When I went to George Colling he had about ten apprentices, including Lionel Browne, Frank Storey, Frank Morby and Tony Shrive. They were all the right size. There's no-one the right size these days. And there are so many girls. The girls are very good but they are not going to stay that long. You're not expecting them to stay to 45.'

George Colling died on the first occasion Barry ever travelled horses to Newbury. Zanzibar won the Newbury Spring Cup and Cutter won the John Porter Stakes. 'We stopped on the way home to see some friends in a cafe at Hatfield and heard then that Colling had died.'

The new master of Hurworth House was John Oxley. 'He came from the West Country and had been with Geoffrey Brooke at Newmarket. He came when John Waugh left to be private trainer to Robin McAlpine after Reg Day retired. He was younger than Colling and did it very differently. I think having seen what he did and what George Colling did, both quite successfully, I learned a lot. I was with John Oxley for 11 years until 1968. He was a very good boss. He never once went behind my back and I've the greatest admiration for him.' As was later to happen to the great Fred Winter, Oxley's career was ended by injuries from a fall downstairs.

When George Colling died in 1959, Lady Halifax, Dick Hollingsworth, Sir Randle Feilden and Archie Kitson bought the yard between them and put John Oxley in to train the horses with the proviso that he could buy them out eventually, which he did. Barry continued as travelling head lad with Oxley, a post he was to hold for ten years, until the gamble on Frankincense gave him the funds to start out on his own. He was certainly not paid a fortune. His income tax assessment for the year 1961-62 shows that his salary at Hurworth House was £726 for the year, with tax assessed at £16 6s.

From the very early days, it was clear to those who knew him that Barry was destined for higher things. Former trainer Neville Callaghan, a friend and then later briefly Barry's assistant in Lambourn, says: 'It was obvious he wasn't going to stay a travelling head lad for ever. He was always going to train and was always going to make his way in life and it's amazing what he has achieved.'

Sir Peter O'Sullevan remembers many years ago being shown round the Windsor Forest Stud stables, where horses were quartered for Ascot races. The travelling lads had little cupboards of their own to stow their gear. Some were scruffy, some were half tidy. "But here, look at this," said the official, opening one to show a gleaming array of perfectly polished, shining bridles and surcingles, arranged with near military precision. "That lot belongs to a Barrington Hills, George Colling's man. I'll bet you anything he'll go on to make a name for himself."

Another friend from those early days was former champion jockey Willie Carson. Willie recalls: 'He was the only travelling head lad I remember who used to drive to the races following the horsebox in a BMW.' (Actually, say the family, it was a 1.5 Riley, then a Fiat).

'He was always better dressed than the others,' says Willie. 'He was always the smartest head lad, the one who looked like a trainer. He always had plenty of patter in him. He chatted everybody up and kept them informed. We were both setting out on the long journey. I used to say to him, "Get your licence and help me to get going." '

It was in those days that Barry earned the nickname 'Sparrow' still used by some of his close friends, such as the leading Lambourn jumps trainer Nicky Henderson. The cheery Willie, who still remembers her lemon meringue pie, says Maureen was a wonderful cook but that Barry earned his nickname by merely picking at his food. 'I was always watching his plate. He would eat a corner and I would eat his steak.'

Theirs was something of a mutual self-help society. When Willie took the job as Lord Derby's retained jockey he had no money and was asked for £200 for fixtures and fittings when he moved into a house owned by another jockey. The Lloyds Bank manager bounced Willie's cheque but Barry set up a lunch with 'Nobby' Clarke, the manager of the Midland, who then managed Willie's profitable account for decades.

Willie is one of those who confirms that the gruff persona Barry often presents to the world is not the full measure of the man. The trainer can be confrontational with the media and tough with staff who fail to live up to his high standards. He does not gush with praise, even with his own family, for a job well done. But most of his staff are long-termers who respect Barry's professionalism and who know that the storms never last for more than a few minutes.

'Deep down,' Willie insists, 'Barry is soft. He is a sentimentalist. He's possibly top of the list of the men I've seen cry. He's got a soft heart and the persona he presents to the racing press isn't quite true. He's very passionate about people and horses. You couldn't ask for a better friend.'

Willie recalls how he and Barry used to go up to London for nights out with 'Kipper' Lynch and Paul Tulk. They were nights out, you gather, which were not always famous for their restraint. 'But Barry always had that air of authority. He's not much older than me but he was my father figure giving me advice. If he likes you and you work for him he'll do anything for you.'

The softer side that Willie Carson acknowledges is not often on view. But Barry admits: 'When horses like Rheingold leave the yard I prefer not to be here. They are wonderful creatures and I can't help getting fond of them.' I remember going up on the gallops with him one morning when he looked back at his state-of-the-art stables, his beautiful house and sculptured garden, and he said quietly: 'Without the horses there wouldn't be anything here.'

As travelling head lad to John Oxley, Barry got on well with the trainer. He respected him. But Oxley was clearly not a man enamoured of officialdom. In 1963 Olgiata, owned by Lady Halifax, won the Wood Ditton Stakes at Newmarket but was subsequently found to have been doped. Barry still has the statement he made to the subsequent investigation, which suggested that it would have been very difficult for anyone to get in Olgiata's box on the morning of the race without being seen by him, the loft man or the gardener. It added: 'Olgiata is a very mean animal. She has to have a head collar left on her all the time to catch her. She kicks and bites and most of the lads in the yard are scared stiff of her.'

He also has a pencilled note signed by Oxley and dated 30 August of that year. It warned: '1. *There were Jockey Club snoopers prowling round the boxes on the way to Sandown today, when they stopped for breakfast. 2. Give whoever you leave in the box (**and you must leave someone**) this rubber truncheon. Tell them to hit anyone who comes into the box hard – and if it is a member of the Jockey Club they must hit **twice** as hard – it is rubber and does not mark!'*

CHAPTER TWO

The First Horses

La Dolce Vita and Hickleton
set the ball rolling

'Everybody had to muck out at South Bank. It wasn't a playpen.
We were on the floor trying to get off it and we could all have sunk.'
FORMER HEAD LAD SNOWY OUTEN.

It took around a year from the win on Frankincense for Barry Hills to be up and running as a trainer in his own right. After searching far and wide, with satisfactory gallops uppermost in his mind, Barry purchased the South Bank yard in Lambourn for £16,000 from Lester Piggott's father Keith, who trained Ayala from there to win the Grand National at 66-1 in 1963. Barry says: 'After I'd paid for the place I had £600 between me and the workhouse.'

The yard had just 28 boxes. Later Barry bought Bourne House as well in Lambourn but at first things were tight. Maureen Hills, Barry's first wife, says: 'We moved in with three small children. The first night we all slept together with the dog. It was freezing cold everywhere and, although we could turn the lights on, none of the plugs were working, so there was no heating. The boys were asking, "Can we go home to England?" '

There was an object like a coffin in a recess by the fireplace. She and owner's wife Dorothy Mills found a sledgehammer and disposed of it. When Keith Piggott came round he said, 'Oh, I see you got rid of my cocktail cabinet.'

The starting staff comprised Barry, Maureen, her father Paddy Newson and his wife and Peter Openshaw, who had been a lad at Oxley's and came with them. Eric Wheeler joined them for a while after leaving Dick Hern's but found it difficult to adjust to a small yard.

They knew what it was to need a winner to be sure of paying the wages at the end of the week and Maureen recalls cooking endless bowls of soup and suet puddings to keep them going. Paddy Newson was a stickler for how things were in the stable. 'Women didn't really go into the yard then. I always used to say to the head lad, "Can I come and see the horses tonight?" '

A popular owner in those early days was Bill Gooch, an East End bookmaker and turf accountant. 'The lads loved him. He would come down with a crate of beer for them, a sack of carrots for the horses, presents for the children.' One owner gave them some special peas for the garden that grew up sticks like beans. The twins, Richard and Michael, used the sticks as mock Grand National jumps. 'Barry was furious and went out with the Long Tom. The twins hid in the hay barn and poor John got caught.'

Sometimes owners had particular requests. Jack Ramsden, the stockbroker and successful gambler whose wife Lynda became a successful trainer, bought a filly called Lovelight, which he eventually sold to Robert Sangster, and Barry laid her out to win a nursery sponsored by the bookmakers Ladbrokes. The target was chosen because Ladbrokes had closed Jack Ramsden's betting account and he wanted to take some revenge on Ladbrokes' boss, Cyril Stein. 'They closed me down but we managed to nick some of their money in other ways.'

Jack Ramsden, whose first horse with Barry was a decent two-year-old called Jacket Potato, says: 'Barry was always going places. He was always going to do well.' He remembers the pair of them having a nice touch on one occasion in a five-furlong race at Newbury when Willie Carson was on the Hills-trained favourite and the less fashionable Bob Street on Lovelight. 'We had a pretty major coup on Lovelight. We'd got her handicapped at around, say, 65 and she went on to be over 100.'

At one stage Jack Ramsden worked for Barry, helping with the entries, effectively as a private handicapper. Smiling, he recalls: 'Barry wanted you there really to agree with him. The job was to agree with him. If you didn't, even if you were proved right on three or four occasions, it was of no interest to him whatsoever.' One of those who succeeded Jack Ramsden in that role was Matthew Tester, now senior handicapper with the British Horseracing Authority. Says Ramsden with mock ruefulness: 'He learned far too many tricks working for Barry.'

Working for Barry, you had to be prepared to face a challenge. 'You'd say to Barry: "Is he sure to stay?" If I said that a hundred times, then ninety-nine times I would have got the reply, "He probably wants further." '

Snowy Outen, Barry's long-time head lad, who still works part time for the yard in his eighties, remembers the early days well. 'We all had to work hard. At Faringdon Place everything is on a plate. Up there it was all much harder. He had put all his money into buying the place and getting it ready and every penny counted. He had a lot of pressures. Everybody had to muck out at South Bank. It wasn't a playpen. We were on the floor trying to get off it and we could all have sunk.

'The horses didn't have mangers, they had buckets for their water. My wife and I used to walk up at 9.30-10pm (Snowy has never driven a car) to ensure that every horse had a full bucket for the night and I would have a pint myself in The Lamb (now closed) on the way home. If they kicked a bucket over and made a noise, it was Barry lying in bed who would hear it and have to go and fill it for them.

'I asked for a rise after a couple of months and he said, "I can't even give myself one yet". He said he couldn't do it until we'd had a few winners. But as soon as he got on, I got on and I got that rise.'

Snowy would be up again in the yard around 5am to give the horses a feed before having a cup of tea and seeing the lads into the yard at 6.30am. 'Sometimes I would do the list (of who was riding what) and sometimes the guv'nor would do it. He would ask about their legs. If he was away I didn't train them. He gave me the instructions. The key in the early days was Paddy Newson. If he got off one and said "this isn't far away from winning a race", it wasn't.

At South Bank, Barry started off training 14 horses, soon up to 22, for which he charged owners £14 a week. In the first year he averaged more than one victory per horse with them, winning 17 races worth a total of £9,525. Appropriately for a man who knows how to celebrate success with a quality glass, the first winner was La Dolce Vita at Thirsk, ridden by Ernie Johnson, on 18 April 1969. Best of the bunch in the first year was the cheaply bought Gay Perch.

'He cost around £1,000,' says Barry. 'He won five races for us in 1969 (including four of his last six runs). La Dolce Vita cost me under £200. Not only was she my first winner but she improved my score shortly afterwards by winning a seller at Wolverhampton. We bought her in for £1,000.

'I think Mile Cross was the dearest horse I had in the first year and he cost 3,000 guineas. Only one other cost more than 1,500 guineas. But we managed to win 17 races.

'There was an American-bred three-year-old called Taxanitania. We bought him through Willie Carson from Mimi van Cutsem, wife of trainer Bernard van Cutsem, for a Mr S Lee who lived at Southport. He wanted to have a bit of a touch, so we gave him his first run in a six-furlong maiden at Thirsk. A month later, ridden by Willie Carson, he won a mile maiden at Ripon at 10-1.'

Golden Monad failed to win in the first season but in the second season he became Barry's first winner abroad, taking the Prix Henri Delamarre at Longchamp, worth almost £12,000, with Lester Piggott in the saddle. The prize was £2,000 more than the stable's total winnings in the first year and it demonstrated early on Barry's shrewd knack of placing horses to his owners' best advantage.

Timeform's commentary on Golden Monad after the 1970 season said: 'Who can blame the owner of a good-class English horse for choosing to run in France? Golden Monad earned less than £3,500 for five fine performances in this country, yet in three races in France in the autumn he picked up well over £19,000 for a first, a second and a third … Why, for instance, should a three-year-old ever take on older horses for about £3,000 in the Cumberland Lodge Stakes at Ascot when he can run against horses of his own age for a first prize of at least four times that amount in the Prix Henri Delamarre at Longchamp the same week?'

Of those early years, Barry recalls: 'In the second year (1970) we had 47 two-year-olds and only 11 three-year-olds, some of them bought the first year I started and they weren't very good. But we had 31 winners. In 1971 we had a virus that didn't help but we finished up with 39 winners of £46,000 in stake money.'

His friend Pat 'P.P.' Hogan, the bloodstock agent who was later Robert Sangster's right-hand man, helped the young trainer to buy yearlings, one of whom was Our Mirage, a muscular Miralgo colt who was one of the best two-year-olds of 1971 and won the Prix de la Salamandre, worth over £15,000, at Longchamp in September. But the biggest bargain was Hickleton, formerly trained by John Oxley, who was bought out of a selling race for £500.

Barry hadn't forgotten going round Oxley's yard one day with Lady Halifax, who had bred Hickleton. In his box she stopped and said, 'If ever a horse needs a mile and a quarter, he does.' Oxley won with the horse as a three-year-old and when Barry was getting going he encouraged one of his owners, who later lost him in a card game, to buy him out of a seller. At only £500 Hickleton was one of the bargains of the year. He was 'done' by an old stable lad called Lou. Lou could do anything with him but if anybody else walked in the box he would kick their eye out.

Snowy Outen recalls: 'Barry never forgets Hickleton. He was only a little horse but when Barry bought him he said, "This one will win us some races, Snowy." Later he said, "I've got a goldmine here." He was only a pony but he won races at two and a half to three miles. He stayed for ever. He wasn't even getting wound up at a mile and a quarter. Barry had him weighed up before he bought him and Hickleton helped to put us on the map.'

Hickleton did not win in 1969 but was responsible for the yard's first prestige victory when he took the 1970 Great Metropolitan Handicap at Epsom. He was a close second in what was to become one of Barry's favourite races, the Chester Cup, and then the bonny little stayer, a chestnut son of Exbury, went on to win the Brown Jack Handicap over two and three-quarter miles at Ascot. The next year his three successes included a convincing victory in the Queen Alexandra Stakes at Royal Ascot when he made up ground smoothly in the straight and sprinted clear to beat Parthenon by five lengths. He was also placed in the Prix Gladiateur at Longchamp. He remains one of his trainer's favourites. 'Not big,' says Barry, 'but the heart of a lion. A very sweet horse.'

Another good stayer in the early years was Colonel I. Chandos-Pole's Proverb. He won the Chester Vase in 1973 and the Goodwood and Doncaster Cups the following year.

The training bill for the month of January 1971 to Hickleton's then owner Bill Ward shows that Barry was charging him £18 per week, up from £16 the previous year. A shoeing bill for the month for Hickleton and the same owner's Courtly Lad (in the yard just 11 days) came to £4 5s 0d and attention to their teeth to £2 10s. Gallop fees for each horse for 1971 came to £25. A notice from Barry to his owners in December

1975 saw him raise the basic keep and training fee in February 1976 to £42 per week and shoeing costs to £1.50 per week. Now it is more like £60 per day.

The young trainer's ascent to the top ranks was remarkably rapid. At the end of the 1972 season Barry was in the top ten in the trainers' table with a total of 55 winners and earnings of £180,000. For the next season he had more than 100 horses in training, worth more than £1m between them, and from the start he was ready to invest in success. He had an all-weather gallop of four and a half furlongs constructed, the ground dug out to ten inches and filled with 127 tons of treated wood shavings.

He told one visitor: 'All my yearlings know their business, due to regular exercise on this new gallop, after spells of roadwork. Even if we have a hard winter the majority of my 50 youngsters should be fit to run in the spring or early summer.'

What had helped him to make such a flying start? 'Being apprenticed to a very good trainer, having the luck to start with a wonderful horse, saving, winning some money and knowing a lot of racing people. I had always been associated with decent horses so I got to know the wheat from the chaff.'

From the start Barry was a trainer prepared to experiment and to travel for the better prize-money beyond Britain's shores. Our Mirage, Hickleton and Golden Monad were early winners abroad along with Rheingold, who has his own chapter in this book. In his third season Barry won a total of £46,000. Among the 39 winners were five foreign victories, including two at Ostend in Belgium.

When Rheingold won his second Grand Prix de Saint-Cloud in 1973, the value of the races the yard had won on the Continent was only about £20,000 less than the total collected by all the winners at home.

Barry's swift ascent of the rungs on the training ladder was confirmed by an intriguing development early in his career. He was offered the chance to succeed Albert Klimscha as the mercurial

Daniel Wildenstein's trainer in France, but he turned down a five-year contract at £50,000 a year, which was big money in those days. He did not want to move at a time when he was much involved in improvements at South Bank and Wildenstein would not accede to his wish that he should take ten horses with him from his Lambourn string. Angel Penna got the job instead, but Barry's refusal confirmed the self-belief of a 'hot' young trainer.

In 1973, the winning total was up to £325,000 from 62 winners, with an equal number of seconds. As well as a second Grand Prix de Saint-Cloud, Rheingold also won the Prix Ganay, the John Porter Stakes at Newbury and the Hardwicke Stakes at Royal Ascot.

Other successes in 1973, proving that Barry was in the top echelon to stay, included the July Stakes at Newmarket and the Richmond Stakes at Goodwood, won by Dragonara Palace, owned by the wife of Ladbrokes' bookmaking chief Cyril Stein. Also noteworthy were the triumph of Straight As A Die in Ascot's Royal Lodge Stakes and Our Mirage's victory in the Jockey Club Cup. By 1974, six years after starting up on his own, Barry had the biggest string of Flat horses in the country.

But there was still time for his favourite country pursuit, hurtling across the Leicestershire countryside perched like a little black wren on some hefty hunter, or soaring over Irish banks with the 'Black and Tans' or the Limericks in company with P.P. Hogan and jockey friends like Brian Taylor and Greville Starkey. The fearless Hogan was a true horseman in every sense of the word. He was a leading amateur jockey, one of the most successful point-to-point trainers Ireland has ever seen and still rode to hounds at 67. His Avondhu 'pirate pack' used to hunt on Sundays. As a young man Hogan was said to have once brought home fifteen horses from the fair of Cahirmee in Buttevant to Rathcannon, a distance of 21 miles, riding one and leading the 14 others on a string.

In 1975 Barry showed that with the right raw material he could do quantity as well as quality. His total of winners rose to 81, with Mrs Charles Radclyffe's three-year-old filly Duboff winning nine races and Nagwa thirteen, a record.

Nagwa's score was remarkable and so was her durability, as she ran in no fewer than twenty races that season. Owned by Khalifa Sasi, the daughter of Tower Walk out of Tamarisk Way did not break her duck until her fourth start, winning over five furlongs at Leicester on 14 June. She was not in the top class but she then collected another twelve victories, over distances from five furlongs to seven furlongs.

Early victories came in the hands of Willie Carson and Ernie Johnson but for the last nine her partner was the then apprentice Ray Cochrane. Apart from being a tough filly, Barry says, she coped with all sorts of going.

Nagwa, who cost 6,300 guineas as a yearling, was only out of the frame once in her twenty public appearances. Apart from her 13 successes, she finished second five times and fourth once. Her last eleven races were over a period of just ten weeks. Timeform declared: 'Nagwa is not in the top flight but for stout-hearted consistency of running and honesty of purpose we haven't had a filly the like of her for years.'

Nagwa's most valuable prize was the £1,335 she collected for winning the Marston Moor Stakes at York in October, though she was beaten only a head in the Princess Margaret Stakes at Ascot.

For her final victory, which made her the most successful two-year-old of the twentieth century, she led all the way to take the Plaistow Plate at Lingfield on 3 November. Under Ray Cochrane's urgings she held off Steel Power, ridden by Frankie Durr, by a head.

Nagwa thus beat the record of 12 wins by Catalogue (1864), Lady Elizabeth (1867) and Semolina (1889). But Lady Elizabeth's record had included two walkovers. Nagwa was sold for export to America at the end of the season but won only one of her six races there.

Duboff, by So Blessed out of Proper Pretty, showed promise as a two-year-old, says Barry. 'We thought she'd win at York when we sent her up there for her third race but the rain came down and it was like a bog. She just couldn't go in it. And as a result she got herself well handicapped, quite by accident.

'The following year she ran at Kempton, in softish ground, funnily enough. Bob Street rode her and I told him to come up the stands rail and get across as soon as he could coming into the straight. She won at about 100-8 or something like that. She continued to improve and she won and won and won. People say it is a good mark for a trainer to keep a filly going so long. But you can't do it without the animal. They've got to be willing partners.'

Duboff won her first race at Kempton on 30 May and her next five starts. She began her season in the lower regions of the handicap and improved 28lb in four months. At one stage she won four handicaps in seventeen days.

She was outclassed in the Irish Guinness Oaks but then came back and easily won the Extel Handicap at Goodwood on 2 August. She then went on to collect the Sun Chariot Stakes, with Willie Carson in the saddle. Even after her formidable programme experts agreed that she looked the pick in the paddock. Duboff won all her nine races in England: she was defeated only in Ireland and in Wales. Timeform called her 'as genuine a filly as one would wish to see'. Placing four-year-old fillies in Britain was not easy then, but Duboff won two of the ten races she contested the next year before being sold for 100,000 guineas at the December Sales.

Willie Carson hasn't forgotten that after Duboff won the Extel Barry was given a 'present' for the jockey and put it in his safe. He then forgot all about it until he left South Bank many years later, but Willie didn't get any interest.

From the early days, say those about him, Barry has always exuded an inner certainty, has always known where he was going. Ernie Johnson, Barry's first stable jockey, recalls: 'When I rode for Sam Hall and was riding some for Barry he offered me the job. Sam Hall's yard was stronger numerically but I realised his owners weren't competing. When they'd been very successful, the money they were spending to buy a nice horse was just the same, they weren't going for a better calibre of horse. Barry was always going to go upwards.'

What gave that impression? 'Professionals will recognise something in a professional. He had it, almost from day one.'

Maureen Hills reflects: 'I always knew Barry would be different, that he would make his mark.'

Her sons testify that Maureen, mother of John and the twins Michael and Richard, was a huge help to Barry in the testing early days. But marriages in racing, as in other fields, do not always last. Barry and Maureen parted and in due course Barry married Penny Woodhouse, a talented showjumper on the fringes of the England team. The pair had met as Barry indulged his passion for country sports with hunts like the Belvoir and the Quorn.

The parting from Maureen was a painful period in the lives of the Hills family, particularly sad for the three elder boys. They praise their mother for keeping things together at a difficult time. But they also pay tribute to Penny, an immensely popular figure in the racing world, for her understanding.

John Hills is a man who looks the world straight in the eye and he says of his mother: 'The reason the twins and I have got where we have is her hard work. She held the thing together at what was the worst time of her life. She'd come from the beginning through all the Frankincense business, buying South Bank, to that mid-Seventies period, which looks like the best thing since sliced bread in training terms. And we were only kids.

'There were times when they didn't know where the wages were coming from. She didn't train the horses. He had the skill and all that. But she helped to get things to that stage and then helped us through that period. We were adolescents and she kept us on the straight track. What she had done for Dad, she transferred to doing for us. She was a jockey's daughter, Newmarket born and bred. Racing is in her blood too and she guided us through that period.'

But it is Penny, mother of Charlie and George, who has been Barry's rock ever since, through his rise to fame and fortune and his battles with cancer, and there is a remarkable family unity embracing her and Barry and all his five sons. John says: 'We were always fond of her from the first day we ever met her. Penny became a friend of the family through hunting, then when things blew up she was very sympathetic and kind – as kind as anybody could be in those kind of circumstances. She made it possible for us all to go forward.' At South Bank, Manton and Faringdon Place, Penny has always been very much involved with the horses too, riding out top-quality animals every day come fair weather or foul.

Staff and children alike confirm that living and working with a genius like Barrington W. Hills can be testing. He is certainly not famed for his patience. Hence the cushion in the elegant living room that bears the emblem: 'Sometimes I wake up Grumpy and sometimes I let him sleep.' Long-time owner Dick Bonnycastle named his Derby candidate Mr Combustible after the man who trained him. So is Barry as fearsome as his image suggests? Perhaps after all their years together the most reliable witness is Snowy Outen.

Has Barry always been that way? 'Yes, he bloody well has, though he's mellowed a bit with age. But he's a fair man. He will give you a right bollocking and five minutes later it is all forgotten and he would offer you a drink. He has never held grudges.

'The guv'nor is as good as anybody but he wouldn't suit all. There's some who say, "Stuff it up your backside." There are times I've picked up my coat and gone home. Barry would come down and say, "What the bloody hell are you doing?" and it would be over. He wouldn't apologise as such. If he said sorry I think the sky would open up.'

But then Snowy concludes: 'He has been a perfect gentleman to me and my wife Margaret … and he always takes his hat off to Margaret.'

CHAPTER THREE

The Great Rheingold

Beaten by a whisker in the Derby, he goes on to win the Prix de l'Arc de Triomphe

'On that particular day I don't think much would have beaten him, not in my lifetime. I think he would have been up to the great Sea-Bird that day – he wouldn't have been far behind him anyway.'
BARRY HILLS ON RHEINGOLD'S PRIX DE L'ARC DE TRIOMPHE.

Probably the best horse Barry Hills has ever trained was Rheingold, the bay colt by Faberge II who lost the 1972 Derby by the width of a nostril in a pulsating finish, the closest in the race since the dead-heat of 1884.

Had the contest been staged on any other track, Rheingold, a 22-1 shot, would probably have won. Had any other jockey been aboard his conqueror, Roberto, instead of the Epsom incomparable Lester Piggott, Rheingold would probably have won. As it was, Barry's stable jockey, Ernie Johnson, rode a great race on a horse unsuited by the Epsom undulations only to face a nightmarish dilemma in the last furlong as his horse hung violently left on the inward-sloping camber of the Epsom course, while the whip-flailing Piggott was driving Roberto inside him.

Had Johnson gone for his whip to inspire one last effort from his mount, he might have surrendered control and could well have lost the race in the stewards' room for interference. As the sage John Oaksey put it at the time: 'In the early stages of a race a tendency to hang can be corrected by pulling the bit through your horse's mouth, slapping him down the neck or even letting the reins go completely slack for a couple of strides. But all such remedies either make the horse go slower or allow him to come off a straight line or both. In the first mile or so of a Derby that might not matter so much but in the last fifty yards it is almost certainly fatal.

'A jockey in Ernie Johnson's position therefore feels something like a driver who, having approached a corner too fast in the first place, finds it going on twice as long as he has expected. A strong sense of imminent disaster is mingled with a feeling of utter powerlessness to prevent it.

'The bad driver's instinctive reaction is to slam on the brakes, the bad jockey's is to go for his whip. Both have the same results, namely loss of control, and if there happens to be another car (or horse) in the vicinity a violent collision. So the only answer, whether you are a driver or a jockey, is to sit very still and pray that you don't run out of road, or in Ernie Johnson's case, that the winning post will come in time.'

As Johnson said after the race: 'The winning post came just a stride too late.'

Sir Peter O'Sullevan noted that day that the Derby stewards had been rescued by the length of a well-smoked cigarette, which decided the photo-finish. If Rheingold had been an inch up instead they might have had to make a disqualification decision involving millions in bets (Roberto was the 3-1 favourite) and bloodstock values.

The head-on camera film showed that Rheingold had veered from a true course, confirming Johnson's claim that on a flat course, given the full opportunity to ride his mount out, he would have won and supporting Piggott's argument that 'Rheingold lay on me all the way up the straight'.

The camera evidence also underlined the words of jockey Pat Eddery, the rider of the third horse home, Pentland Firth, who caught a bump from Roberto as the two principals drove past to fight out the finish three lengths ahead of him. He declared: 'It only affected me by a length and it happened because Rheingold bore in on Roberto.' He added emphatically: 'It wasn't Lester's fault.'

For once, though, victory for Piggott was not well received by the Epsom crowd, most of whom were full of sympathy for Australian rider Bill Williamson, who had been due to ride Roberto but who had been 'jocked off' in Piggott's favour by American owner John Galbreath 48 hours before on the grounds that Williamson would not be fit enough, having injured a shoulder in a fall at Kempton ten days earlier. The Australian had been passed fit by the doctors and underlined his point by riding two other winners on the Derby Day card. At least he had the compensation that Galbreath had promised him the same winning percentage as Piggott if Roberto won. Williamson admitted later that he could not have ridden with the force Piggott used to get Roberto home and that he was delighted that Lester had managed to win him so much money.

So close was the Derby result that neither jockey headed for the winner's enclosure. Johnson simply could not say if he had won. Piggott dismounted from Roberto a long way away and told onlookers as he headed for the weighing room, 'I don't think I've won.' After surviving a long-delayed stewards' inquiry for bumping, he didn't smile until he heard the 'placings unaltered' announcement as he emerged from the weighing room for the next race.

With good grace, Barry Hills told reporters: 'That Lester is just the most super ever,' adding: 'But Ernie Johnson rode a really fine race.'

It was fair comment given that rider and trainer both felt in their hearts that their horse was unsuited by the course on which he had come so close to clinching a famous victory for his young trainer.

Barry has not changed his opinion but he adds now: 'Piggott always said Ernie Johnson should have given Rheingold a couple of good smacks, rather than try to keep straight, and won the race and then argued it out in the stewards' room. In other words he should have made sure of winning the race first and argued about it afterwards. It was a short head. It was very close.'

But might he not have lost it then in the stewards' room? 'Of course, especially in those days. They don't sling them out as easy these days.'

Owner Tony Shead, who had a stake in Rheingold, takes a similar view. 'Ernie Johnson rode him well in the Derby but he concentrated on keeping him straight at the end as the horse was leaning heavily to the left. Johnson was just praying he could hold on. He didn't dare touch him. I've never held it against him but maybe he should have taken the risk of giving him one good clout.'

Holding out his hands a few inches apart, Shead says: 'When they went past me (in his brother-in-law Michael Gee's box) Rheingold was that much in front. You could say it would have been better to have won the Derby and been disqualified than to have finished second in a Derby.

'Who would have objected? Piggott would have wanted to but I very much doubt if the rather patrician American owner of Roberto (John Galbreath) would have objected to an English winner in England's biggest race. Would the stewards have objected? Doubtful. They'd have probably thought "six of one and half a dozen of the other". But that never entered my head at the time.'

Ernie is a thoughtful and articulate man who, in his sixties, still rides out twice a week for Barry through the racing season: 'I wouldn't enjoy it at a lower level but Barry has good horses.' He admits he would like to ride that race again. 'Even if you got beat again you would like the second opportunity.' But he says of Rheingold: 'He was basically a horse that was never made for Epsom. He was a big, leggy type of horse, he wasn't an Epsom horse.'

It is often forgotten that Barry's other runner in that Derby, Our Mirage, ran a cracking race too to finish fourth at 100-1 after nearly being pulled out because the ground was much firmer than he liked. Our Mirage went on to be second in both the English and Irish St Legers. Again Barry knew early on what he had got for the 6,200 guineas the son of Miralgo had cost. When he made his debut in the Beacon Maiden Plate at Newmarket in August of the previous year he, like Rheingold on his debut, was the subject of a significant punt, being backed down from 12-1 to 11-2. He never gave his supporters a moment's worry, taking the lead a furlong out and stretching comfortably clear of his field. In only his second race Our Mirage won a tough contest for the Prix de la Salamandre at Longchamp, beating a Gimcrack winner despite losing four lengths at the start.

*

Rheingold's story was a remarkable one all through. Although he ran in the name of Henry Zeisel, the talkative owner of a London nightclub who claimed to have been the former leader of the Vienna Philharmonic Orchestra (the horse was named after a Wagner opera), he was in fact owned by a syndicate.

Barry says: 'I met Henry Zeisel in a box at Royal Ascot one day three months before the sales and he said, "I want to buy a horse, I've got £3,000." Two days later he gave me a deposit of £1,500 – in cash.'

Rheingold was finally bought a few months later at the Newmarket October sale by Barry and bloodstock agent Pat Hogan. They secured a horse who was to prove a remarkable money-spinner for just 3,000 guineas.

'Pat said to me. "I know of a nice horse. He's owned by a fellow called Dr Jim Russell from Bansha in Tipperary. There's plenty of improvement to be had if he gets fed a bit better." We bought Our Mirage off Bob Donworth for £5,200 at the same sale. (The good-looking Our Mirage was placed in the King George as well as coming fourth in the Derby). We won the Prix de la Salamandre in France with him for Nat Cohen and Sonny Enfield. Lester Piggott got off him and they said, "Thank you very much Lester, we'll give you a present." ' True to form, Lester replied simply: 'Make it a big one.'

Remarkably Athene, Rheingold's dam, once changed hands for £1. The small-scale Newmarket trainer Peter Poston bought her for 140 guineas at Tattersalls' yearling sales in 1961 for two reasons.

'First,' he explained, 'No-one else wanted her except a buyer whom I believed to be a horse slaughterer. Second, she had been beautifully reared and was within my price bracket.'

Athene was sold on and purchased by the organisers of the Saints and Sinners charity meeting at Sandown to be given as a raffle prize. The holder of the winning £1 ticket then put her back into training with Poston but the results were disappointing and she was sold off at Ascot sales to Freddie Maxwell for 300 guineas before being acquired by Rheingold's breeder.

The breeder, Dr James Russell, kept only two mares and the results Rheingold achieved won him an official vote of congratulations from the local county council. They have a proper sense of priorities in Ireland.

Barry and Henry Zeisel were not the only people, however, who did well out of Rheingold. In a deal concluded just 48 hours before he finished second in the Derby, six others bought into the colt.

Lloyds underwriter Tim Sasse, who had persuaded Barry to take on his son Duncan (whom he later set up with his own yard) as an assistant, had been convinced by Duncan of Rheingold's potential. He persuaded Zeisel to sell 80 per cent of Rheingold on a valuation of £50,000 (which on an average earnings comparison would be £774,000 today).

Tony Shead, who was to become one of Barry's long-term owners and who was a friend of Sasse, takes up the tale: 'Henry Zeisel kept 20 per cent, Tim Sasse took 20 per cent and the others – me, Sir William Pigott-Brown, Charles St George, John Weller-Poley, Paddy Bowen-Colthurst and an F.W. Wicks – had ten per cent each for £5,000. (Neither Shead nor Barry ever met F.W. Wicks).

'None of us were all that affluent and £5,000 was a lot to find in cash in those days. But Tim Sasse was a very persuasive man and he got us all to cough up.

'I think Henry Zeisel regretted it later but it's not bad turning £3,000 into £40,000 and at the same time keeping 20 per cent of the horse.'

Zeisel, says Shead, was a charming, amusing man with a tall mistress who tried to restrain his volatile character. The Rheingold Club, which Zeisel ran in a little alleyway off Oxford Street, he says, wasn't very smart but it was popular. 'There was a live band. It was always crowded, more beer than cocktails. We called him a London nightclub owner but it wasn't exactly the Mirabelle or the 400 Club.

'Henry was there every single night. He liked to be in charge of the takings. Credit cards hadn't been invented. He didn't take cheques, so it was all in cash. He was always the last to leave when the club closed and he went home with a nice suitcase every night. I know he used to pay his training bills in cash.'

That is confirmed by Maureen Hills, who recalls Zeisel arriving at the yard with bundles of fivers stuffed in a Marks and Spencer carrier bag, handing over the bundles of notes and exclaiming: 'How much you wish? How much you wish?'

*

Rheingold made a winning racecourse debut at Newcastle in August 1971. Barry recalls: 'The day before that first race he got his nose caught in a bucket hook and the vet wanted to put half a dozen stitches in it. I said, "He's running tomorrow, you can't do that. Just clean him up and I'll send him." I said to the vet, "He won't need more than one nostril to win. As long as he can breathe out of one he'll be all right." Anyway he went up to Newcastle and won, beating a horse of Sam Hall's.'

The normally cool and restrained Timeform annual noted that in the Newcastle race Rheingold was backed down from 4-1 to 11-8 favourite. 'Rumour has it that his trainer Barry Hills had had a nice touch. No wonder. With a horse of the quality that Rheingold showed himself to be subsequently, at least two stone above the standard one expects to see in ordinary maiden events in the north, Hills could have mortgaged his stables, horses, house, car and other valuables and won all the money on Newcastle racecourse. It's better than winning the pools.' Had Timeform's man had a little on himself? one wonders.

Barry says: 'After that he was second in the Champagne Stakes to Crowned Prince. He was second to him again in the Dewhurst. Then he and Our Mirage were eighth and ninth respectively in the Observer Gold Cup (these days the Racing Post Trophy).'

That race led Timeform to downgrade its enthusiasm for the horse, commenting that, although he was genuine, he was 'unlikely to secure success in a Classic race. Almost certainly his position at the finish – eighth of 13 – was as near as his ability could take him. Rheingold is a good horse but he is not as good as all that.' Horses can make monkeys of even the shrewdest judges.

As a three-year-old Rheingold ran in the Blue Riband Stakes at Epsom, an early Derby trial. Although he was to go on to win the Dante at York before the Derby, in the Blue Riband Rheingold was beaten into fourth place by John Dunlop's Scottish Rifle. 'Ernie Johnson came back and said he didn't go one yard on the track. He didn't handle it at all. Of course what happened was that he learned to handle the track by going round it.'

Early in the summer Barry rated Rheingold as inferior to Our Mirage. But he kept on improving. 'Between the Dante Stakes, which he won at York in May, and the Derby Rheingold improved by stones.

You could see at exercise every day how much he was coming on.' So, despite the Blue Riband experience on the course, the connections felt they had to go for the Derby and Johnson chose to ride Rheingold rather than the higher-rated Our Mirage.

Tony Shead, who had a happy association as an owner with Barry for thirty years, recalls their first meeting, about a week before the 1972 Derby when the syndicate was still trying to clinch the Rheingold deal.

'He arrived very early one morning on Epsom Downs with his two Derby horses. Getting out of an expensive car and wearing what seemed to be an ordinary suit, he got up on Rheingold. With a work rider on the other horse he went up to the Derby start, cantered to the top of Tattenham Hill and then came down the hill and round Tattenham Corner at full pelt. "He'll handle that all right," he remarked after the two horses had jogged up the straight.'

Barry says: 'When he ran in the Derby I said to Ernie Johnson, "Whatever you do he's a big, long-striding horse. Keep him out of trouble and let him use his stride right throughout the race," which he did. He rode him beautifully, to be fair. The bad luck was that Piggott had jocked Williamson off to ride Roberto and that made the difference between winning and losing. Charles St George always said, "It's better to have Piggott with you than riding against you," and it's very true. Of course if Williamson had ridden Roberto we'd have won.'

Racing is a tough business and when Rheingold next came out in the Grand Prix de Saint-Cloud in France the owners dispensed with Johnson's services and put up French rider Yves Saint-Martin. 'Rheingold was a much better horse that day,' says his trainer, 'and he hacked up.' So he did, by five lengths.

Was it hard for Johnson watching others win on Rheingold? 'It's always tough. But it happens to a lot of people.' You can see why he and the gritty, undemonstrative Hills worked so well together.

After that Rheingold ran in eight more races and won five of them. His only bogey race was the Benson and Hedges at York, for which he twice started favourite and in which he was twice beaten. (In 1972 he fell victim to a brilliant front-running ride on Roberto by Braulio Baeza, when the Panamanian scorched off from the start and made all, leaving everything except Brigadier Gerard, who had won his previous fifteen races, struggling behind him in what was undoubtedly the best performance of Roberto's career). But probably a mile and a quarter was a little short for Rheingold in the very best company.

In the yard Rheingold was something of a character through his racing days. Snowy Outen recalls: 'You had to feed him first before the others. He used to flick the door with his foot until his food arrived and we would worry that he would hurt himself. So we got his ready first. He would eat his food and then we'd have peace.'

Rheingold was the first horse Geoff Snook, one of Barry's travelling head lads since 1976, 'did' in the yard. Then an apprentice, Geoff had been promised a choice when the next batch of horses arrived. When they did, Snowy reckoned Rheingold was so big that one of the paid lads ought to have charge of him. But none of them wanted him, so Geoff got his wish. He says: 'Rheingold was almost human. He used to play with his water bucket, kicking it around the box, so we put it outside. When he wanted a drink he would bang on the door until he got it.

'What made Rheingold so good was his devastating turn of foot. He had a high knee action but when you asked him to pick up he would double the length of his stride. Others with similar breeding had the same knee action but weren't the same when they were let down.' The Benson and Hedges, he reckons, came at what was never Rheingold's time of the year. 'But there was time after that to bring him back for the autumn races.'

The York race was Rheingold's last as a three-year-old. He was later cast in his box and injured and it was a huge relief to his owners when he came out as a four-year-old, with Yves Saint-Martin keeping the ride, in the John Porter Stakes at Newbury and won in emphatic style, streaking home lengths clear of the field. He then won the Prix Ganay in France and the Hardwicke Stakes before returning to France to collect a second Grand Prix de Saint-Cloud.

Then came the Benson and Hedges once more, and a severe embarrassment for the trainer.

Barry tells it like this: 'Tim Sasse, Charles St George, John Weller-Poley and William Pigott-Brown all got on the train at King's Cross. By the time they got to York Lester Piggott had persuaded them to let him ride the horse and not Saint-Martin. It caused a frightful row. I had to declare Piggott for the horse and of course the stewards hauled me in and asked me for an explanation and I didn't have a lot to offer. Anyway he got beat and he never ran again until the Prix de l'Arc de Triomphe.'

He says the 'jocking off' should never have happened, particularly because Saint-Martin got on very well with the horse and had ridden a brilliant race on him in the Prix Ganay.

Maureen Hills, who had driven up with assistant Duncan Sasse, says they hid in the Silver Ring in their embarrassment as the Press hunted for them. Tony Shead was on holiday in Majorca at the time of the York race and was amazed to discover from his newspaper that Rheingold had been ridden by Piggott. 'Tim Sasse always vehemently denied to me that he had any part in it. It was all St George, Piggott's great chum. Sasse said he did all he could to prevent St George having his own way but St George was a very strong, domineering character.

'St George argued, "If you want to win the Arc you've got to have Piggott riding him today," because I think that – and this is one point in St George's favour – owing to his own contractual arrangements Saint-Martin was unlikely to be available at Longchamp.'

Who had to tell poor Saint-Martin? Tim Sasse told me: 'Who do you think? He wasn't going to do it himself. Barry refused to do it. St

George said to me, "You're the only one who speaks French." '

Saint-Martin, says Shead, was a charming man and when Sasse expressed his embarrassment, the jockey contented himself with the comment, 'Ca n'est pas tres gentil', which you might call a masterpiece of English understatement by a Frenchman.

Shortly after the Arc, Shead spoke to St George about the jocking off of France's leading rider at York. 'St George was totally unrepentant. He put me in my place. He said, "It was the cleverest thing I did in all my life." '

Shead reckons Rheingold was beaten at York partly because Piggott was trying out a way of riding the horse in preparation for the Arc 'because despite the York performance Lester remained extremely confident about winning the Arc'. Barry doesn't agree.

But the Benson and Hedges jocking off may have had one curious effect. Although French writers had no hesitation in naming Rheingold as the best in Europe after his scintillating Arc performance, surprisingly few British racing commentators voted for him that season as the Horse of the Year, many plumping instead for the French mare Dahlia, who had beaten him in the King George at Ascot. Timeform was among those who publicly expressed puzzlement at the English scribes' refusal to take their chance of waving the national flag.

Rheingold seemed to have lost his sparkle when beaten by Arc rival Dahlia in the 1973 King George VI and Queen Elizabeth Stakes at Ascot and he looked a Longchamp no-hoper when struggling home in third place at York in August. But that is where faith and remarkable skill entered the equation.

Barry and Zeisel still believed the colt to be a world-beater. Barry took the horse back to Lambourn faced with the tricky task of rekindling Rheingold's enthusiasm and faith in his own ability and he planned a meticulous Arc preparation.

He later told John Rickman: 'It was one of the best things I have ever done in my life with horses. He had been quite busy and needed building up again. I hate letting horses down, giving them virtually nothing to do. Of course you can give a horse a rest but you must keep the wheels turning. This I did with Rheingold and he just built up and regained his strength. He came right back.'

At one stage during Rheingold's preparation for the Arc, Barry's friend Syd Mercer crucially 'charmed' an awkwardly placed wart off Rheingold. Mercer had a remarkable knowledge of lotions and potions for tackling horses' ailments. Maureen Hills recalls that he came down one day when Barry was at the races and they had a number of horses in the yard afflicted by ringworm. He handed over a mixture to Snowy Outen and said, 'Wash all the horses with this.'

Maureen says: 'It included, I think, sperm oil and sulphur and paraffin. All the horses went bright yellow and when Barry came back from the races he was shouting, "What the f*** have you done?" But it worked like a dream, all the ringworm dropped off.'

Ten days before Rheingold's big race, when Piggott came down to partner the horse in a final gallop, the 37-year-old trainer realised how well his work programme and psychology had succeeded. 'Rheingold showed me then that not only was he as good as ever, he was actually better. It was then that I knew we could win the Arc.

'Lester came down and rode him work and he broke two blood vessels before he ran in the Arc. He didn't break them in both nostrils, only one nostril, and he did a good bit of work. I had a good bet on him with Ladbrokes about ten days before the race and it would have taken a very, very good horse to beat him that day.'

That bet was another £1,000 at 12-1 and it came after what Ray Cochrane, later a top jockey but then an apprentice in the Hills yard, remembers as a brilliantly planned gallop. 'It was a very well-executed piece of work. Avon Valley led the first four furlongs and then spun away as Galiano (with Paddy Newson up) jumped in at the four pole. He led from there and Proverb (with Derby-winning jockey Ernie Johnson riding) took over for the final four. Rheingold went by him in the last couple of furlongs as if he were standing still and everybody knew he had got a major chance in the Arc.'

Piggott, of course, was desperate to ride an Arc winner. The race in which he had ridden unsuccessfully fifteen times had become a jinx for him. He had finished second in the Arc on horses as good as Sir Ivor, Park Top and Nijinsky. But this time the result was rarely in doubt.

Rheingold was in the first half-dozen throughout the race and Piggott took him to the front soon after rounding the home turn to lay down his challenge. Allez France went with him as the pair left the rest of the 25-strong field for dead and in the end Piggott drove home two and a half lengths clear of Yves Saint-Martin on the classy local favourite, with the previous year's French Derby winner, Hard To Beat, third. At that stage only Mill Reef among English-trained horses had won more career prize-money. Geoff Snook recalls Piggott saying that on his day Rheingold was the best he had ridden and Christopher Poole reported: 'Lester's ice-cold reserve cracked into an ear-to-ear grin as thousands packing round the winner's enclosure cheered and counter-cheered the world's greatest race-rider.' The dapper trainer's smile was twinkling too.

Barry says: 'He beat Allez France nearly three lengths and Allez France won the race the next year. On that particular day I don't think much would have beaten him, not in my lifetime. I think he would have been up to the great Sea-Bird that day – he wouldn't have been far behind him anyway. He was a very, very good horse but if he was just a bit weak, a bit off-colour, he could run a really poor race. He would improve with the weather. He came to top pitch around midsummer. Obviously the older he got the stronger he became.

'Rheingold got a leg in the Arc and was then sold. Tim Vigors bought him to go to Coolmore. But he didn't have a very good pedigree and he wasn't much of a success at stud.' Rheingold's owners, though, some of whom retained breeding rights, did not do too badly. For his stallion career Rheingold was syndicated for a million pounds.

CHAPTER FOUR

Barry and the Derby

So nearly there so often

'The thoroughbred exists because its selection has depended not on experts, technicians or zoologists but on a piece of wood – the winning post of the Epsom Derby.'
ITALIAN BREEDER FEDERICO TESIO.

The Derby is a special experience, even for those who have little knowledge of horseracing. Writer Bill Bryson likened it to his first experience of sex: 'Hectic, strenuous, memorably pleasant and over before you know it.' For racing aficionados the mile-and-a-half 'scurry over Surrey', the Blue Riband Classic, is the ultimate test. The illustrious Italian breeder Federico Tesio once declared: 'The thoroughbred exists because its selection has depended not on experts, technicians or zoologists but on a piece of wood – the winning post of the Epsom Derby.'

Some trainers would like to see the ultimate test for the three-year-olds of the Classic generation run on a flatter, more even course. But Epsom is special. To triumph around its uniquely testing undulations a horse needs not just speed, stamina and physical dexterity but the character to cope with the big-day buzz of a 100,000-plus crowd.

The pack of trained-to-the-minute thoroughbreds, nerves jangling, set off from a low point on the Epsom Downs, beyond the funfair occupying the centre of the track. Many watching will be carrying memories of the great horses they have seen sweep to victory in the past, like Sea-Bird, Nijinsky or Mill Reef.

For four furlongs the horses climb uphill, streaming round a gradual right-hand bend. Then they need to settle as they switch left to the inner rail and head up to the top of Tattenham Hill. There follows a pell-mell dash down the slope to the sharp left-hand bend round Tattenham Corner.

Lester Piggott, winner of a record nine Derbies, says of the potential Derby winner: 'Size is less important than the manner of racing. You need a horse that can lay up handy, a few places behind the leaders. Getting too far back at Epsom can be disastrous as there is no part of the course where you can readily make up ground forfeited early on. You have to get into a reasonable place and keep out of trouble as beaten horses fall back on the downhill run.'

Even when Tattenham Corner has been negotiated, the horses face a further test in front of the stands. The finishing straight is nearly four furlongs long and as they reach the final 200 yards the tired three-year-olds, running through a wall of noise, face not just a further lung-bursting rise to the finishing post but a camber that tilts them in towards the inside rail, making it hard for their riders to keep them on an even course and avoid impeding others.

For Barry Hills, so painfully close to winning the Derby with Rheingold and also second in the great race with three others – Hawaiian Sound, Glacial Storm and Blue Stag – winning the Derby has become a quest. So what sort of a horse does he believe triumphs at Epsom, a speed horse or a stayer?

'The old adage used to be "fourth in the 2,000 Guineas, first in the Derby" but times have changed. The trials are still there but if you've got a horse that's going to stay the Derby distance he should win the Guineas if he's good enough. They've got to have speed. A lot of mile-and-a-quarter horses have won the Derby – horses like The Minstrel, Nijinsky and Mill Reef. Mill Reef was fast enough to win

Ascot's six-furlong Coventry Stakes as a two-year-old. They've got to have speed to keep them out of trouble. If you've got a horse that gets a mile and a quarter then there's no reason in a normal Derby year you can't win it.'

*

Barry's association with the Derby, and with bad luck in the big race, began when he was a lad at George Colling's Newmarket yard. 'When the yearlings came into the yard the senior lads picked the ones they wanted to do and I got left with a big, gawky animal that nobody else wanted. I rode that horse out for two years, every day, and it was like having a Rolls-Royce. He was an absolute machine called Acropolis and he could beat the rest out of sight.'

The pictures of Alice, Lady Derby's Acropolis in Timeform's *Racehorses of 1955* and *Racehorses of 1956*, which described him as 'a talking horse before he was a racehorse' show a diminutive lad holding him. It is the young apprentice B.W. Hills.

Barry says: 'He was winter favourite for the Derby but he went lame setting a course record at Newmarket and that ruined his preparation, though he still finished third.

'Ever since riding him I've always been able to tell whether I was sitting on anything good, even if I'm only walking or trotting up the road. If someone blindfolded you and put you in a Rolls or a Mercedes you'd know you weren't in a Mini, wouldn't you? It's the same sort of thing.'

Acropolis, a brother of the very good stayer Alycidon, was known to Barry and the lads as 'Willie'. Leased by Lady Derby, then 93, Acropolis was a very good horse but an unlucky one, who as a three-year-old in 1955 ran in a two-horse race for the Newmarket Stakes against Lord Rosebery's Rowland Ward. The Rosebery horse ran out, off the course. Anxious his mount did not do the same, jockey Doug

Smith rode Acropolis so vigorously that his horse broke the course record.

The impeccably bred Acropolis, described in the Press at the time as 'the most valuable colt in the world', had a near-perfect conformation and an impressive stride. Although he had never been fully tested in public, Acropolis was a long-time ante-post favourite for Epsom, even after My Babu had won the 2,000 Guineas. A week before the big race, one contemporary scribe quoted the verdict of his then 18-year-old apprentice work rider, Barrington Hills: 'He was the first to throw a leg across the colt as a yearling and after he had achieved his third personal riding success on stable companion Peter Pan at Hurst Park he said, "Willie is the kindest but laziest horse I have ever done and I don't see how he can be beaten next Wednesday." '

But that record-breaking run at Newmarket had jarred Acropolis's joints and he had had to be rested. The 11-4 favourite entered the Derby short of work and in the event finished third behind Phil Drake. Barry says: 'He didn't stay beyond one and a quarter miles and didn't have the ideal preparation. His work was held up by a jarred joint. He could well have been a Derby winner – he had a lot of speed.'

*

Rheingold's loss by a nostril in 1972 has been described in chapter three. Only six years later Barry lost another Derby in a photo-finish with Hawaiian Sound.

This was the year he really thought he had won, in what would have been an astonishing achievement both for him and the horse's jockey, the diminutive American Willie Shoemaker.

After Hawaiian Sound was beaten a neck by Icelandic in that year's Chester Vase, one of the traditional Epsom trials, Barry began to wonder if he would stay the trip at Epsom. Stable jockey Ernie Johnson elected to ride their other Derby entry, Sexton Blake, in the big race and both Lester Piggott and Pat Eddery turned down the offer of the ride on Hawaiian Sound after partnering him in work on the Lambourn gallops.

Barry and majority owner Robert Sangster consulted and decided on the bold stroke of engaging Shoemaker, the 46-year-old American rider, who had never before ridden on Epsom Downs. On his first experience of Tattenham Corner, Shoemaker declared: 'It's like coming down a ski slope without skis.' The Derby was his first horserace in England and yet he failed by only a nose to make it his 7,451st winner, being thwarted in the dying strides by Barry's old friend Greville Starkey on Shirley Heights, trained by John Dunlop.

The trainer gave the American veteran a free hand over his tactics, although he did not really want him at the front too soon. In the event Shoemaker found the pace slower than he had expected and he did take an early lead. Once round Tattenham Corner, initially running straight as a tramline, he beat off challenges from Julio Mariner, Remainder Man and Pyjama Hunt. Barry insists that Shoemaker rode a marvellous race. 'He imposed his authority on them and had them stacked up behind him like a pack of cards coming round Tattenham Corner.'

In his typically undramatic and rational style, Hills adds: 'Shirley Heights just collared him and that was bad luck.'

Owner Robert Sangster and Barry watched the race from either side of the winning post. When they found each other, Sangster commiserated: 'Bad luck, Barry. Just beaten.' Barry looked at him in astonishment. 'Don't be silly,' he said. 'We've won.' When the judge's verdict on the photo-finish was announced, Sangster recalled, the colour drained from his trainer's face, leaving it ashen.

Barry says now: 'The horse didn't quite stay the trip but he came off the rails to block Remainder Man and that let Shirley Heights through on the inside. I thought we'd won.' He calls it the perfect example of a horse that didn't quite stay one and a half miles.

'The plan was not for the horse to make the running. He was to sit handyish but basically Willie Shoemaker couldn't hold him for a while. He came off the rail to try to block Remainder Man, who at the time was the only challenger. The other horse (Shirley Heights) came up the inside having run across the camber – you could have driven a double decker bus through the gap – and swooped and beat him on the line. Tactically Shoemaker made exactly the right move. It just didn't quite come off.'

Some say that, ridden again by Shoemaker, Hawaiian Sound should have won the Irish Derby, in which he was once more beaten by Shirley Heights, to whom he also finished third in the King George and Queen Elizabeth Stakes at Ascot, again ridden by Shoemaker.

'I don't think you can really say that. I don't think the horse was quite as good that day in Ireland as at Epsom. Shirley Heights had more stamina than Hawaiian Sound, that's the simple answer to it. He truly got one and a half miles, whereas our horse didn't. That's why we brought him back in distance for the mile-and-a-quarter Benson and Hedges, which he won. In fact he won over nine furlongs the next spring.'

Shoemaker was harder on himself after his second race on Hawaiian Sound. He had wanted to hold up the colt or at least drop him in behind the leaders in Ireland, but he let him run along and nothing left him alone. Although he kept on being taken on through the race, he was only a head and a neck behind Shirley Heights and Exdirectory at the finish. Barry says: 'Shoemaker came back very annoyed. He thought he had made a mess of it.'

You could certainly call Hawaiian Sound unlucky in missing the Derby by a head and the Irish Derby by a head and a neck, but he confirmed his quality by getting within two lengths of the winner in the King George and winning the Benson and Hedges. He finished the season with a second to Swiss Maid in the Champion Stakes. Certainly he was a horse who stood his racing well.

Hawaiian Sound had opened his Derby season by winning the Kosset Carpets Stakes at Kempton Park. Among the prizes offered by the sponsors to the winning jockey was a white cat (the company's advertising emblem) or £150 worth of carpets. Spotting that the prize moggy had drawn blood already while struggling with the managing director of the sponsors, the canny Ernie Johnson, who had ridden Hawaiian Sound, opted for the carpets. Asked what he would have chosen, Lester Piggott typically replied 'a monkey', slang for £500. No cats or carpets for him, he was always a hard cash man.

Would Piggott have won the Derby on Hawaiian Sound? He did take over from Shoemaker for the two-furlong-shorter Benson and Hedges Gold Cup at York that August and won the race from Gunner B. On that occasion, when Robert Sangster asked him in the winner's enclosure what he would like for his 'present', Piggott sarcastically replied: 'Just give me what it cost to fly Shoemaker over here twice.' But that was hardly fair. Lester had been offered and had turned down the Derby ride on Hawaiian Sound.

*

As well as those close finishes involving Rheingold and Hawaiian Sound, Barry has also filled the runner-up spot in the Derby with Glacial Storm in 1988 and Blue Stag in 1990. In 1993 he was third with Wafic Said's Blues Traveller, a 150-1 shot in the race won by Commander In Chief. Ever the realist, Barry says Glacial Storm and Blue Stag were sub-standard Derby horses.

The 1988 Derby in which Glacial Storm was second was won by Luca Cumani's Kahyasi, ridden by Barry's former apprentice Ray Cochrane, now Frankie Dettori's agent after a long and successful career in the saddle.

Cochrane had asked for Lester Piggott's advice on riding the Derby from prison, where Lester was serving a three-year sentence for tax evasion. The great jockey's advice for the 13 draw was 'Let him flow along with the leaders up to the first turn and take it from there'.

Cochrane had served a five-year apprenticeship with Barry, during which he rode the remarkable filly Nagwa to eleven of her thirteen victories in 1975. While he was recovering from a broken leg he became too heavy for the Flat and joined Fred Winter as a stable lad, riding five winners over jumps. Then Ray moved to Ron Sheather's stable and got kicked on the head by a horse. During his recovery 'the weight just fell away from me' and he returned to the Flat, winning the Lincoln on Saher in 1981. Cochrane won the St James's Palace Stakes and Sussex Stakes in 1984 on Chief Singer and had a highly successful spell as Luca Cumani's retained jockey.

In the 1988 Derby Michael Hills on Glacial Storm set sail for home from Unfuwain soon into the finishing straight. For some two furlongs his father and owner Robert Sangster must have felt they had the Derby in their pockets as he fought off challenges from Kefaah (John Reid) and Doyoun (Walter Swinburn). But then in the last furlong Kahyasi hit the front, going on to win by one and a half lengths in the fastest Derby since electrical timing was introduced.

Michael Hills said of Glacial Storm: 'He acted all right up to the top of the hill but the problems started coming down. I made the best of my way home as soon as we turned into the straight and the horse just kept picking up and picking up. If he had acted all the way round I don't think Ray Cochrane and Kahyasi would have got to us.

'I was up there all the way and hit the front two out. About a furlong out it looked as though I was going to win and then Kahyasi came looming up with Ray Cochrane and got me on that last fifty yards. When he went by me he was laughing his head off that Ray: "I've got you, I've got you, I've got you." ' As Cochrane dismounted Kahyasi after the race, he said: 'He's always been an idle bugger but now he's a good idle bugger.'

Michael Hills's reflections show just how painful the experience was for his father. 'Dad didn't even come to the winning enclosure and I don't think I spoke to him for about two weeks after that. He was gutted.'

Did he blame you? 'I don't think so. It's just that he thought he was going to win. It took the pleasure away from him. It was not that he thought I had ridden a bad race. It was just that the Derby is so important to him. It has been his mission since Rheingold was touched off. Winning it would mean everything to him.'

Glacial Storm finished third in the Irish Derby under Steve Cauthen. The respected commentator Richard Baerlein wrote that some were suggesting it was a case of Barry jocking off his own son Michael because he had not won at Epsom. He added: 'Nothing could be further from the truth. When Cash Asmussen turned down the Manton job, Robert Sangster and Barry Hills gave Michael a golden opportunity to make a name for himself, with one of the best retainers in the business for such a young man.

'At the same time it was agreed by Michael himself that if Pat Eddery or Steve Cauthen became available in any of the Classics or top races they would take over and Michael would get the same present. Steve Cauthen could have had the ride on Glacial Storm in the Derby had he so desired but he preferred to be associated with the Dick Hern stable.' There was, he pointed out, absolutely no disgrace in a jockey being replaced by Eddery or Cauthen.

Sangster said: 'I discussed the situation regarding rides with Michael Hills before the start of the season. Michael rides superbly but Steve Cauthen is champion jockey after all and it wasn't a difficult decision.'

Michael was back on Glacial Storm for the King George VI and Queen Elizabeth Stakes at Ascot. Later the horse went to the USA to be handled by D. Wayne Lukas after finishing a distant third in the Ormonde Stakes at Chester as a four-year-old.

Richard Baerlein criticised Barry for running Glacial Storm in the Derby, saying later: 'A year ago he told me that nothing would persuade him to run Glacial Storm in the Derby. "He is a great big backward baby and a run at Epsom could put him back for the season, if not for life." ' Baerlein added that precisely that had happened and that a horse with ideal breeding and a good record as a two-year-old had gone downhill with each succeeding race, going through the season without a victory. (He did not win again until April 1990). Baerlein commented: 'They all break their pledges as the big day draws nearer. Those fatal words, "There is only one Derby", have proved the downfall of many a promising thoroughbred.' Barry insists he still has no regrets about running Glacial Storm.

*

Two years later at Epsom, in 1990, it was the turn of the 8-1 shot Blue Stag to fill second place in the Derby for Barry and for Robert Sangster.

A Sadler's Wells home-bred from Sangster's Swettenham Stud, Blue Stag had been working lazily at home but when he went to Epsom for a gallop regular work rider Billy Nicholson reported that he had 'completely come to life'.

In the race, on a wet and windy Derby Day, Treble Eight, ridden by Bruce Raymond, led for most of the way, closely attended at Tattenham Corner by the Khalid Abdullah colt Quest For Fame. At the two-furlong marker Pat Eddery took Quest For Fame into the lead and there he stayed to run out the winner by three lengths, Eddery's third success in the big race.

Blue Stag was ridden by Cash Asmussen, who appeared to give the colt plenty to do. He made up a lot of ground in the closing stages to finish in a clear second place, with Willie Carson's mount, Elmaamul, in third, but Blue Stag never looked like troubling the winner.

The Sadler's Wells colt went on to finish fourth in the Irish Derby but Barry never rated him as one of his better Derby horses. 'Blue Stag had won the Dee Stakes but didn't do a lot after that. He lacked a bit of constitution and didn't stand up to it. They need a good constitution these good horses – like people.' Both Blue Stag and Glacial Storm, he believes, ran above themselves at Epsom.

Some pundits believed Blue Stag, a true galloper, would have a good chance in the concluding British Classic, the St Leger. Barry was reckoned to have scored a coup by securing the services of Willie Carson to ride him in the Doncaster race. But then, without any advance notice to Barry, Robert Sangster sold a half-share in the colt, together with eight others in a package deal, to American interests and he was sent off to be trained in California by Gary Jones.

Barry had much more regard for Storming Home, who did less well at Epsom in the 2001 Derby. 'Storming Home was an exceptionally good horse. He was a bit of an Al Capone. If Storming Home had produced his best ability he would have been one of the best horses I'd had. But he was a playboy. He didn't really concentrate. He certainly had plenty of ability. He proved that when he went to the USA. He was one of the best in America later. He got better with age.'

Storming Home, by Machiavellian out of Try To Catch Me and owned by Maktoum Al Maktoum, won the Blue Riband Derby Trial Stakes at Epsom in April 2001. He did not look comfortable coming down the hill to Tattenham Corner and still won by four lengths. But that year Barry was spoiled for choice after the Classic trials.

Bill Gredley's Chancellor won the Group 3 Classic Trial at Sandown, Dick Bonnycastle's Mr Combustible won the Chester Vase and Khalid Abdullah's Perfect Sunday won the Derby Trial at Lingfield, settling their worries about whether he would cope with the hill at Epsom. Sir Ernest Harrison, chairman of the long-time Derby sponsors Vodafone, had a stake in Chancellor. But even with four strong entries, a quarter of that year's Derby field, Barry was not convinced he had a horse to beat Golan.

Mr Combustible's name, of course, was something of an in-joke.

Barry's affectionate nickname among family and friends is 'Mr Grumpy'. Dick Bonnycastle had wanted to call the horse Mr Grumpy, but that name had already been claimed by someone else and they had to settle for Mr Combustible. Barry said in a Derby preview interview: 'People say I've mellowed but I've not changed very much. I can still be quite stroppy at times.'

Barry was not exactly stroppy about his four intended Derby runners that year but he certainly did not let on which of them he fancied the most, telling reporters: 'They're all entitled to be there and it would be folly to go elsewhere with them. They might all be very good and I'd give anything finally to win this race.' Winning no prizes for political correctness, but in all truth, he added: 'Well, it wouldn't mean very much winning the Italian Derby, would it?'

Barry told one correspondent: 'Because of the wet spring we don't really know the pecking order of my four runners and I'm certainly not going to work them together before the Derby, because there's no prize-money paid out on home work. I've told Michael he isn't coming down here to have a feeler on the gallops so that he can sort out the best one. We'll find that out at Epsom.'

In the event the horse Barry had feared the most in the 2001 Derby, Golan, was beaten into second place by Galileo, with Tobougg third. But Barry's horses filled three of the six prize-money places. Mr Combustible was fourth, Storming Home fifth and Perfect Sunday sixth. Richard Hills, who rode him, afterwards called Mr Combustible 'a proper St Leger horse'. Perfect Sunday didn't handle the camber. Michael said Storming Home could not get out from his stall one draw to pick up the pace: 'I had a lot of horse at the end but it was just a three-furlong sprint. I feel my horse is going to be good.'

Michael was right. Storming Home won the King Edward VII Stakes at Ascot, traditionally a grave for Derby runners, passing six horses once they were in line for home. He then finished fourth in the King George VI and Queen Elizabeth Stakes. On 20 October Storming

Home finally came good as he powered to success in Newmarket's £424,000 Champion Stakes, wearing sheepskin cheekpieces. It was the most high-profile victory yet for a horse in that particular form of headgear and Barry declared: 'The cheekpieces have made this horse run sweeter and he's easier to ride a race on.'

Later in his career Storming Home had an extraordinary near-miss. Then trained in the US by Neil Drysdale, he was coasting home as winner of the Arlington Million, ridden by Gary Stevens, when, 50 yards short of the post, he jinked right and tried to pull himself up. Something about the boarding near the winning post seemed to upset him: he had jammed on the brakes at the same spot when working earlier in the week. Drysdale said the horse was too intelligent for his own good.

Storming Home passed the post still in front before dumping Stevens in the path of oncoming horses. Because he interfered with Kaieteur and Paolini, who dead-heated as third finishers behind Sulamani, Storming Home was disqualified and placed fourth, handing the race to Godolphin's Sulamani. Stevens suffered a collapsed lung and a broken vertebra.

There was booing from the crowd throughout the prize ceremonies, partly because Storming Home had been backed down to favourite and, although Sulamani's 'victory' brought up the century of Group One/Grade One winners for Godolphin, their manager Simon Crisford said: 'We'd have much preferred not to have won in this manner.'

Of Barry's other Derby runners in 2001, Perfect Sunday finished second in the Group One Grand Prix de Saint-Cloud. Mr Combustible, who was sixth in the Irish Derby behind Galileo, won the Geoffrey Freer Stakes at Newbury in August, beating Millenary, the winner of the St Leger the year before. In the final Classic Mr Combustible finished third to Aidan O'Brien's Milan and Demophilos.

In August 2002 Chancellor won the Royal Whip Stakes at the Curragh. It was the first victory at the Irish track for owner Bill Gredley since User Friendly won the 1992 Irish Oaks. He said Chancellor had had colic a fortnight before the Derby and this was the first time he had really seen him looking right.

He added: 'The way he runs would give you heart failure. If he finds himself in front too long he won't do it. He needs a battle.'

Few people in racing would begrudge Barry Hills an Epsom Derby victory. Few results would be more popular, and the quest continues. As he says philosophically: 'There is always next year … That's the good thing: they run it every year.'

The race still excites him as much as ever and he doesn't want to see too much changed. 'These days the course is in much better shape than it was in those days. They don't do as much damage. It is a good test of a thoroughbred, up and down, round bends, that's part of it. It wouldn't seem the same race anywhere else.'

But he reckons the race is less of a test of a horse's temperament than it used to be. 'Now they go down the track 200 yards and canter away. Before, they used to go down, come back, go round that bend and then across the course. It's not anywhere near as pressurised as it used to be. I've never been a fan of parades but you can argue it is part of the test of a horse.'

Barry would like to see the Derby moved back to a Wednesday and made into a national holiday. 'When they took the gypsies away they took away the soul of the place.'

BARRY HILLS'S DERBY RECORD

1971	Meaden	W Carson	00-1	9th
1972	Rheingold	E Johnson	22-1	2nd
	Our Mirage	F Durr	100-1	4th
1973	Natsun	G Lewis	11-1	11th
	Proverb	E Johnson	40-1	17th
1974	Regular Guy	W Pyers	66-1	10th
1975	Royal Manacle	W Carson	16-1	7th
1976	Danestic	E Hide	50-1	9th
1978	Hawaiian Sound	W Shoemaker	25-1	2nd
	Sexton Blake	E Johnson	9-1	15th
1979	Cracaval	W Shoemaker	22-1	8th
	Tap On Wood	S Cauthen	15-2	12th
	Two Of Diamonds	E Johnson	25-1	14th
1980	Saint Jonathon	S Cauthen	33-1	13th
1981	Kind Of Hush	S Cauthen	25-1	16th
1982	Father Rooney	S Cauthen	28-1	13th
1983	The Noble Player	S Cauthen	16-1	11th
1985	Royal Harmony	M Hills	40-1	9th
1987	Sir Harry Lewis	J Reid	66-1	4th
	Water Boatman	B Rouse	150-1	16th
1988	Glacial Storm	M Hills	14-1	2nd
1990	Blue Stag	C Asmussen	8-1	2nd
	Missionary Ridge	M Hills	50-1	10th
1991	Arokat	P Eddery	250-1	12th
1993	Blues Traveller	D Holland	150-1	3rd
1996	Busy Flight	C Asmussen	25-1	18th
	Prince Of My Heart	B Thomson	100-1	19th
1997	The Fly	R Cochrane	12-1	5th
	Musalsal	M Hills	40-1	8th
1998	The Glow-Worm	D Holland	20-1	6th

1999	Through The Rye	M Hills	100-1	16th
2000	Zyz	J Fortune	100-1	9th
2001	Mr Combustible	R Hills	20-1	4th
	Storming Home	M Hills	14-1	5th
	Perfect Sunday	R Hughes	9-2	6th
	Chancellor	T.Quinn	25-1	10th
2003	Dunhill Star	M Hills	50-1	15th
2004	Coming Again	M Hills	80-1	12th

CHAPTER FIVE

An Oaks Hoodoo Too?

The misfortunes of Dibidale
and Durtal

*'About six furlongs out the reins seemed to be getting longer.
I couldn't understand why her head was getting further away.
Then the shock hit me. I was becoming unstable.'*
WILLIE CARSON ON DIBIDALE'S OAKS.

There is a story in US racing circles of an unfortunate punter, Hymie, who has been fired from his job. His wife and children have left him, his house has been reclaimed and he goes to a seaside racetrack with his last fifty dollars. He invests it on the jackpot, sees all his six selections come up and, as he goes to the pay window to collect, a sudden gust of wind seizes his ticket and blows it far out to sea. The raincoat-less unfortunate drags himself back to the car park in the rain to see the tyres of his vehicle let down and the petrol gauge flickering on empty. Sinking to his knees in a puddle, he inquires aloud: 'God, just what have I done to deserve all this?' At which, the story goes, an Almighty head appears in the clouds and a voice thunders: 'I really don't know, Hymie. There's just something about you which pisses me off.'

Barry Hills is the last man on earth to indulge in self-pity but he could be forgiven for assuming that lurking in the chalk of the Epsom Downs there is some malign presence that has it in for Barrington

W. Hills and is determined to deny him success even when he has the raw material trained to the minute to achieve it. To what else can we attribute the ill luck that has not only twice denied Barry a Derby victory by the smallest of margins, but has also cruelly robbed him of the success he should have had in the Oaks, the fillies' equivalent of the great race, with two outstanding prospects. On both occasions he was frustrated not by jockey error, a failure to last the distance or his filly finding herself up against a faster competitor on the day, but by sheer bolt-from-the-heavens misfortune.

In 1974 Barry was training an attractive filly called Dibidale, by Aggressor out of Priddy Maid, for his friend Nick Robinson, who had bought her from Robert Sangster. Robinson, the former *Pacemaker* publisher, says: 'Willie Carson rode her first in a big maiden at Newmarket and finished sixth. I'll never forget the huge grin on his face when he came back. His face told the whole story and Barry and I knew we had something to look forward to.'

For Dibidale's next race Carson was claimed by Bernard van Cutsem, whose stable jockey he then was. With another jockey aboard, the filly, who Barry had thought was unbeatable, was beaten a head. She started her three-year-old career as an odds-on favourite at Haydock with Lester Piggott in the saddle. In a ding-dong finish she was just edged out by the Carson-ridden Scientist. Piggott was dismissive about her future prospects. Barry wasn't. Next time out he ran her in the Cheshire Oaks at Chester. With Carson making the pace on her, Dibidale won easily on the soft ground she needed, and from then on she was his ride.

The next target was the Oaks. Dibidale was the third favourite at 6-1 with Polygamy, also trained in Lambourn by Peter Walwyn, the favourite and Piggott's mount, the Queen's Escorial, the second favourite. But with Dibidale's prospects dependent on soft ground, the weather turned against them in a sunny week. The Epsom ground was firm.

Nick Robinson takes up the story. 'We were at Epsom the day before and Barry said, "I'm afraid the ground is going to be no good and we won't be able to run. Never mind, come up to Haydock. We're staying with Robert (Sangster). I've got a plane and a horse that's going to win." '

Nick's objections that he hadn't even got a toothbrush with him were brushed aside. 'We got in the plane and we never saw a cloud in the sky from Gatwick to Haydock.'

Barry remembers: 'We trundled off to Haydock and Danum duly obliged at 4-1. Robert was stewarding. He won the fifth race with Puritan at 10-1 and then asked us to supper in the stewards' room. We got stuck into the port there and stayed the night with Robert, having a few jars to drown our sorrows over Epsom.'

Trainer and owner were both woken around 4am by the welcome sound of heavy rain lashing at the window panes. Barry says: 'I rang (Epsom trainer) John Sutcliffe because I knew he always got up early and he said it was raining heavily at Epsom and had rained all night.' Sangster came into Robinson's room and told him he had already called the pilot and put him on standby. And then, says Barry, they attended to the essentials. 'When we came down to breakfast we all got on Dibidale ante-post.'

Having taken the 10-1 that Heathorns were offering, the trio flew down to Gatwick in Sangster's plane, not exactly oblivious of the buffeting it was taking but heartened by the amount of rain that was bucketing down. A car met them at Gatwick and Barry asked the driver to go via Tattenham Corner. 'When we got there,' says Robinson, 'he told the driver to stop. He got under the rails, put his heel in, turned round to me and said, "We run." '

There was a different reaction to the weather back in Lambourn, where Dibidale's rival Polygamy had been prepared for the Oaks by Peter Walwyn. When it began raining in the night, Walwyn woke up and said to his wife Virginia (known to all as 'Bonk'): 'Bonk, it's f****** raining. Barry will run that filly of his.' To which Bonk replied: 'What do you want me to do about it? Run up and down the racecourse with an umbrella?' Bonk confirms: 'Peter was a box-walker all that night.'

The ground, it turned out, was the least of Dibidale's problems. For the first half of the race the filly was travelling beautifully. Carson was very happy with her. But then, he says, disaster struck. 'Between the six and five furlong poles I began to think there was something wrong. About six furlongs out the reins seemed to be getting longer. I couldn't understand why her head was getting further away. Then the shock hit me. I was becoming unstable. I felt the saddle move. Only my balance was keeping me there. Here I am, in the Oaks, I look like riding the winner and all the time my saddle is slipping. Any sharp movement and I'm a goner.'

The most crucial thing, Carson thought, was to maintain a good rhythm. He took hold of Dibidale's mane and put his feet right at the end of the stirrups.

'It is dangerous to have your feet in the irons if the saddle does go and coming round Tattenham Corner it took me about half a furlong to get my toes to the edge of the irons. About two furlongs out I got my toes to the edge and jumped forwards. I thought, "God, this is all right." I realised I could still win and started to ride a finish. We finished third and I was quite pleased. It wasn't until I pulled her up that I realised the lead cloth and weights weren't there. The saddle was under her belly but there was no lead cloth, so that was it. She finished third behind Polygamy but she should have won.'

Even the third place, of course, did not count. Fellow jockey Tony Murray helped Carson to pull up but as the relieved jockey slid off Dibidale's back the realisation dawned and he threw his whip down in frustration. When he got back to the weighing room, the clerk of the scales said: 'Weigh in, Carson,' and Willie simply replied: 'What with?' With no lead cloth and weights his filly had to be disqualified.

Up in the stands in Robert Sangster's box, Nick Robinson was numb with shock. 'I didn't realise what was happening at first. Three furlongs out she looked a certain winner. But just as we were taking the lead I saw things flying off. The saddle flew up in the air and ended up under the filly – and that was that.' It wasn't much consolation that as jockey Brian Taylor came in after riding another filly in the race he told Robinson: 'You would have won five lengths.' Carson, says Robinson, was in tears despite his marvellous ride.

Willie and Barry were great friends, making their way at the same time and, with the ground in her favour, the jockey believed Dibidale was unbeatable. The memory is still painful: 'That was in our early days. A Classic, of all the races for that to happen. It was a huge disappointment.'

In public, of course, Barry was unmoved. Carson says: 'There would have been nothing shown at the races but there were tears behind closed doors, I would imagine. In racing we all put brave faces on in public.'

But what caused Dibidale's saddle to slip? How did it happen? Carson says: 'Dibidale was deep-girthed, with a lot of heart room, but she tapered away pretty quickly. They didn't have chamois and slip pads then.'

Barry doesn't believe anyone was to blame. 'She was saddled properly and checked at the start. They couldn't fine me or anything like that. I know what happened. She jumped a path at the top of the hill. In doing so she stretched right out and, as it were, jumped through her girths.' Nevertheless, he says, 'Dibidale was the unluckiest loser of a Classic I have seen. She was a very special filly and there is no doubt she would have won had her saddle not slipped two furlongs out. Perhaps justice was done when she gave me my first Classic winner in the Irish Oaks.'

Peter Walwyn agrees that he was perhaps fortunate to win the Oaks with Polygamy, who was 'only a pony', but reckons he was due some luck because she had lost the 1,000 Guineas to Highclere by just a head. 'It was a case of unlucky in one, lucky in the next.'

As for Barry's consolation for his ill fortune, it had rained hard in Dublin before the rematch with Polygamy. Dibidale was wearing a breastplate to anchor the saddle, as she always did after the Epsom disaster. Barry was telling his friends that she was in the same bracket as Rheingold. When Nick Robinson asked him in the parade ring at the Curragh whether he should back her, Barry replied: 'Back her to win by five lengths.'

The Hills's stayed the night before with Paddy Prendergast and Barry recalls that he had given the same advice over the dinner table to several Irish racing folk. One of them, Brucie Alexander, said he would be getting the hay in the next day and wouldn't be at the races. Then at the Curragh they saw him rushing up and down the bookies' stands getting the prices. 'Thought you were getting the hay in?' Alexander replied: 'If this filly is as good as you say I can pay for hay later.' After the event the Irishman would surely have agreed with Nick Robinson, who says: 'Barry is a very good judge of a horse.'

Willie Carson put Dibidale on to the heels of the leaders round the turn. Two furlongs out he pressed the button and she stormed into the lead, going clear of the field to win by the predicted five lengths. As commentator Peter O'Sullevan told the crowd: 'She's flying in and there's no saddle slipping now.' Timeform called it the most impressive Classic win of the season.

Dibidale went on to win the Yorkshire Oaks, making all the running this time, although she only just scrambled home from Mil's Bomb. She was then aimed at the Prix de l'Arc de Triomphe, where she would almost certainly have got the ground that suited her. But, unlucky as ever, she developed a hairline fracture of a pastern and had to miss the rest of the season.

Worse was to come when she stayed in training as a four-year-old in 1975. First Dibidale ran disappointingly in France, then she played only a minor part as a 33-1 shot in the epic King George that saw

Grundy and Bustino locked together down the Ascot straight in the 'Race of the Century'. Dibidale's last race was the Geoffrey Freer Stakes at Newbury. She was going well and then, Nick Robinson recalls, she suddenly gave a great leap in the air. Clearly she was badly injured, on a different leg to the one that had given trouble before. Willie Carson slipped off her back and when the vet advanced on the filly, gun in hand, he pleaded with him not to shoot her.

He recalls: 'I was pulling her up. I think they could have saved her. But then Frankie Durr on Ravi Tikkoo's JCB hit me up the backside as I was pulling up. She put her weight on the injured leg. Nowadays they might have been able to save her. She would have been a good mare. It was very sad. She was unbeatable when the ground was soft.'

Even then they tried hard to save her. They put Dibidale's leg in a fibreglass cast and took her back to Barry's yard. Operations and anaesthetics followed for three weeks but it was clear the filly was in distress. Finally they resolved that the only decent thing to do was to end her life. When they did so, the full extent of her horrific injury was revealed.

Dibidale's leg was, says Barry, splintered like a box of matches. 'If you had hit an oyster with a ten-pound hammer you would not have found so many pieces.'

Nick Robinson believes Barry always had an especially soft spot for Dibidale. 'He said she was the only horse he knew that could be ridden to a cocktail party, tied up to a tree and after two hours would still be standing there waiting.' Perhaps the best filly Barry ever trained, Dibidale was buried under a grassy slope in the South Bank garden.

During her racing career Robert Sangster, who had sold Dibidale to Robinson as a yearling, took a half-share in the filly, reportedly for a six-figure sum. And it was Sangster who owned another filly with whom Barry had expectations of winning the Oaks: Durtal.

As a two-year-old in 1976 Durtal, a bay filly by Lyphard out of Derna II, showed great promise. Most eye-catching of her three victories from five runs that year was her three-length success in the Cheveley Park Stakes at Newmarket. Lester Piggott, who had eagerly sought the ride on Durtal, jumped off in front and made all. Durtal also won the Rose of Lancaster Stakes so emphatically that her jockey took three furlongs to pull her up. She was second in the Lowther Stakes at York and in the Laurent Perrier Champagne Stakes at Doncaster over seven furlongs.

Aided by the Guinness and an occasional glass of white wine with which 'lower yard' head lad Hughie Heaney used to supplement her diet to keep her relaxed, Durtal had clearly trained on as a three-year-old. She won the Fred Darling Stakes, trouncing Miss Pinkie, and dead-heated for second place in the Poule d'Essai des Pouliches in France. Not surprisingly, after that she started as the heavily backed favourite for the 1977 Oaks. But once again the papers the next morning, celebrating a royal victory at Epsom, were full of dramatic stories of a different kind. Durtal never got to run in the race and several reported that in the preliminaries she nearly killed Piggott.

Durtal was in a highly excitable state, sweating and dancing nervously on her toes as the field paraded before the stands. Then suddenly she took off at a furious pace, oblivious to all signals and urging from her rider. Willie Carson, riding the Queen's Dunfermline for Major Dick Hern, recalls that she was totally beyond Piggott's control as he tried to slow her by pushing her against the rail. As they reached the bend near the paddock, with Piggott fighting desperately to stay on board, the saddle slipped right underneath the filly.

Onlookers recalled how Piggott was dragged, head along the ground, until Durtal suddenly lunged right and smashed through the rails, badly injuring herself. Fortunately for the rider, at that terrifying moment Piggott's foot came free. Contemporary reports said the stirrup leather snapped. But Piggott later insisted that it was actually his stirrup that broke, not the leather – a several thousand to one chance. Mercifully he was left stunned on the turf instead of being hurled through the splintered wood and iron supports. Typically, although he declared himself lucky to be alive, he rode in two races later on the card.

Durtal was given an anaesthetic by the racecourse vet, who stitched up a nasty gash in her near-hind leg. He said: 'Another half-inch and a vein would have been severed. She would have had to be put down.'

Many believed on the day that had Durtal participated in the race she would have won. Intriguingly, Barry told me he did not share that opinion – and that Piggott, ironically, had ruined Durtal's chances before she ever set off for Epsom.

Barry says: 'Durtal was favourite when she was withdrawn after staking herself on the way to post but, though I have never previously said so, she would not have won anyway. Lester had revved her up in a gallop beforehand. He blew her brains out and then had the cheek to get off and declare: "She nearly killed me." She was a million to one from that point.'

Barry's trainer son John was a witness to the gallop and he describes it like this: 'Robert (Sangster) had decided he wanted Lester to ride Durtal in the Oaks. There's a gallop between Faringdon Road and Wantage called Moss Hill. It's got this sharp, left-handed bend. It's like a Derby trial gallop. I don't think Dad ever wanted Lester to ride the filly in the race and the last thing he wanted was for him to come and have a feel before the race but all these things had to happen, so Lester came down to ride this filly work before the Oaks.

'I went up in the car with Lester in front to watch the gallop. When we got up there Dad was on his hack, and the horse was taking a turn and he put Lester up on the filly. I remember him saying, "Now look, this filly is very temperamental and wants to have an easy bit of work. Don't go too fast."

'There were two lead horses. When they started Lester went straight off and shot about ten lengths clear of the others and went up the straight – basically to "have a feel", to make sure that he was on the right one for the Oaks. The shouting and the noise and the howling was incredible. I've heard Dad give some very loud bollockings in my time but he was apoplectic bollocking Lester.

'Lester never said a word. He got off the horse and jumped in the car. You could still hear the old man shouting as we drove away. We were stunned. The driver was stunned. I was stunned. On the back shelf was a box of Romeo y Julietas, great big Havana cigars which in those days Dad used to smoke one after the other. "Any in there?" asked Lester, looking back over his shoulder at me. I wasn't saying a word. So I passed him this box of cigars and he grabbed himself a handful. No-one said a word all the way back into Lambourn. That was the end of that. The outcome was that the filly nearly killed him in the Oaks.'

It wasn't just Barry who was angry with Piggott's selfish behaviour, his staff were too. Former jockey Ray Cochrane, then working in the yard, says the gallop was a massive mistake. 'Durtal was very edgy and the boys had done a great job from the autumn all through the winter to keep her organised and relaxed. She was a very good filly. The one thing she didn't want was somebody getting on and kicking her in the guts just to have a feel of her.'

Another witness to the trial gallop was Lambourn trainer Peter Walwyn. He says: 'I remember that morning. I was on my hack and I saw it all going on from the other side of the road. I remember saying, "God, that's a very odd bit of work." '

Barry's good friend Jimmy Lindley, a top jockey in his day, also recalls Barry asking him one day if he would mind riding a bit of work in which Piggott, notorious for wanting to find out everything about his mount's capacity, was participating. Another long-experienced rider was involved too. 'We lined up and away goes Lester, jumping off ten lengths clear. His filly goes through the wood like a rocket and out the other side. I was supposed to jump in for the last three furlongs but it was all over. By the time she got to me we were walking and we trotted past Barry, who said: "What the f*** is going on?" By then there was no sign of Lester. Finally, when we got back to the house, Barry said, "What happened, Lester?" and he simply muttered, "Them two old f*****s have lost their nerve." '

Barry had the greatest respect for Piggott's race-riding abilities, but he was much less enamoured of his behaviour when coming down to ride work on potential racecourse partners. Of Durtal's infamous gallop, the trainer says: 'He made a complete mess of it. He set off at five-furlong pace and accused everybody else of not trying. They never even got to the end of the gallop.

'Lester would try anything. He'd want to try and find the best horse to ride and if he didn't think it was any good he'd get off it.

'He'd ring up on a Sunday morning. In those days you could pick your rides and then you could stop other horses running. The system's different now. If he decided he wanted to ride one of mine in some race Lester would stop Helen Johnson Houghton or Jeremy Tree or others he rode for from running their horses against it. He farmed it and controlled it. But Lester rode me a lot of winners.'

Durtal ran only once more after the Oaks, trailing in last at Ascot that October and being retired to stud. As Barry puts it: 'She cut herself to ribbons and that was the end of her.'

Whatever had spooked the temperamental filly, Barry was, one way or another, denied his chance of winning the Oaks with Durtal. But he did not lose his sense of perspective, or sportsmanship. Among his papers I came across a letter from Buckingham Palace, thanking him for the letter he wrote to the Queen congratulating her on Dunfermline's success in the race.

CHAPTER SIX

The Man the Bookies Fear

The secrets of Barry's betting success

'You can't make betting horses, you come across them.
All of a sudden you get a horse that improves, goes through the
handicap and goes on to something better. They are the joys of life.'
BARRY HILLS.

The American Blues composer W.C. Handy once wrote: 'While it may well be that "true riches are laid up in heaven" it is sure nice to have a little pocket money on the way there.' Like ninety per cent of the people who go racing, Barry Hills likes a bet, as is only to be expected of the man who founded his training career by winning £60,000 on Frankincense. Unlike the rest of us, however, Barry usually ends the season with a profit. He reasons it this way: 'It's about the only thing left that's tax-free. I've got all these horses and I know more about them than most people. So I have a slight edge. Why not make use of it and earn some pocket money?'

He told *Pacemaker* in 2006: 'I have maybe ten decent bets a year, in handicaps mainly, but it depends on the odds. I like value for money, so I don't back at short odds. Two or three grand would be a reasonable bet for me.'

The first Hills coup as a trainer was one that he and recently retired Newmarket trainer Neville Callaghan still chuckle over. In fact it was only his second winner.

'Neville Callaghan was my assistant. We had an owner called Sam Lee from Lytham St Annes who owned Golden Mean, which won the Royal Hunt Cup, and who liked a bit of a punt. He was a pal of Willie Carson's, that's how I got him, and we bought Taxanitania for him. First time out he ran at Thirsk. Kipper Lynch rode him. He had a nice run and finished twelfth or thirteenth. Kipper said he could have been third and that he wanted further. The day came about six weeks later.

'Neville and I went to Ripon, staying on the way with friends in Derbyshire. The plan was not to get there too early because someone might ask you about the horse and you didn't want to be telling a lie. In those circumstances the best thing is not to be there.

'At that time Neville's great ambition was to have £1,000 on a horse. I was going to back it as well. We went though the turnstiles about twenty-five minutes before the race. Then there was the owner facing us and saying, "If you pinch my price I'll chop your knees off. After I'm on you can do what you like."

'It was pouring with rain and, with Willie Carson up, Taxanitania won three-parts of a length. He was always going to win. I think he was 9-2. Neville got his £1,000 on and I had a decent bet too.'

Carson remembers it well. He had bought two horses off Bernard van Cutsem for £200 and £500 and he went to Sam Lee and offered him the choice of the two. 'I'll have the expensive one,' the owner said. That one was Taxanitania.

'For Barry in his first year Kipper Lynch rode Taxanitania and came back with a thoughtful look and the comment, "He ran okay." So we worked him and when we reckoned he was capable of winning we went to Ripon. The story went about that he wasn't "off". It was a gull and he was 10-1 and it came off at 10-1. We had a few like that.'

Sam Lee complained later to Carson because the £200 horse was Scoria, who went to Colin Crossley with another owner and won the Cesarewitch. But he had had the choice.

Barry can play his cards close to his chest even with good friends like Carson. The former champion jockey recalls with his trademark cackle of amusement: 'I went into the paddock one day at Newbury. Barry had two runners. I was on the favourite and Robert Street was on the other one, an outsider. He looked at me and smiled. "You're on the wrong one. You're on the wrong one." And the other one duly won – at 33-1. You have to laugh, don't you?'

Lester Piggott, too, found himself used as a distraction on one occasion at Sandown when the money was down on a Hills outsider, the grey Royal Pinnacle. Stable rider Bob Street says: 'Those were the good old days. Barry called me down to the office and said: "Don't tell anybody else but you're on the best one." Piggott was on the other. We got down to the start and one of the other jockeys said to Lester, "Who's going to win this?" Lester, whose horse had won at Windsor, I think, said, "That one there," pointing at my horse.'

Royal Pinnacle duly won at 25-1, after opening at 33-1. Not surprisingly, says Bob Street. 'We'd galloped them together and we knew.'

Jimmy Lindley also has a memory of that day. 'Walking down the rhododendron walk Barry said, "You can have a tenner on mine." I said: "Thanks Barry but I only bet in tenners and it's a 6-4 on shot." Barry said: "Not that one, you bloody fool, the other one, with Robert Street on." I put on £20 on the Tote. The horse bolted in. I was just saying thank you afterwards when Lester came by on the defeated favourite. "I hope you put me on," was all he said to Barry.'

Sometimes, though, plans go awry. In the early days Barry ran Sam Lee's Gay Perch in a mile-and-a-half maiden at Pontefract. 'It was just to give it a run, get a race into him. I felt the best way to get beat was to put on a jockey who couldn't ride a winner. I put on a fellow called Dennis Ryan, father of Willie. He f****** won six lengths at 20-1, not off. The owner went bananas. Anyway he then won five races that year. Paul Tulk broke the Newmarket Sefton course track record on him.'

Another one that got away was Trampship. She was in a valuable Ascot handicap at the QEII meeting. Everyone in the yard had backed her heavily ante-post at 10-1 and in the meantime she had landed the Park Hill Stakes at Doncaster.

That success in a Group race had prompted the handicapper to raise her by no less than seventeen pounds, but the conditions of the Ascot race stated that horses were only to be penalised for winning handicaps. So there it was: Trampship was at the top of her form, she was seventeen pounds well in and the money was on at 10-1. By race day she was 6-4 favourite in what would otherwise have been an extremely competitive handicap.

But then nature stepped in. Trampship came heavily into season. When she got down to the start she 'planted', refusing to move. When the stalls handlers put the straps round her bottom, says one observer of the scene, it looked as though she was expecting the stallion next and she would not go anywhere. The handlers were unable to cajole Trampship into the stalls, the race was run without her, and since all the money was on ante-post the bets were lost.

*

In those early days there was a sense of fun about training and betting that Barry feels is missing today. Bob Street remains a highly valued work rider at Faringdon Place and, with jockeys barred from gambling, Barry was much amused by Street's response to a *Racing Post* profiler who asked him if he was a profitable punter. 'Yes, over the years I've been in front,' said Bob.

'This was in 2004,' Barry says. 'He had his last riding licence in 2000. It's like the fellow who went up to Scobie Breasley's wife, complimenting her on a winner he trained and suggesting he must have done well backing it too. "Oh no," she said, "Scobie hasn't had a bet since he stopped riding."

'That's what racing is lacking these days. The sheer fun. You can't police it too heavily. They go overboard if anybody tells someone a bloody winner. To tell them a loser, that's wrong . . .

'I've always liked the lads to be punters. They work harder. They get more interested in what's going on, in looking for success. They need to get some money, don't they? What's the matter with tipping a winner if someone puts a tenner on for them? Plenty of people used to put me a score on, like Lord Wigg or Sir Randle Feilden. Phil Bull used to talk about "betting as the pursuit of pleasure". Racing should be about pleasure, it's a fascinating, intriguing business.'

Not all of Barry's bets, of course, were on little races. 'I had £8,000 with Ladbrokes on Rheingold before he won the Prix de l'Arc de Triomphe, about ten days before the race. He did a bloody good gallop. Piggott came down and rode him. It was one of the times when it did go right when he came down to ride work. Normally when he came down it went wrong.'

The only other time Barry backed Rheingold before the Arc, he once said, was when he ran in a maiden at Newcastle. Rheingold started at 13-8 but Barry had sent one of the lads round the Silver Ring with £50. 'He got 7-1 and 6-1 and came back with bundles of readies.'

Barry admits he gets enormous pleasure out of having a successful bet. But he warns: 'You can't make betting horses, you come across them. All of a sudden you get a horse that improves, goes through the handicap and goes on to something better. They are the joys of life, the Duboffs of this world – she won nine of her ten races in 1974.

'Indian Trail was one of my favourite horses. He is the only horse since Frankincense that I knew exactly where he was.'

Indian Trail, who won a series of handicaps, was a source of considerable profit for Barry and his great chum Robert Sangster, who also loved a tilt at the ring. With Steve Cauthen aboard, the Sangster-owned Indian Trail won a massive gamble in the Extel Handicap at Goodwood in July 1981. It was the third time he had hit the bookies in a big way and one pressman recorded that day that he had been approached by the amiable Malcolm Palmer of Corals, who was visibly shaking as he inquired: 'Did Barry Hills say where the horse was going next?'

Sangster, says Barry, went off one day to Thirsk when Indian Trail was running. 'For some reason the horse started to sweat and he didn't like the look of him, so he didn't back him. From then on when the horse ran we took particular notice of whether he was sweating. We took him to Newmarket in the July meeting and Robert had about four men lined up from the paddock so that when he put a sign up, having satisfied himself that the horse wasn't sweating, it was like a chain link that went all the way down to the ring. There was an army of people standing about two strides off the bookmakers and when they got the signal they were to go in to each individual. Of course, when the bookmakers started laying off all the price had gone.

'Robert had a £2,000 double that day with a horse called End Of The Line, owned by Dick Bonnycastle, which won the July Stakes, and he won a lot of money. I think it was Fred Binns who never paid him. After the last we were all drinking champagne and I was short of cash, I hadn't got any readies. But I'd got plenty of credit with Colin Webster, the on-course bookmaker, so I went to go and get a few quid off Webster to pay for the champagne and he said, "Why don't you f*** off." '

Ebor winners Further Flight (1990) and Sanmartino (1995), Cambridgeshire winner Risen Moon (1990) and Goodwood Golden Mile winner Strike Force (1988) were other hugely successful gambles. Barry still has the confirmation slip from Victor Chandler on which he laid him £20,000 to £1,400 against Sanmartino.

Sanmartino, who started at 8-1 and was ridden by Willie Carson, won the Ebor Handicap as part of a 30-1 Hills treble on the day. He beat Midyan Blue by a short head. The contemporary reports said: 'Hills, who won the Ebor five years ago with Further Flight, had the smile of a man who has just netted £35,000 from the layers. He revealed: "I backed Sanmartino at 16-1 and again at 14-1 and first approached Willie about the ride three weeks ago." '

Further Flight's win is described by Barry as 'one of the biggest gambles I had apart from Frankincense', adding: 'The horse would have won the Melbourne Cup if he'd gone that year.'

It was the old firm of Hills and Sangster who brought off what some layers said was then one of the biggest touches since the Second World War with Strike Force, the 8-1 winner in 1988 of the £75,000 Schweppes Golden Mile, then the richest handicap in Europe, from Foreign Survivor and Hoy. He was ridden by Michael Hills.

'I've had a nice little touch,' said Hills at the time, 'and I got 25-1, which makes it all the sweeter. There's no mystery about it. Strike Force is an improving three-year-old who had won well at York last time out.' Sangster told the Press: 'My sons nicked all the long prices but I certainly got involved in the action as well.'

Geoff Lester reported in *The Sporting Life*: 'Sangster said: "I rang up William Hill's from my car phone and asked for £2,000 for myself at 25-1, £2,000 for my wife and £1,000 for Barry. They came back and told me that my wife and I had the bet but that Barry would have to be content with £500." With a wry grin, Sangster added: "It's a case of the working man losing out." '

Barry complained to William Hill's and still has a copy of a rather sniffy letter from the bookmakers' Len Cowburn, which offers an illuminating insight into bookmaking practices. Cowburn concedes: 'In view of the fact that the race was an extremely competitive handicap I feel that you should have been laid your bet in full.' But after an apology, he adds: 'This is a commercial operation and the management make their decisions based on their knowledge of the client, his type of bet and how often he favours us with his business. In your case I believe that the person responsible was influenced by the fact that the last bet you placed with this office was on Bold Citadel. I feel sure Barry that, as a businessman, you realise that I cannot give you or any other client a guarantee that in future you will be laid your bet in full. This particularly applies when a price is requested.'

Barry's reply stated: 'I do not bet every time I go racing and I haven't had an ante-post bet since Bold Citadel (a Newmarket winner) ran in the spring, so there is nothing odd in that. I too run a commercial operation and enjoy a bet from time to time. But I don't intend over a long period to be giving my life savings away to bookmakers.'

Barry says that, with Robert Sangster away in Australia, he had £5,000 on Bold Citadel without his patron knowing. But Risen Moon's victory in the Cambridgeshire was a truly bold stroke for both of the deadly duo. Barry says: 'We backed him to win the Cambridgeshire with Steve Cauthen riding him. About ten days before the race somebody offered a very big price for him and we sold him. The vet came and "spun" the horse and said he had a cracked cannonbone, a hairline fracture of the cannonbone. I rang Robert up and I said, "This horse has failed the vet. If you'll take my advice you'll have another thousand on it." I had another thousand on it. I don't know what he had on.'

Risen Moon was backed down to 7-1 favourite and it did not worry Barry that the previous twenty-one favourites in the race had all been beaten. He had £1,000 on Risen Moon at 16-1 and then another £1,000 at 8-1 the day before the race. It was one of those occasions, he believed, when everything had fallen into place.

Risen Moon was weak as a youngster and hadn't shown his form as a two-year-old. In August of his three-year-old season, when the stable had fancied him for the Bradford and Bingley at York, he ran too freely. But he had got himself well handicapped. 'After that I got Pat Eddery to hold him up at Doncaster and he flew home. From that moment he was a good thing in the Cambridgeshire, providing he stayed.'

The 7-1 chance looked to be well out of it halfway through the Cambridgeshire, with Steve Cauthen right at the back and seemingly trapped behind a wall of horses. Many punters must have assumed that another Cambridgeshire favourite was doomed but Barry was not worried.

He explained afterwards: 'Risen Moon needs to be behind for as long as possible so I didn't start shouting until two out. Steve rode him perfectly and I was never worried.' The favourite threaded his way through his 39 rivals, passed the northern challenger Mellottie and won by a length and a half going away, in the process giving Barry his 100th winner of the season. Cauthen said it was difficult finding a way through with horses being blown around in the high wind but his mount had picked up well. 'It's nice to win a good race for a good friend.'

Sangster used to rave about Risen Moon's victory as a great training performance. It was hardly surprising. He won £300,000 on the result.

Barry had another couple of thousand on Further Flight to complete the Autumn Double by winning the Cesarewitch, a feat last achieved by Sam Darling in 1925. He came close, running second to Trainglot.

How successful a gambler was Sangster? Barry shrugs with the air of a man who does not want to criticise a friend but who would not have done it his way. 'Because he had quite a lot of horses he would put them together in combinations and the bookmakers would take him on. Because they took him on he lost quite a lot as well.

'Robert loved to gamble. He had a horse one day at Newmarket called Observation Post. He ran in a maiden at the back end, big field of runners. Michael rode him and I said to Michael in the paddock, "If it's close you can just give him a couple," (i.e. a couple of smacks with the stick). Robert said, "Give him six." In other words he'd had six grand on.

'Robert was a big player. He always liked an angle to things, a bit of skulduggery or a bit of fun attached. That's the way it should be. Not bloody boring like a lot that goes on.'

So how successful is Barry as a punter? In the 1990s he used to tell reporters that he reckoned to supplement his training fees by winning £50,000 to £60,000 a year. In April 1996 he told Richard Evans of *The Times* that he had taken £66,000 off the bookmakers the previous season and added: 'I'll try to make it £100,000 this year.'

Barry's comment in an interview with the *Racing Post*'s Alastair Down summed up his attitude: 'At heart this is a game of intrigue and fascination. It is respectable skulduggery – you don't have to cheat with them but the way people run horses perhaps over the wrong trip or at the wrong time is all part of the skill. This shouldn't be a game designed for idiots.'

One to rank with the big handicap gambles was a bet Barry landed at Newbury on 13 June 1996. On course he found that his Fun Galore, entered in the Kingsclere Conditions Stakes, was available at 12-1. Barry admitted to 'having a few quid on'. It turned out later this meant £2,000. Joe Mercer, racing manager for Maktoum Al Maktoum, the owner of Fun Galore, said at the time that the trainer won enough to buy a new car. And Barry doesn't drive utility models.

The trainer's comment was: 'You've got to set one up sometimes.' Pat Eddery was on the stable's other entry Peartree House, which was shorter in the betting and finished fourth, but Barry could argue that he had put the Derby-winning jockey, son Michael, on Fun Galore!

One of the more recent Hills successes with the money seriously down was the victory of Desert Dew in the Esher Cup at Sandown in April 2007. Desert Dew was showing himself to be an improving horse in his homework and Barry knew he had him ready. In the morning Desert Dew was available at 17-1 on Betfair. On the course his price evaporated to 7-1 and in the race, ridden by Michael Hills, he burst clear in the straight to beat Aegean Prince and Zaham. Job done. Barry did not lack for re-stocking funds at that year's Chelsea Flower Show.

Former jockey Brent Thomson says of Barry: 'He could see a nice horse and if that horse showed him enough he would place it in the right race and he would have a bet.' He is convinced Barry had a nice win on one he rode. 'We were heading to Newmarket. There were no mobiles then, only car phones. A mate of mine rang me up and said: "You're riding a horse called Sure Blade. How does he go?" I told him I'd never sat on the horse. He said: "Well, Michael Stoute's got this Green Desert, the best horse he's had for some time." I said, "I'm sorry, I can't help you. I've never seen Sure Blade, I wouldn't know what he looks like." Maybe Barry purposely never let me look at him. In the race he went by Green Desert on the fly and won by about a length and a half. Then he went on to Royal Ascot and won the Coventry. Barry knew what he was doing there all right. I'm sure he'd had a good touch, but he certainly didn't include me.'

What, one wonders, does it feel like in the yard when Barry has a well-backed horse coming up? Does it show? Most say not. Derby-winning trainer Peter Chapple-Hyam, one of Barry's assistants at Manton, says: 'You wouldn't know if he had a fiver or £5,000 on. If you didn't ask you didn't know. He's a very private sort of person. He'd be a very good poker player.'

Bob Street says: 'He doesn't tell you he has backed it. He just says, "Go out and win." I used to ring up and say, "How do you want me to ride this?" and he would say, "Just win." '

Son Richard says: 'He'd more likely tell you afterwards, especially if you got beat on the thing. You'd hear the sharp end of his tongue if he thought it should have won. When you walked in the paddock he wouldn't tell you.'

But it is stable jockey Michael who is most likely to find himself on a fancied Hills runner and he admits that it is the one pressure which can get to him. 'When he's had a bet he will tell me six or seven times before I go out in the paddock how much it means. It can be quite unnerving. A lot of trainers would never mention it. He would want you to know how much it meant.

'The first time round when I got sacked it did hurt, it did matter, because Sangster was doing it and other people were involved and they'd all had their money on. The second time I went back to him I knew how to handle it. He has had some touches and he's pretty good at it. But he doesn't do it that much now. Basically he won't back one unless he really thinks he's getting value for money.'

So what are the B.W. Hills rules for sensible betting? What can the rest of us learn? The first thing is that most of his bets are on his own horses. 'I rarely back other people's horses. Sometimes I feel I don't know enough about my own.

'You can't win backing bad horses because most bad horses have a problem – they bleed or they won't do it or they need blinkers. You're far better off backing one good horse against other good horses than a bad one against other bad horses.' Also, he says, it is easier to make money in the second half of the season when there is more form in the book.

Any other golden rules? 'Never bet odds-on. If you could buy money they would sell it at a shop down the road. Never back each-way. And don't be frightened of a long price – the longer the odds the more you should have on.'

An intriguing Hills theory was outlined one day to J.A. McGrath, who noted in *The Daily Telegraph* that Barry reckoned he could spot future winners by watching horses after the finishing line as they began to pull up, instancing that The Glow-Worm had been upsides High-Rise fifty yards beyond the winning post in the 1998 Derby. 'You'd be amazed the numbers of winners you can find,' Barry told him.

You can see why Barry gets on with owners who like a gamble, like lucky Tony Shead. He was only ever interested in a good bet if the odds were decent. Like Barry, he says he would not back a 4-7 shot.

'If you do, it's the relief you feel at not losing the £700, not the joy you get in winning £400.'

Tony tells a tale of one winner that Barry might not have backed. At one Epsom Bank Holiday meeting the trainer was elsewhere and it was up to him, he reckoned, to give suitable instructions to the jockey riding his horse. To his surprise, the jockey told him in the parade ring: 'I spoke to Mr Hills on the telephone this morning. He told me you've got a nice horse here but she's only run once and to give her a nice race and get as close as I can.'

The response from the startled owner was: 'What are you talking about? None of the other runners are much good. I fancy her to win. I've backed her and I've put on £25 for you.' The jockey did not waste much time getting his mount into the lead and was never headed. Shead says: 'All he had to mutter as he unsaddled was, "Will you be seeing me later, sir?" It must have been a popular win, too, because I still remember the roaring cheers as they came up the straight.'

The days of the old-fashioned coup, Barry suggests, have largely gone. 'It's different now because horses have to run on their merits. You've got to find one who's improving fast.' His betting winnings these days are down to about £15,000 a year, although he did have that good touch in Desert Dew's Esher Cup.

As a man of strong views, Barry certainly has some on the betting industry too. He doesn't like the exchanges. 'I'm very much against Betfair. I think it is terrible to lay horses to lose. The Levy should be based on turnover, not on the bookmakers' profit. Bookmakers will cheat on it. They've always been classed as the enemy.'

Barry's main complaint is that, while punters are better informed than ever, it is harder for them to back winners for one simple reason. As his friend Phil Bull, the Timeform founder, used to argue, the going is the most crucial factor, yet 'the officials responsible for watering racecourses do whatever they like. As a result punters never know what the ground is going to be and for that reason they're doing their money and bookmaker profits are soaring.

'Years ago you'd be able to whittle down a race to four runners with a serious chance. That's no longer the case because we're all in the dark over the state of the going. So many odds-on shots are getting beaten due to the ground.'

Interestingly, one big victory that looked like a Barry Hills betting coup wasn't. Not for him, anyway. Having launched his career with Frankincense's Lincoln Handicap victory, he was thought by many to have landed another touch when 35 years later Barry won the 2003 Lincoln with Pablo in the gold and black checks of Yorkshire owner Guy Reed, with Michael Hills riding. But, although the horse was backed down from 9-1 to 5-1 favourite on the day, it was not with Barry's money.

Barry didn't back him because Pablo was not certain to run until the last few days. He reckoned him an improving horse who would go up to Listed class and had thought at the back end of 2002 that he might be a Lincoln horse. But there was not a laid-out plan. He was not trained especially for the race. 'I've done what I thought I'd do with him,' said Barry. 'I've got him fit and he's come to himself.' Guy Reed, who later fell out with Barry over horse sales commissions, had, however, backed his horse for the Lincoln at 33-1 'with a run'.

Gambling for Barry Hills is an added element in his profit-making. So it remains an activity largely confined to horses, almost always his own. Playing cards does not attract him. 'I was never really interested. If I play cards I do it in a casino, not with friends. If you play with friends and you are losing you never want to back off and if you are winning you can't back off.'

But every man, it seems, has his weakness. Barry does not play golf any more and that may be a good thing. Says his friend Bobby McAlpine: 'Barry is a good loser on the racecourse but he was a terrible loser on the golf course.'

"FRANKINCENSE"

Turf Pictures

Lincoln Handicap, 1968.

Wallis, Photographers
Doncaster.

Frankincense wins the 1968 Lincoln and lands a hefty gamble

Apprentice jockey B.W. Hills riding Yes Tor to victory on Cesarewitch day 1954

Barry's mother Phyllis and father Bill lead in one of Bill Hill's winners at Northolt Park

Barry as a schoolboy: he had other priorities

The always immaculate young trainer in early days at South Bank

Barry Hills with Lester Piggott at Longchamp. To the left is the film mogul owner Nat Cohen with a lady friend. Unsaddling Our Mirage is assistant trainer Duncan Sasse and behind Barry is jockey Sanday Barclay

The multiple winner Duboff with Willie Carson aboard is led in after another victory. With Barry are owners Sir William Pigott-Brown and Mrs Charles Radclyffe

*One of the closest-ever. Roberto wins the 1972
Derby by a nose from Rheingold*

*Lester Piggott rides Rheingold to victory in
the Prix de l'Arc de Triomphe in 1973*

*Dibidale (second from left) in the 1974 Oaks: Willie Carson clearly without any means of support
(Gerry Cranham)*

Willie Shoemaker on Hawaiian Sound is narrowly beaten in the 1978 Derby

Glacial Storm: runner up in the green and blue Sangster colours to Kahyasi in 1988 Derby (Pascal Rondeau)

Blue Stag runs second in the 1990 Derby (George Selwyn)

Bobby McAlpine's Cormorant Wood is led in the winner of the Champion Stakes at Newmarket in October 1985 (Gerry Cranham)

Royal Ascot 1985, Gildoran (second left) wins one of his two Gold Cups, Brent Thomson aboard (Mark Cranham)

Tap On Wood wins the 2,000 Guineas in 1979, Steve Cauthen's first British Classic
(George Selwyn)

Sure Blade (Brent Thomson) takes the St James's Palace Stakes at Royal Ascot in 1986
(Mark Cranham)

The founder of a dynasty:
Barry with his five sons
Richard, George, Michael
Charlie and John

The main yard at
Manton, a very
special place (Gerry
Cranham)

Barry Hills wins a
Derby – with John Reid
up Sir Harry Lewis takes
the Irish Derby at the
Curragh in 1987 (Mark
Cranham)

CHAPTER SEVEN

Further Flight's Famous Five-timer

*'He is so game, so courageous. He is just a pleasure to ride. He
sticks his old neck out and always gives me 120 per cent – I've won
so many photo-finishes on him. He's by far my favourite horse.'*
MICHAEL HILLS ON FURTHER FLIGHT.

If ever there was a horse who was special to the Hills family, it was
Further Flight, a grey by Pharly out of Flying Nelly, who ran in
the apple green, with black sleeves, of Simon Wingfield Digby. They
didn't just love him because Barry brought off a few good touches
with him. Further Flight was one of the most durable, consistent and
courageous staying handicappers seen on British tracks in the post-
war years, going on racing on the Flat to an age when even many
jumpers have retired. He won races in ten consecutive seasons.

Being a grey, he was one of the most identifiable characters on the
racecourse, and Barry's team say he was an absolute gem at home,
more like a friendly old Labrador curled up on a mat in front of the
fire than the high-mettled racehorse he was on the track.

Snowy Outen, head lad throughout the grey's time in the yard, says:
'He was a gent. If you had put the brush in his mouth he would have
groomed himself. If you had opened the stable door and said, "Go
to Newmarket", he'd have gone. There was only one Further Flight.
Every time when I went in he'd be looking out of his door with his
ears pricked.'

Sheena Grierson, Barry's former joint head lad, used to say: 'The only time you get any trouble with him is when his brothers, Busy Flight and The Fly, are around. For some reason he doesn't get on with them.' Travelling head lad Ian 'Scan' Willder says the horse 'knew his job so well'.

Although Further Flight won a couple of early races in the hands of Pat Eddery and Willie Carson, his regular pilot and deepest admirer was Michael Hills. After the pair won their fourth consecutive Jockey Club Cup together at Newmarket on 1 October 1994, Michael put into words how he felt about the gelding whom race crowds had come to adore. 'I love him so much and I don't think we'll ever find another one like him. He's not a horse with sheer natural ability or who shows a tremendous turn of foot, though he does have a turn of foot over two miles. But what he's got is that he is so game, so courageous. He is just a pleasure to ride. He sticks his old neck out and always gives me 120 per cent – I've won so many photo-finishes on him. He's by far my most favourite horse.'

*

Further Flight made his racing debut at Chepstow on 17 October 1988 in the Whitsbury Manor Graduation Stakes over seven furlongs. The ground was soft, which did not suit him, and with Michael Hills aboard he finished unplaced. His seventieth and last race came ten years later at Newmarket, in the NGK Stubbs Rated Handicap on 30 October 1998, when he was again ridden by Michael, as he was in sixty-four of his contests. In between Further Flight won twenty-four times and was placed on another fourteen occasions, collecting over £510,000 in prize-money. His record included five consecutive Jockey Club Cups, making him the only horse ever to win the same Pattern race that many times.

After his single run at two, Further Flight was gelded. In 1989, as a three-year-old, he had four runs, at Newbury, Epsom, Ayr and

Windsor. On the first run, in April, Bob Street was instructed to try to beat a couple home in a big field. About ten days later, says Barry, he rang up Simon Wingfield Digby to say he wanted to run the horse at Epsom in another maiden and had engaged Greville Starkey to ride. 'If I were you I wouldn't bother to come, if you see what I mean,' Barry remembers telling the owner. 'The job will be completed, I think, if he finishes ninth.'

Further Flight, running off a mark of only 56, opened his winning account at Ayr on 7 August, in the ten-furlong Oronsay Handicap for horses rated 0-70. He was soon to dwarf the £2,742 earnings for that success and it was his four-year-old career in 1990 that demonstrated Further Flight's quality.

He made his seasonal debut at Bath in May, picking up a prize of £3,218 for winning the 0-80 Empire Handicap over 1m3f in Pat Eddery's hands. Then came victory with Willie Carson nine days later in Chester's 1m4f Eaton Handicap. On firm going at Royal Ascot, with Gary Carter riding, Further Flight was out of the money in the Bessborough Handicap. Then, reunited with Michael Hills, he was second in a 1m4f handicap at Haydock in July.

After that came the start of a glittering list of successes. Ten days later, back at Ayr and stepped up in distance to 1m7f for the first time on good to soft going, Further Flight won the Tennent Trophy and the £15,400 prize that went with it. The gutsy grey turned Scotland's oldest sponsored race into a procession. Initially tucked in behind by Michael, Further Flight moved up at the three-furlong marker, collared the leader and went away to win by four lengths, proving Barry with his fiftieth winner of the season.

It was about this time in 1990, Barry recalls, that Pat, the lad who looked after Further Flight, noticed one morning at Manton that a beautiful rainbow had appeared. 'He said, "Where there's a rainbow, there's a pot of gold," and I said to him, "Don't worry about the rainbow, you're sitting on a pot of gold, you fool." '

How right he was. A month later in 1990 Further Flight won what is always one of the season's most hotly contested prizes, the Ebor Handicap at York over 1m6f, triumphing with his usual rider at 7-1. Barry declared after Further Flight had added £69,893 to his winnings: 'I thought he had a right chance and had two grand on him, though I wasn't greedy and didn't get the fancy prices his owner had.' Wryly, he pointed out that he hadn't won enough to be able to buy the Manton stable he was then struggling to find the money to purchase from Robert Sangster.

Pacemaker reported: 'The crowd gave Michael Hills a huge cheer as he was led into the winner's enclosure and the glint in his father's eye was as much a sign of parental pride as an acknowledgment that a nice touch had been landed.'

Commentators were swift to point out that the jockey's Ebor victory, his biggest up to then in a handicap, was one in the eye for the owners in the Hills yard who had pressured Barry into dispensing with Michael's services as stable jockey. Certainly there had been no sign of nerves as Michael took Further Flight into the lead two furlongs out and held off the fast-finishing Bean King at the death by one and a half lengths.

John Garnsey's story in the *Daily Express* was headed 'Sacked Hills answers critics with Ebor win' and the reporter declared: 'How Michael Hills must have wished yesterday's victory with Further Flight in the Ebor Handicap could have happened several months earlier. Then the much-publicised split which cost him his job as first jockey to his trainer-father Barry might never have taken place.

'Amid a throng of well-wishers in York's packed winner's enclosure father and son congratulated each other as if there had never been any strain between them.'

Barry says now that Further Flight had beaten better horses in other races the year he won the Ebor. 'He could have gone to Australia and won the Melbourne Cup that year.'

Further Flight's final race of that 1990 season was the 2m2f

Cesarewitch at Newmarket on 20 October, the last big handicap of the year. He was strongly backed, partly because Barry had already won the Cambridgeshire, the other half of the Autumn Double, landing a hefty gamble for Robert Sangster and himself in the process, with the Steve Cauthen-ridden Risen Moon.

In the Cesarewitch Further Flight, carrying 9st 1lb, was beaten only by Trainglot, carrying just 7st 12lb, trained by Jimmy FitzGerald and ridden by Willie Carson. Perhaps if he had been partnered by the trainer's son who knew him so well, Further Flight would have brought it off. But on this occasion he had a different pilot. Barry says: 'Steve Cauthen rode him and I'd given him far too much confidence that he could go on when he liked. He went far too soon. Further Flight didn't get home. He didn't truly get two and a quarter miles, that's the answer to it. I thought he was a certainty that day. I'm certain I was to blame for giving him too much confidence.'

Did he back him? 'I had a fair bit on him.'

*

In 1991 Further Flight had a busy and highly successful season, running in eight races and winning five of them as he graduated to Pattern events.

The victories started with his opening race of the season, the Yorkshire Television Handicap at York in May, in which he scored an easy victory under 10st, and ended with the St Simon Stakes at Newbury at the end of October. In between came an unplaced effort in the Prix Gladiateur at Longchamp and a second in Deauville's Prix Kergorlay. In that race Further Flight was actually first past the post, beating Turgeon by a head in a rough race, but the French stewards reversed the placings.

By now an established favourite with the crowds, Further Flight also took his second successive Tennent Trophy at Ayr. But his most lucrative victory that year, and his first acquisition of black type, was his success in the Group Three Goodwood Cup over two miles, which netted his connections another £37,994.

Barry had regretted the reduction in distance for the Group Three race from 2m2f to 2m but it still took a rugged stayer to win the contest after Khalid Abdullah's pair Play Games and Silver Rainbow had set a fast early pace.

Michael Hills was able to track Pat Eddery on Great Marquess and press the button for a surge from the grey at the right stage. Sadly the 7lb penalty he acquired for that success ruled Further Flight out of the Ebor, which was why Barry then tried him in the French races. He was also at that stage planning a later hurdling career.

The trainer said: 'Racing should be fun and I get a great kick out of the winter game too. I'd like to think that Further Flight could win the Supreme Novices' Hurdle next March and return to Cheltenham a year later for the Champion. I've had more pleasure out of Nomadic Way running second in two Champion Hurdles than out of many other things in life.'

The 1991 season also saw Further Flight win for the first time in Newmarket's Jockey Club Cup, the race he was to make his own, before he concluded the year with victory in the St Simon Stakes.

*

The hurdling career never took off but Further Flight was back on the Sussex Downs the next year, 1992, to become the first horse since Le Moss in 1980 to win the Goodwood Cup two years in a row. This year he also joined The Hero, Brown Jack and Isonomy as the only three horses to have won the three stayers' 'classics': the Goodwood Cup, the Doncaster Cup and the Ebor.

In his Goodwood victory Further Flight clipped a second and a half off the course record, even though most of Barry's horses had been suffering with a virus at the time. Further Flight's 1992 season had begun with unplaced runs in the Yorkshire Cup and the Curragh Cup. When the grey ran in Ireland he could hardly raise a leg as much as seven furlongs out. But Barry had ridden him the week before Goodwood and reckoned him ready to do himself justice, if perhaps short of a gallop. Entering the Goodwood race, Further Flight was 7lb or 8lb above his usual racing weight and he was last turning for home but in a battling finish Michael Hills got him up in the last few strides. At that point in his career Further Flight had won nearly £250,000 after starting his career in a 0-70 handicap at Ayr.

Further Flight went on to take the Listed Lonsdale Stakes at York and then there was rematch with Witness Box, whom he had beaten by a short head at Goodwood, in the Doncaster Cup The distance was two furlongs further than at Goodwood, but Further Flight was two pounds better off and the result was exactly the same: he beat Witness Box by a short head. The third horse, Hieroglyphic, was eight lengths behind. Further Flight came through on the bridle and forced victory on the line, with Michael Hills paying tribute to Steve Cauthen on the runner-up. Another course record, it was Further Flight's 13th victory from 25 runs and took his total winnings to nearly £300,000.

After those three victories in a row, it was back to Newmarket for another attempt at the two-mile Jockey Club Cup on 3 October. A popular favourite, Further Flight won again, at 4-6, from his stable companion Supreme Choice.

*

In 1993 the grey's season took a slightly different shape. It began with his trainer dropping him back to 1m5f for the Ormonde Stakes at Chester, in which he was fourth. He then ran unplaced in the 2m Henry II Stakes at Sandown and the 2m4f Ascot Gold Cup. In August he was back on more familiar territory, once again taking the £12,000 first prize in the Lonsdale Stakes at York.

After the race, in which Further Flight went on two out under Michael Hills and stayed on strongly to beat Silverdale, his trainer confessed that he might have got it wrong by not running him in a contest carrying five times that prize. 'I think I have run him in the wrong race. Tomorrow's Ebor is not a good race by any means and he would have been running off 9lb less than his best mark. He would have trotted up.'

It was proving a difficult season and Barry said: 'Our horses have been so out of form you start to lose confidence. That was one of the reasons I strayed towards the easier Lonsdale.' He had also feared the ground would be puddingy. Further Flight had missed that year's Goodwood Cup because Michael had told his father he did not feel right on the gallops. 'But he came down on Saturday and sat on him and said he was a different horse.'

After the Lonsdale Further Flight went north again for another Doncaster Cup attempt, this time finishing second, before returning to Newmarket for his third Jockey Club Cup. In what was by his standards a disappointing season, which concluded with a predictably unsuccessful run on soft going at Longchamp in the Prix Royal-Oak, Further Flight once again delivered the goods at Newmarket.

That already put Further Flight into a significant category. The only other horses to have won the same Pattern race three times in a row since the system started in 1971 were Sagaro (Gold Cup) and Sharpo (Nunthorpe Stakes).

*

The 1994 season was an eight-race campaign for the durable Further Flight, who seemed to be enjoying his racing as much as ever but was taking longer to get to his best. Starting with an unplaced run in the

Yorkshire Cup over 1m6f, he then ran unsuccessfully at Sandown, in the Northumberland Plate at Newcastle and in the Goodwood Cup. Two third places followed in his 'regulars', the Lonsdale Stakes and the Doncaster Cup. But the season ended triumphantly once again with two Newmarket victories, the first in the Jockey Club Cup and another in the George Stubbs Rated Stakes, again over two miles.

In the Jockey Club Cup Further Flight was still detached from the leaders with seven furlongs to run but he was travelling well. Three furlongs out Michael Hills began his move and it was clear he would win from a long way out. The crowd sensed it and cheered him on to beat Capias by seven lengths. Even his rider, not one given to displays of emotion on the course, clapped Further Flight into the winner's enclosure.

In the George Stubbs Stakes he showed all his old determination, edging into the lead one furlong out and making it clear there was no way he was going to let the second horse, Tree Of Life, get past him. At the line he had half a length to spare.

*

Further Flight began his 1995 campaign with a victory, in Haydock's Easter Conditions Stakes. He then ran at Ascot, York, Sandown and Doncaster, where he won, before once again contesting the Goodwood Cup, in which he was last of nine. As usual he showed his best form in the autumn, finishing second in the Doncaster Cup before heading for Newmarket on September 30 for his attempt to win an incredible fifth consecutive Jockey Club Cup.

Every eye was on the grey among the good-class field of eight and when their hero began his effort half a mile out the 16,000 crowd, many having made the journey especially to see Further Flight, were already willing him on. As he hit his stride running down into the Dip, every yard of his gallop into the history books was cheered. He responded gamely to Michael's urgings to go clear in the final furlong for a two-and-a-half-length victory over Assessor, with Double Eclipse third.

Travelling head lad 'Scan' Willder travelled Aldaniti to win the 1981 Grand National in his time with Josh Gifford, but he never forgets his days taking Further Flight to the races. That day he was outside the stands. 'There was a head-to-head battle. I could hear the commentator's voice rising and I could see that great big grey head creeping into the frame on the TV sets. I looked at him as he came in and my eyes just filled with tears.'

Five consecutive victories in the same Pattern event. No other horse had achieved anything like it. Nobody made a fortune on Further Flight's five Jockey Club Cup victories, which were achieved at prices of 7-4, 4-6, 2-1, 11-8 and 5-2, but he was one of those horses loved for what he was, not the profit he brought to punters.

When Michael rode the old grey back into the winner's enclosure, both his hands raised skywards, he conducted the crowd into a still greater volume of applause. The two were led round the parade ring in a lap of honour. Barry was in tears as he patted the veteran's neck. 'This is his finest hour,' he declared.

'Racing,' he said, 'is all about characters and he is one of them. Arkle and Desert Orchid were characters you would dream about and this fellow is another.' Having declared that he didn't know what to say, Michael then put it perfectly: 'This is what a racehorse is all about – wanting to win.'

*

Further Flight ran once more in the 1995 season, finishing unplaced in the St Simon Stakes, Newbury. But he had lost none of his enthusiasm and, now almost white, he made a winning reappearance at Nottingham in April 1996 in the Michelozzo Conditions Stakes. Although he failed to win again that year in his four other races, he twice finished third.

In 1997 Further Flight was campaigning as an eleven-year-old. But he was, as assistant trainer Kevin Mooney says, 'the most competitive eleven-year-old in the country' and the veteran ran in eight races. Although he was a fast-finishing fourth in the Ebor, only one of those races brought a victory, his 23rd, when he triumphed in very testing ground in the Listed Chester Rated Stakes on 30 August. That day the ground was officially rated 'soft with heavy patches', which had not always suited him, but on one of his trainer's favourite tracks Further Flight travelled sweetly and had the field well strung out behind him as he won by ten lengths from the useful stayers Kutta and Grey Shot.

The *Sporting Life* report said Grey Shot had set out to make all, while Further Flight was hunted along by Michael Hills, 'tactics that have become the hallmark of the old-stager through the Nineties'.

The report added: 'Further Flight steadily picked off the opposition on the second circuit and a throaty roar rose from the packed stands as it became obvious that nothing short of a landslide would stop him from yet another triumph as he cruised into the lead two furlongs out.'

A beaming Barry declared: 'Further Flight has enjoyed a lovely summer. Nobody has had to do anything to him. He has stayed fit all season and retains enough zest at home to match strides with the five-furlong specialists. Look at him. He is a sight for sore eyes. You get a horse like him once in a lifetime and he is still loving every moment.

Simon Wingfield Digby, by then an 87-year-old confined to a wheelchair and watching at home, declared: 'I was thrilled with the way the old boy broke from the pack ... He's too good not to train ... he has the most wonderful temperament and enjoys his racing. That's his secret.'

In his last race of the year, the Group One Prix Royal-Oak at Longchamp, Further Flight could finish only ninth. But his remarkable consistency was still there. His form figures for the year were 22441339.

Further Flight's final racing season was in 1998. Amazingly he began that too with a victory, once again taking the Michelozzo Conditions Stakes at Nottingham.

There followed races at Chester, Royal Ascot and Newbury (twice) before, fittingly, the old boy completed his career at Newmarket by taking fourth place to Etterby Park in the NGK Stubbs Rated Stakes on 30 October. As Michael Hills rode him into the winner's enclosure for the last time, Barry told the media with tears in his eyes: 'That will definitely be his last appearance. He was changing his legs in the race. You can't go on for ever. We were very lucky to have had a horse like him.'

He explained that Further Flight would be kept in training the next year because he so loved what he was doing but he wouldn't be asked to compete on the track. He would be responsible for leading up the yearlings.

When Simon Wingfield Digby died, Further Flight was given to his trainer. He used to go to Michael in Newmarket for his summer holidays and his long-time partner never wanted to give him back. Eventually Michael took Further Flight home permanently and he lived as a family pet with his jockey's family. Ironically it was Michael's wife Chris whom he seemed to love, rather than his regular rider. 'I could never catch him,' says Michael. 'I don't think he liked men.'

Further Flight, he says, 'was a horse in a lifetime. He was a very strong puller who would race with his head on the ground. But when you put him back into a race he was so aggressive at the end. He would fight back against any horse trying to come by him. He would always find another length. Only a handful ever did that for me.'

Sadly Further Flight did not live to a ripe old age but had to be put down after suffering an injury, aged only fifteen, in 2001.

CHAPTER EIGHT

Manton: The Hopes and the Heartbreak

How Barry rescued Robert Sangster's biggest project but still lost out

'The gardener said to me once: "Mr Hills, if you don't beat this place it will beat you." And I think he was right. It's the sort of place you've got to get up every morning and hit with a stick — you've got to make it work.'

BARRY HILLS ON MANTON

B arry Hills is a 'get on with life' man who puts the focus on the future, not the past. But those close to him acknowledge that if there is one big sadness in his life it is summed up in the six-letter word 'Manton', the magnificent training facility on the Wiltshire Downs. Barry trained there with conspicuous success for four years from 1986 to 1990 but when his patron Robert Sangster decided to put the estate up for sale he was unable to raise the purchase price of more than £10 million and was forced to leave and return to Lambourn.

Sangster had amazed and fascinated the racing world when he appointed the young jumps trainer Michael Dickinson, then only 35, to take over and develop the Manton estate, which had been acquired by his Swettenham Stud from a London property developer in 1984.

'I am a competitor, always have been,' said Sangster, 'and my aim is always to endeavour to be number one. It was with this as my objective that I started my search for a trainer. Michael at his age, with all that he had achieved in such a short National Hunt training career, his boundless enthusiasm and dedication to detail, had to be the man.'

Dickinson had been champion amateur rider at 19 and rode 378 winners over jumps. He was three times National Hunt champion trainer before his mid-thirties. On Boxing Day 1982 the trainer who listed his recreation as 'work' sent out twelve winners across the country. In 1983 he performed the extraordinary feat of training the first five horses home in the Cheltenham Gold Cup won by Bregawn. Every summer he went to Ballydoyle to learn about Flat racing from Vincent O'Brien.

The Manton that Dickinson took over was a place with a deep racing history. The main yard was built in 1870 and Alec Taylor senior trained twelve Classic winners there before his death twenty-four years later. His son, 'Young Alec', known as 'the Wizard of Manton', took over and did even better, with twenty-one Classic triumphs, including the 1917 and 1918 Triple Crown winners Gay Crusader and Gainsborough. He was champion trainer twelve times.

Alec Taylor junior was a strict disciplinarian who discouraged visitors. Lads were locked in at night, their mail was censored and mantraps were scattered on the gallops to discourage local touts from watching the horses work. Following Alec junior's retirement in 1927, his assistant, Joe Lawson, then enjoyed twenty years of similar success, saddling ten Classic winners.

George Todd, who took over Manton in 1947, had only one Classic victory, with Sodium in the 1966 St Leger. But he turned out many brilliant stayers including Trelawny, who twice achieved the Ascot Stakes/Queen Alexandra Stakes double. In all, forty-three Classic winners had been trained at Manton before it was purchased by Sangster.

When Dickinson moved in there was a frantic flurry of activity with a massive building programme initially completed in nine months. Thirty thousand trees were planted and twenty-five miles of barbed wire removed. The new trainer installed a permanent security staff of nine with walkie-talkies and had closed-circuit TV scanning the approaches. Typical of what some would call Dickinson's attention to detail and others would dismiss as obsessive fussing, the feed oats were rolled daily because research had shown they lost five per cent of nutritional value every day after being rolled. Each animal's daily water consumption was automatically monitored. No racing stables had ever seen expenditure like it.

Michael Dickinson took in his first yearlings on 1 July 1985. Sangster declared: 'Michael the Yorkshireman and myself the Lancastrian have created here in the Wiltshire Downs a training establishment which we know to be the most progressive in the world. To me the wonderful thing is that Manton is a privately owned and funded British enterprise from which we are going to challenge the best in the international racing world. I find this exciting in these days of multi-million-pound takeovers and the large foreign investment that is finding its way into British industry.'

Intrigued by his friend's decision and Dickinson's secretiveness about much of the project, Barry Hills hired a helicopter to fly over the complex and take a look. When he told Sangster, who always appreciated style, the millionaire roared with laughter.

'Nothing is guaranteed in this life,' said Sangster in 1985, 'but I do know that everyone concerned with Manton is giving it their best shot and it won't be for want of trying if the Manton horses don't greet the judge.' Sadly, despite the trying, very few of them did. In the first season at what was being described as a £14 million training establishment the prize money won by the Dickinson-trained horses amounted to just £14,000. Of the total of just four victories two came from an older horse brought in to teach the blue-blooded two-year-olds their job. The sequel was inevitable.

On 25 November 1986 the *Racing Post* reported: 'Michael Dickinson has been sacked as private trainer to Robert Sangster. Sangster blames a clash of personalities for the dramatic split. He said in a specially prepared statement from his Isle of Man home: "We do have fundamental differences of opinion which have made things very hard for both of us." '

Sangster told journalists: 'You could say it was a personality clash, an irretrievable breakdown in relations. I love my racing and I enjoy my relationships with my trainers all over the world. When I signed Michael I considered myself lucky to get a genius. But we cannot communicate any more and that takes all the fun out of it. I don't blame Michael for everything. He works very hard and he's got his own ideas. He says he will win seven Derbys and show us all. I hope he does – really I do.'

The face-saving formal statement declared: 'Michael has done a wonderful job in creating such a magnificent training establishment,' and his four-year contract was to be honoured in full.

Sangster said later that the sacking was the hardest decision he had to make in his life. He said that Dickinson, who later proved himself in the United States with Breeders' Cup victories before retiring early to concentrate on track surface development, was trying to run before he could walk. 'If he had just experimented with ten per cent of the horses and treated the rest traditionally that would have been all right. But as it was there were an awful lot of blood tests, an awful lot of measuring horses' strides and a lot of work that quite frankly might have suited eight-year-old geldings but wasn't much good for two-year-old colts."

Dickinson's replacement was Sangster's old friend Barry Hills, a man never far from topping the trainers' list who had won both the 1,000 and 2,000 Guineas and who had secured two Ascot Gold Cups for Sangster with Gildoran.

Sangster's chum and gambling companion Charles Benson made the first approach. Barry says: 'He rang me and said he had something to talk about. We met on a Sunday morning at a motorway junction.

That's how it started. Then we all had lunch the following day or two.'

The deal was clinched by 25 November after a lunch in Scott's restaurant in Mount Street, Mayfair, attended by Sangster, Barry and Penny and Ken Paul, the financial director of Swettenham Stud.

Barry says of his swift acceptance: 'It was difficult in one sense because I owned everything at South Bank. It might have been different if I'd been at Newmarket and hadn't been used to training on downland. But I knew I could do it because I'd trained 1,062 winners at Lambourn. It was the challenge of a lifetime.'

Barry had 130 horses at South Bank. 'I had to study the financial angle carefully with my accountant because my future and the future of my family depended on my decision.

'No trainer could possibly afford such an undertaking on his own and I was only able to accept because Robert Sangster allowed me to lease on very generous terms. When I found my wage bill was £15,000 a week you can understand my worries. Another worry was the enormity of the undertaking. There had been nothing like it in my world before – the place is so vast.'

At the time of Barry's 1987 open day, with part of the proceeds devoted to the Radiotherapy Research Fund at the London Hospital, where he had first been treated for cancer seven years before, the Manton estate covered 2,300 acres, with 500 acres devoted to racing. There were five areas of grass gallops divided into eleven separate gallops, two all-weather shavings gallops, one of nine furlongs and one of six (both with their own automatic sprinkler systems), a one-mile straight 'Derby gallop', rising 150 feet in seven furlongs, a semi-automatic irrigation system for six gallops and six miles of stone dust roads connecting the gallops and for exercising.

The New Astor yard comprised sixty-one boxes, forty-one in conventional European style and twenty within two US-style barns, a veterinary area including weighbridge, solarium and darkroom, two fully irrigated lungeing areas, a horse walker and a one-and-a-half-furlong covered ride.

The Barton yard, originally designed for yearlings, had become a fully integrated racing yard of forty boxes, four external isolation boxes, a veterinary area, feed and storage barns and an indoor school.

The Manton House yard comprised thirty-nine conventional boxes, a museum and a pub. The staff facilities included two hostels, twenty houses, the 'Trelawny Club' with snooker, pool, table tennis and disco, a tennis court, and football and cricket pitches.

To run the enterprise with the Hills's, there were three assistant trainers, three head lads, two travelling head lads, three second head lads, six work riders and fifty-three stable staff. In addition, there were three office staff, four gallopsmen, two maintenance men, a gardener, a farm manager, four tractor drivers, a shepherd and two gamekeepers.

In the official exchanges in late 1986, Sangster declared: 'My lifelong friend Barry Hills has agreed to take over the supervision of the training at Manton. He will start immediately.' Barry responded: 'I am delighted to reinforce my relationship with Robert, but I shall be continuing with my own yard. I intend to move some of my current string to Manton and will be discussing the situation with my owners as soon as possible.'

He added that it was a wonderful opportunity but he was sorry for Michael Dickinson. After touring Manton, Barry said: 'Michael has done a wonderful job. It may have cost a lot of money but none has been wasted. There is a reason for everything that is there.' Later he paid tribute to some of Dickinson's ideas such as the 'American bend' he built on the gallops to help prepare horses to run in the US.

On arriving in Manton, Barry declared he wanted to be champion trainer. 'I have been in the top ten for the past ten years but now I am aiming to be number one.' Had he stayed there long enough, there is every likelihood he would have been.

Barry, who ironically got off the mark at Manton not with a Sangster horse but with his rival Sheikh Mohammed's Accompanist, ridden by Brent Thomson, told the *Sunday Express*: 'If I am ever going to get to the top Manton is my one chance. There is everything I want here.' In a *Sporting Life* profile at the time, he noted, looking around him at the splendours of Manton: 'Not bad when you look back to the days when I ran a three-speed bike, was paid five bob a week and got £25 a year clothing allowance.'

Swiftly he decided it was not feasible to run two yards and his son John Hills took over at South Bank in Lambourn with a licence in his own right. Sangster had wanted Manton to be a private operation for Swettenham Stud, but Barry's owners included Sheikh Mohammed and Khalid Abdullah. By bringing with him from South Bank a number of owners and horses he had a mixture of older horses, handicappers and early two-year-olds to balance the homebreds. Crucially, the sociable Barry also had the energy to drink late into the night with his patron and an understanding of his passion for the betting ring.

Sangster set a new target for Manton. He declared: 'I want at least seventy winners next year and Barry's the man to do it. In fact, he was the first and only man to whom I offered the job once I had parted with Michael.' Barry, who had been sixth in the previous season's trainers' list with fifty-five winners worth £350,000, comfortably beat the target. In the 1987 season he had 101 winners, seventy-three of them for Sangster, worth £468,000.

His three assistants at Manton were George Foster, Peter Chapple-Hyam and Joe Naughton and the bulk of Dickinson's staff stayed on. The gallops were not a problem for the new man. He said: 'Because I have been used to training on the Downs for eighteen years I will have no problems with the gallops here, which are also undulating. If I had come from Newmarket, which is flat, I would have been inclined to over-work the horses.' As for jockeys, Sangster had an arrangement with the American Cash Asmussen to ride any of his horses when free from commitments to his first retainer Vincent O'Brien. Asmussen had a flat at Manton and was supposed to spend two or three nights a week there.

On 27 June 1987 came Barry's first Classic success at Manton when Sir Harry Lewis, who had been fourth to Reference Point in the Epsom equivalent, won the £329,000 Irish Derby at the Curragh. The horses were kept sweating at the start for fifty minutes because of a bomb scare. In muddy conditions jockey John Reid kept Sir Harry Lewis, owned by American Howard Kaskel, in the first three all the way. Just over a furlong and a half out, he sent on the 6-1 chance from Vanvitelli. Ray Cochrane gave chase on Naheez but never looked like catching him. 'The moment I picked him up it was all over,' said Reid.

Barry loved Manton. He says: 'It was a romantic place. It was the best place in the country to train horses. It had everything. I was once there for six weeks and never went off the estate. It is so lovely there is no need to go anywhere else.' But he was a realist too. 'The gardener said to me once: "Mr Hills, if you don't beat this place it will beat you." And I think he was right. It's the sort of place you've got to get up every morning and hit with a stick – you've got to make it work.'

Barry says now: 'I knew my playing field. I knew what I could do and what I couldn't. There was never a cross word about my way of running the place, although on open day Susan Sangster may have been a bit that way …"

There was one unhappiness at Manton, when Sangster and other owners pressured Barry to dispose of his son Michael as stable jockey, a painful decision discussed elsewhere in this book. John Hills says of his father: 'In Manton he found a challenge and a match. He was tremendously successful – 400 winners in four years.'

Not all of them were for Sangster, who had hoped at Manton to have an edge over Arab owners like Khalid Abdullah and the Maktoums. But Barry insists that was not a problem. 'When I was approached it was agreed I should take horses with me. I didn't take them all. I left

John about 20, including some of Robert's. There wasn't much of a battle with the Arab owners then. They and Sangster got on pretty well. He was probably quite keen to get them involved.'

Soon after Barry took over at Manton, world economic circumstances and Sangster's own finances began to deteriorate. Stavros Niarchos, who had joined forces with Sangster as bloodstock prices spiralled, pulled out of their syndicate. Sangster was only sixth in the owners' list in 1988, his worst position since 1980. Ballydoyle was plagued with a virus for two seasons and Sangster, who had pioneered the concept of making big money not from prize-money but from syndicating successful horses as sires, was finding it harder and harder to meet the competition of Arab owners for whom money was no object. Some suggested the drop in sale prices had brought him cash-flow problems, instanced by his sale of a half-share in *Pacemaker* magazine to Michael Smurfit for £1m and of his Swettenham Stud in Cheshire, although Nick Robinson, who owned the other half of *Pacemaker*, says he was the keener of the two on selling.

Reports that he would be putting Manton up for sale were at first debunked. Sangster insisted: 'It is not on the market at the moment.' However, he added, 'Everything is for sale at the right price," and before long he did put Manton on the market, a massive blow to his successful trainer. How did he tell Barry? 'He didn't. He got Bill Gredley, who I was staying with, to tell me. Robert was a shy person and didn't like confrontation. He used to put other people in to bat.'

Faced with the prospect of losing his racing paradise, Barry moved into action with planners, property people and fellow trainers to try to find a way of remaining at Manton.

Among those he sought to bring into play was Sheikh Hamdan, for whom he was training. Barry still has the draft of a letter he sent to Sheikh Hamdan admitting that he was at his wits' end trying to solve the Manton problem and keep his staff together. In the letter he outlined his plans for creating a 'mini Newmarket' by expanding the existing yards and creating new ones, together with two new all-weather gallops.

'Specially selected trainers (those he had in mind included Nicky Henderson, Charlie Nelson and Richard Hannon, "who at the time was being pressed by the people on Salisbury Plain to vacate the gallops")' would have been able to buy the freehold of a good yard along with the right to use the common facilities. The team would have included son John, who says: 'He tried everything possible to get a deal together. We were all going to have a yard.'

In addition, Barry planned a series of 'nursery yards' to be let on a minimum rental basis to young start-up trainers. Part of the project was to be financed by the purchase of additional land on the outskirts of Marlborough that was suitable for residential development, plus a hotel and golf course. Kennet District Council was supporting his application for planning permission.

Could Manton have gone to the Maktoums? Was Hamdan seriously interested? Barry says now: 'He made a bid. Some people have said they were within half a million of doing a deal and that he had put in Colin Hayes (the legendary Australian trainer) to buy it.'

The letter to Sheikh Hamdan included an intriguing 'special offer'. 'Robert, as you know, has been a friend of mine for many years and always will be whether I am training for him or not. When I was discussing Manton with him he indicated that if £11 million were offered he would throw in two Sadler's Wells nominations in 1991.' But the deal was never completed.

The long period of rumours and Press speculation about the future of Manton at times strained the long friendship between the would-be seller and the would-be buyer. In March 1990 reports from the *Observer*'s Richard Baerlein and others that Barry had bid £8 million for the property angered Sangster, who saw it as undermining his asking price. The tycoon, who seems to have been two million out in what he thought was the figure used by Barry, fired off a sarcastic fax to Barry from the Mandarin Hotel in Hong Kong. It read: 'Thanks a million (sorry six million) for your press conference. I could almost hear the various uncalled-for whingeing here in Hong Kong.'

Barry replied: 'I am very sorry if the articles which initially appeared in Sunday's newspapers have caused you embarrassment in any way.' Explaining that Press speculation at the season's start was inevitable, he said: "Richard Baerlein came up with a figure of £8 million, which we both know was not the amount of the offer. No figure had been mentioned to Baerlein when we talked.' Other headlines, said Barry, had 'annoyed me immensely'.

Ending by saying that he had always had Sangster's best interests at heart, Barry showed his own irritation by signing the letter formally 'Barrington'.

Speaking from the Mandarin, Sangster told reporters he was in no hurry to sell. 'Manton is a lovely country estate and I would be quite prepared to run it on that basis with the emphasis on hunting and shooting rather than training horses if the right offer did not come along. I could have a lot of fun with thirty or forty horses in training there instead of all this hassle. I could install a young trainer with my son Ben as assistant.

He described Barry's alleged bid as 'completely uncalled for' and added: 'The asking price is £15m minus ten per cent. I never even considered Barry's bid, but do not want to say any more than that. I do not want to get into a slanging match.'

Charles Benson declared: 'Robert and Barry are old friends. Robert would be delighted to sell to a consortium of trainers headed by Barry but the two offers in January (the second apparently for £9m) were a farce. The fact they have become public and undermined the asking price has put a serious strain on Robert's friendship with Barry.'

The end of the affair came with a formal statement on Robert Sangster's behalf 'to dispel the endless conjecture' and to confirm the estate was back on the open market. Put out by estate agents

James Laing, it announced: 'The two parties who had options on the property have been unable to take these up. Therefore the property will be available from 31 December with vacant possession.' Scratched out on the original draft were two sentences which said, 'Now that it is generally known that the property is NOT under offer, new interest will be generated. As Barry Hills will be leaving at the end of December, Robert Sangster will be making new arrangements for the training yards for next season.'

Barry's disappointment was little veiled in his own press release: 'My attempt in conjunction with others to purchase the Manton House estate has failed, primarily because of the current economic climate and the present state of the bloodstock industry. After exhausting and lengthy discussions I had hoped that Mr Sangster may extend my lease for a period of one year in order to enable both parties to reflect on the situation, but this is not to be and thus I have no alternative but to vacate Manton by the end of this year.

'My ninety-five employees have been told of the position this morning and, like myself, are bitterly disappointed that, after four years and 358 winners, including thirty-two Group wins, at Manton, a happy and successful team will be broken up.

Whether I return to the property I own in Lambourn or to another location has yet to be decided. My options are still open. It is my intention, however, to continue training at the same level as at present.'

Robert Sangster never did succeed in selling the Manton complex at a time which was, said John Hills, 'one of the biggest property slumps in living memory'. Instead it was kept within the family and turned over to Peter Chapple-Hyam on Christmas Eve 1990. He, too, made good use of the fabulous facilities. Within eighteen months he had won the Derby with Dr Devious and the English and Irish 2,000 Guineas with Rodrigo De Triano to silence those who said he had got the job only by marriage to Jane Peacock, Sangster's stepdaughter.

'I know what they were saying," Chapple-Hyam said. 'When I started out a lot of people were waiting for me to fall flat on my face but I didn't take any notice. As they say in Australia, I just let it go through to the keeper.'

Chapple-Hyam rebuilt the stable strength from a low of sixty to 125. But in August 1999, after a slow start to the season, he was dismissed by Sangster, although it was dressed up as being by mutual consent. 'Making these decisions is never easy. However, during the last year or two things haven't gone as Peter and myself would have liked and we both felt a change was in our interests.' After a disappointing spell in Hong Kong, Chapple-Hyam returned to Britain and has re-established himself at the top of his trade, notably with the Derby victory of Authorized in 2007.

When Chapple-Hyam left, the new master of Manton was John Gosden, whose association with Sangster started when he was based in Los Angeles and won the 1984 Breeders' Cup Mile with Royal Heroine. But he, too, has since switched to his own premises in Newmarket and nowadays the advancing Brian Meehan is the man in charge at Manton.

Did Barry see the problem coming at Manton? How close was he to putting together the deal to buy the complex? He says he hadn't really expected Sangster to try to sell off the estate, although he knew he was under a lot of pressure at the time. 'But we did come quite close to getting it. Several people were involved and Robert wanted to keep a quarter of it. It was a lot of money but I had got the necessary planning permission.'

So was he burned by the experience? There you meet the more typically taciturn Hills. 'You win some, you lose some,' he replies. But even with a man who does deadpan as well as Jack Lemmon you can see the pain behind the eyes.

Barry's jockey sons know how he felt. Richard puts it this way: 'Manton was his dream. He had it. He was going to buy it and they snatched it away from him. It really hurt him. He'd have been nearly sixty. To pick himself up and to build what he's built since is unbelievable. I give him a lot of respect for that.'

Michael says: 'He put his heart and soul into it. He never thought he would train at a place like that ... the thought of losing it hurt. I remember them building little copses and him saying, "They'll remember that. Barry Hills built that copse." He wanted to make his mark. He'd changed little things in how the gallops were sorted. He'd say: "I've done that." That's how he wanted to be remembered.

'To train a hundred winners at three different yards – I can't remember anyone else doing it.'

CHAPTER NINE

The Faringdon Place Years

The master builder creates his
own state-of-the-art yard

*'Throughout all his life he's always had to have some scheme to
better himself and his surroundings.'*
WILLIE CARSON ON BARRY HILLS.

The sadness that Barry and Penny felt on leaving Manton was characteristically coupled in Barry's mind with a clear new aim. As they departed, Michael Hills declared: 'Manton needs a trainer like my father to realise its full potential. But he'll bounce back and he'll be twice as hungry. He could train winners from a garage.'

Few doubt that. But Barry had something more than a garage in mind. The property developer Bill Gredley, a long-time owner in the Hills yard, reckons his friend would have made a successful builder. Willie Carson says: 'Throughout all his life he's always had to have some scheme to better himself and his surroundings,' and Barry's new project over the next few years was to create a state-of-the-art training complex in Lambourn, absorbing the lessons of Manton and the rest of his experience. He has spent more than £3 million designing and building his Faringdon Place yard, just along the road from his friend Nicky Henderson at Seven Barrows.

First came a game of planning poker, and most of us would be ill advised to take on Mr Inscrutable with cards in his hands.

As the only Lambourn trainer then with more than 100 horses, Barry simply could not squeeze comfortably back into the precariously sloping South Bank premises, which had been taken over by son John. While he gained some extra capacity by renting John Francome's yard and building a new gallop there, Barry needed to move on.

Francome, the former champion jump jockey and now a TV racing presenter, says he might be training still if Barry had not moved back from Manton when he did. He says Barry's return was a big boost for Lambourn, which could ill afford to lose someone of his stature. 'Everything he does, he does properly. When he came up here there was never any question of cutting corners. Everything he did up here has lasted. Fred Winter was the same: doing it properly is always the cheapest way in the end.'

The coolly irreverent, wisecracking Francome and the traditionalist master trainer, perhaps to the surprise of some, are good friends. One day Francome noticed around forty deer on Barry's gallops as he passed on his way back from Wantage and called in to report them. Instead of sounding pleased at his trouble, Barry barked: 'They're always up there.' Not only that, but Francome learned from Penny the next day that Barry had walked out of the door muttering, 'Does that so-and-so think I never go on those gallops?' The grudging response to an act of friendship merely causes Francome to chuckle, saying: 'You wouldn't want to spend a month with him. He'd drive you mad. But you can't help but admire him, not just in where he's come from but in what he's achieved, having had cancer for twenty years.

'He's always been one for the history books, for tradition. Every time he trains a winner it means something to him. So does having his boys be successful. He expects high standards of others and he expects high standards from himself. He'd have been wonderful in the Army.

'All the trainers here like him. He's straight to the point, there's never any bullshit. If he says he will do something he does it. You can deal with people like that."

Although Barry didn't have much formal schooling, he combines a sharp intelligence with a deep intensity of focus. Jimmy Lindley says: 'He just looks one way. You tell him that Paul Cole or somebody has got a really good two-year-old and he says, "I'm not interested in other people's horses, I've got a hundred of my own." He is just fixed on what he is doing.

'When you think how he has hacked his way in life there are not many with a success story like it. I used to look after Sir Ernest Harrison's horses and I spent a lot of time with them both. Sir Ernest used to say, "If Barry hadn't been a trainer he'd have made a damned good prime minister." Business tycoons like Sir Ernest Harrison and Sir Eric Parker thought the world of Barry. They didn't just respect him for his training skills but would seek his advice on other things too.'

On his return to Lambourn, Barry had some horses at South Bank, some in the Francome yard and some in Eric Wheeler's old yard. He wanted to acquire and develop ten acres along the Faringdon Road (where he already owned another yard close to his private gallops) and to help to fund that he needed planning permission to develop the South Bank yard for housing.

John Hills says: 'When he came back to South Bank he had outgrown it, not just in size but in the conditions he was prepared to train under. Being inside the village, the roads to cross, the traffic to cope with, he had moved forward from there. At that time he had to do what he was going to do with Faringdon Place. If he hadn't got planning permission I think he'd have said, "Bugger it ..." '

Such a development would have been a severe blow to local employment opportunities and, whether or not John's assessment was correct, Barry was certainly happy to plant in the minds of Newbury District Council and the planning authorities the possibility that he would simply up sticks and walk away if he did not win approval for his plans. He told *The Times*' Richard Evans in August 1993 that if the planners refused him he would retire from training. 'I am not going to continue as it is because I am not happy with the situation. Things have not gone right recently with the health of the horses and I want to get them right. I have wonderful gallops and I want to build a yard to cope with the modern needs of racing and to get ahead of the game.'

At that stage Barry was employing fifty-seven staff and had an annual wage bill of over £1 million and, although he had to battle, he secured his planning approval. It wasn't just a matter of 'where' but 'how' to train in a manner appropriate to the then beckoning 21st century. As Barry argued at the time: 'It's hard to make money out of training. It's an expensive business if you don't do it right because you have to employ a lot of people. We are outdated. Our premises are outdated. They all need knocking down and rebuilding closer to the gallops. We should pay lads more and charge owners less, like every other industry in the country. Racing has not adapted.'

Charlie Hills says: 'The facilities were bad at South Bank. We simply haven't got the staff now to take an hour and a half getting to the gallops and back. If you had to do four lots of that we wouldn't have finished until 2pm.'

Admitting that he had been spoilt by the facilities in Wiltshire, Barry set about adding to his set-up initially a pair of Manton-style barns, each housing forty-one horses. 'I want everything under one umbrella where I can control things much more closely myself. We are now moving towards the next century and things have got to be modernised. The day of paying people to take buckets from here to there has gone.

'The Manton bottom barn is pretty well identical to the ones I'm building. Ventilation by louvres will allow us to keep a constant temperature with a temperature gauge inside. I think horses that get stressed can't cope with a rapid change in temperature.'

Who was the architect? I inquired naively one day over lunch. 'I was,' said Barry. But to provide a low-stress environment that protected horses from seasonal extremes, there was consultation with the vet Frank Mahon, horse physio Mary Bromiley and experts from Bristol University's animal husbandry department.

At the time Barry explained to visitors: 'The aim is to get a lot more light to the horses and there will be extra windows in the roof. The extra light gives the horses extra vitamin D – if you get a lot of sunlight you don't feel tired. If it is dark you want to go to sleep.'

There was to be a Polytrack indoor riding school and there were other examples of a long-time practitioner's joined-up thinking, like rubber non-slip floors in the boxes and a rubber 'shelf' to help horses cast in their box to regain their feet. Another of Barry's ideas was 'a lagoon to collect all the rain water off the barn roofs so that I can use a bowser to water my all-weather gallop'. When I asked him recently why no swimming pool was included, the reply was vintage Hills. Insisting that horses don't get as many bad backs as they used to, he declared: 'I put one in at Manton. But they're supposed to run, not swim.'

When work started in 1991, local residents might have assumed it was a new industrial estate going up on the Faringdon Road site rather than the latest Barry Hills winner factory. Some 20,000 cubic metres of subsoil were removed as the trainer swapped his more traditional headgear for a builder's hard hat. 'We dug so much chalk it looked like the white cliffs of Dover. We've turned it into a sort of mini-Down.'

But, while supervising the building work over six months added to the myriad worries of a modern trainer, there was a relish in it. 'This is my chance to get things exactly right, so it will be nobody's fault but my own if it is not.' And not only has Barry got the concept right, unlike many others in racing he seems to have got the finances right too. The Faringdon Place complex, owned by a man who was once pleased to earn £25 a year, is not on any bank's books. 'You have to borrow, don't you? But it's all paid for now.' Willie Carson says: 'He deserves everything he's got. Everybody knows Barry as a worker. He's clever. He's worked for it.'

Barry carries through in the detail. He does immediately the bits others might postpone. As former Lambourn trainer Charlie Nelson says: 'When Barry gets it in his mind for something to happen it doesn't just happen – it happens with landscaping.'

Barry's results since have paid testimony to his careful planning of the new premises, and to his foresight long before in acquiring the extensive gallops between the Faringdon and Wantage Roads. Son John says: 'The Faringdon Road gallop has stood the test of time. It has hardly changed since it was built. I think Dad paid Charlie Nelson £90,000 for it and it was one of his best day's work ever. The word around the village at the time was that Dad had gone off his rocker. He'd paid this ridiculous sum. In fact, it was the cheapest thing he ever bought.'

Nelson, whose father Peter trained Snow Knight to win the Derby and who himself himself trained nineteen Group winners, says: 'It was a very good deal for both of us. It was great for me too because I'd just bought Kingsdown Stables. I needed the money and it enabled me to close that deal.'

As the lists appended at the end of this book confirm, over his career Barry has won a total of 214 Group One, Two and Three races including eleven Classics. Once established, he has been out of the trainers' top ten only once in thirty years.

In the new century, against ever-hotter competition, Barry has continued to churn out winners in both quantity and quality. From 2003 to 2007, for example, the winner totals were 81, 101, 103 and 91. In 2008, when the horses were sick for much of the year and Barry underwent a further series of major operations for throat cancer, the total dropped to 70. It is a mark of his incredible consistency that 2008 was the first year since the Pattern began in 1971 that Barry had failed to send out a Group winner, although even then Captain Marvelous and Royal Confidence won Listed races.

In racing anybody can have a tricky year and the stable's response was to make 2009 one of its best seasons ever, with a Royal Ascot championship, Ghanaati's 1,000 Guineas success and a string of top handicap victories. In 2009 the combined efforts of father Barry and son Charlie and their well-practised team at Faringdon Place took the winners total back up to 88, with prize-money won just short of £2 million at £1,951,093.

Of course, there are other key factors beyond the gallops and the training premises which have contributed to Barry's success. First among those is the support he has had from a remarkable family and the loyal team of long-serving professionals he built up around him. Perhaps the perspective on his achievement is best supplied by the international star who worked with him as stable rider for several years, American champion Steve Cauthen.

'I very much admired Barry for his achievements. In America it's much more easily done. Anyone can set up in a barn at the track. Setting up an operation in Britain is a major business. You have to know and understand that. He is a grafter, he motivates everyone around him. Lots of lads who were around him became good trainers. He would always give somebody the opportunity to get off their butt and work to make something of themselves.'

To confirm that, you have only to look at the the list of those who have spent varying periods of time as pupils or assistants to Barry. They include Ralph Beckett, Michael Blanshard, Neville Callaghan, Peter Chapple-Hyam, Paul D'Arcy, George Foster, Duncan Sasse, Ron Sheather, Tor Sturgis, Mark Usher, Chris Wall, John Warren, Robert Williams and Venetia Williams.

The late Ron Sheather, Barry recalls, was at South Bank for some time. 'Ron knew exactly what the two-year-olds could do. The time he was here as assistant trainer he was always riding the youngsters and if he stopped on one for a week you automatically knew the thing could bloody well run. You couldn't get him off it.'

However brilliant a trainer may be, however, it takes more than genius with horses to succeed. The one-time NATO Secretary General George Robertson once described his job as like trying to push a wheelbarrow full of frogs from Point A to Point B without losing too many in the meantime. Training is much the same. It is a multi-faceted business in which something is always likely to spill out of the barrow, and teamwork is crucial.

Barry's style is not one of gentle restraint. All family members have had to survive the famous bollockings of the man they refer to affectionately as Mr Grumpy. So have others. One jockey who came in to ride work and received a typical Barry roasting for some perceived misdemeanour muttered to the driver of the car ferrying him back to the yard: 'How long have you worked for this cantankerous old bugger?' 'Ever since I married him,' replied Penny Hills.

The staff in racing stables, particularly big yards like Faringdon Place, can be famously transient. But when Barry once asked secretary Debbie Bracewell to work out how long on average their employees stayed, the answer was that they either stay less than six months or more than five years.

Typically, she herself has stayed for sixteen. 'It's because I respect him. He works very very hard. He has achieved so much and sired five brilliant sons. He is very, very hard. You certainly know when you've done wrong, you might not know when you've done well. But he's fair and I respect him.

'He has very high standards. If you've made a mistake once you'll never make that mistake again. He's old school. He's a very respected person. He knows what he wants. You do what he wants and you'll work here many years. If you don't, you'll be out on your ear. "

'Respect' is the word that keeps coming back when you talk to others who have stayed ... and stayed. Kevin Mooney, apart from a few years off riding winners over jumps for Fulke Walwyn, has been with Barry since he was a teenage apprentice and is now in his mid-fifties. Former head lad Snowy Outen started with Barry in 1968 and formally retired in 1994 at the age of seventy. But he has been back in the yard ever since. Travelling head lad Geoff Snook and head groom Steve May have been there forever too.

Top work rider and former jockey Bob Street, who rode more than 100 winners, has worked for only two people in his life: Noel Murless and Barry Hills. He joined the South Bank enterprise in 1974 and is still riding out. Former stable jockey Ernie Johnson still comes back to ride work in his sixties. At Faringdon Place they know the value of experience.

As for those famous bollockings, Peter Chapple-Hyam's recollections are typical: 'Mr Grumpy? Oh God, yes. I think he must have been given a lot of bollockings as a child. He could give a bollocking like nobody could. But ten minutes later he would be your best friend. He didn't ever hold a grudge.'

If some of the assistant trainers were learning on the job, supplying energy and effort in return for their initiation, Barry always made sure that he had experienced hands in the saddle who could help educate his horses. Ex-jockey Ray Cochrane remembers from his time as a stable apprentice: 'So many professional stablemen. They were all very accomplished work riders who knew whether a horse needed a pat on the neck or a slap up the arse or just needed riding properly. If you couldn't learn off them to improve yourself you had no future anyway.'

Working for Barry, he says, was a wonderful grounding for a young rider. 'Even when he had that great all-weather put down on the left of the Faringdon Road we never worked them hard. Everything was done by feel. You didn't need to push the ears off them. Swinging half speed. Swinging half speed. You learned how to ride proper work. Now the feeling is if you're not pushing the lugs off them you're not learning, which is absolutely stupid.'

He recalls the likes of Edward Hide, 'a beautiful jockey', Kipper

Lynch and Ernie Johnson riding out. 'All proper horsemen. Great to ride work with. Some of them today are nightmares, they're just jockeys, they're not horsemen at all.'

It is a team effort. But the most crucial person in Barry's drive to success is his wife Penny – work rider, elegant hostess, mother hen, problem-sorter and supplier at the crucial moments of quiet afterthoughts. The word that so many use instinctively of the woman who has been by Barry's side through a series of crises with throat cancer and then the septicaemia which kept him in hospital for weeks and nearly killed him in in 2009 is that Penny is Barry's 'rock'.

The former Penny Woodhouse, a show jumper who first met Barry in the Leicestershire hunting field, has been with him through the elegant whirl of life with the Robert Sangster crowd and through the long, painful days in hospital. She was with Barry as they built at South Bank, as they prospered at Manton and as they turned a dream project into successful reality at Faringdon Place.

Throughout she has been entrusted with riding some of the best horses in the yard. It is Penny who drives the wives of injured stable lads to see them in hospital. She has entertained the cream of the international racing set as they came to see their horses. She provided a home for Steve Cauthen when the precociously talented American youngster came to Britain. Her happy relationship with John, Richard and Michael has been crucial to family unity. And as the mother of Charles and George, Barry's last two sons, she has set the seal on the Hills dynasty.

In recent years, through Barry's battles with cancer and other medical setbacks, Penny has played an even more essential role beside him. Owner and friend Bill Gredley gives the picture of the man: 'The resilience of the guy is incredible. Never ever have I heard him complain. It almost brings tears to my eyes to think how resilient the guy is. He'll say, "I've got to go to hospital and do this and do that." He just goes in and does it.'

Margaret Spittle, Barry's oncologist, has seen how many cope with the painful treatment to tackle the throat cancers he has suffered. She is amazed by his fortitude and by Barry's insistence, despite the pain and discomfort it must have given him, on wearing a collar and tie to take her and others out to lunch in the middle of his treatment. For Barry there is a right way and a wrong way of doing things, and no such thing as mitigating circumstances.

The racing world has grown used to Barry making light of his afflictions. He has never been one for talking about his travails. But one remark after his two winners at Royal Ascot in 2010 sums up his approach and what he has been through. 'It's nice to be back,' he said. 'Someone asked me what the best part of my day is. I told them: "Waking up in the morning." '

Gredley says: 'He's an extremely intelligent person. The way he deals with life and the way he deals with anything, you'd want him on your side, whether you are sorting out tactics in a tank battle or placing horses, whatever. He gives a lot of thought to everything he does. He's so organised that he comes down to breakfast with his slippers polished and his dressing gown ironed. You feel you should have had the *Racing Post* ironed for him.'

But to be as organised and as brave as that, you need an organiser and a rock beside you. Debbie Bracewell says: 'In the summer of 2008 what he went through was just horrendous. You wouldn't wish that on anyone. When he had that surgery you couldn't help but feel for him. For a man who speaks so much it was awful not being able to do so.

'When he first came out of hospital he put on a brave face and he seems to have adjusted to it. Even when he was in hospital he was a little devil because Mrs Hills is just amazing. She used to go in every day because he still did the entries and declarations from hospital. Obviously he couldn't talk because he had no voicebox. It's quite a long process to get a new one put in. I would ring the details through and Mrs Hills did it all.'

Also, says son George, Barry is not someone who takes easily to being given orders by nurses, and Penny dealt with that too. 'She had to negotiate co-operation. I don't think a trainer can train without a good trainer's wife. Dad is useless on his own even for an hour. I don't think he could be what he is and do what he does without her.'

CHAPTER TEN

Moonax's St Leger

An occasion that defined the words 'mixed feelings'

*'I thought I had the race won and then I could feel this horse
coming. I knew it was probably going to catch me just before the
line. You have that feeling, you're slowing up and it's coming.
When I saw its white face I could not believe it.'*

MICHAEL HILLS ON THE 1994 ST LEGER

In 1994 Barry Hills won the St Leger with Moonax. Behind those ten words lies an extraordinary tale of chances taken and lost, a considerable training feat with a rather less than loveable horse and a maelstrom of emotions which affected most of the racing dynasty Barry has created.

Anyone as competitive as Barry Hills would relish winning the ancient race with a 40-1 outsider. But in doing so Barry snatched away from his trainer son John what had looked to be for most of the race John's first Classic winner, on which another son, Michael, had ridden a courageous and well-planned race. And the irony was that it had been in considerable doubt whether Moonax would run in the race.

Moonax's participation was a matter of sheer instinct. Barry just had a feeling about the race. He had had that same feeling once before, in 1988, when he decided to run Scenic in the Dewhurst Stakes. That resulted in a 33-1 dead-heat shared victory, but only after Barry had 'gone missing' from his office a few minutes before declaration time in case Sheikh Mohammed, who had several better-fancied horses in the Group One event, wanted the colt pulled out.

The year of 1994 had looked like being a breakthrough one for John Hills, a talented trainer who has never quite had his father's ammunition to fire. At Epsom in June, John had serious hopes of an Oaks/Derby double with Wind In Her Hair and Broadway Flyer. But, with what seemed to be the family's ill luck at the Surrey track, Wind In Her Hair finished second to Balanchine in the Oaks and Broadway Flyer ran inexplicably poorly.

In the St Leger, John's luck seemed to have turned. Broadway Flyer was a true stayer with plenty of courage and a brave horse was given a brave ride from the front by John's brother, Michael. A furlong out they looked to have the race at their mercy. Ionio and Double Trigger, who finished third, were in trouble. But still to play his hand was Pat Eddery on Moonax.

Commentator Alastair Down said of Michael's efforts that day: 'This was a ride you could only give to a tough horse. Broadway Flyer never wavered or flinched as Michael Hills did everything he could to maintain momentum, while on the outer Eddery, at his most powerful, forced Moonax to dig deep and fight hard in order to gain the upper hand inside the final unforgiving furlong.'

Told by Barry to 'go out and have a hunt', Eddery had waited at the back. Even as he made progress through the pack Eddery didn't much fancy his chances of catching Broadway Flyer. But under a typically strong Eddery drive, Moonax responded and they forged ahead in the final hundred yards in one of the most exciting finishes to a St Leger.

Michael says: 'I thought I had the race won and then I could feel this horse coming. I knew it was probably going to catch me just before the line. You have that feeling, you're slowing up and it's coming. When I saw its white face I could not believe it . . . I could not believe it.

'I was gutted for me and for John and then pleased because Dad had won another Classic. It was hard to swallow at the time. Dad was great. He didn't really say anything. We all said "well done" and all that and I don't think he knew what to say. He knew how much it meant. He never really commented on it. But the horse did justify itself later.'

By another cruel irony, Michael had ridden Moonax regularly. 'I'd been on it all year. And then I got on Broadway Flyer and they were both being aimed for the Leger. But Moonax wasn't really going to run in the St Leger. In fact, Dad booked me to ride him in the Troy Stakes a fortnight before. But plans changed."

It was only at the previous day's final declaration stage that Barry definitely decided to run Moonax, his first Classic winner for Sheikh Mohammed. The colt was highly regarded at the start of the season but injured himself on a trip to Rome for the Italian Derby.

Barry says: 'Rainbow Heights, my other horse, upset Moonax, who got a hind leg jammed between the stall partitions. He took all the hair off his leg. I got him back to run in the King Edward VII Stakes at Royal Ascot (where he finished fifth to Foyer) but he wasn't at his best. Then he finished almost last in the German Derby. He had a long layoff and people like Mary Bromiley treated him. He only really came back to himself just before the St Leger. It took a lot of perseverance. I had a gut feeling he was coming back to himself. He was entered in two other races the previous day, but I thought I might as well have a go at the big money in the St Leger.'

Before the St Leger Barry had been struggling, sending out thirty-two runners without a winner. One of his best friends, the top jumps trainer Nicky Henderson, says: 'Where Barry is so good is that he weighed up the race absolutely right and wasn't frightened to tell Pat Eddery to go out and ride such an unorthodox waiting race in a Classic. But then he has never been frightened to do anything at any stage of his life.'

Charlie Hills was with his father in a box high up in the Doncaster stands as the drama of the last two furlongs unfolded. 'I remember walking down the steps with him and he was in tears,' Charlie says. As Moonax was led in, those were tears of sadness as much as joy. Barry declared: 'It's great to win a St Leger but the last thing I wanted to do was to beat John and Michael.'

John, a popular figure in Lambourn, took his defeat in typically sporting fashion. He insisted then: 'I was chuffed for Dad. The horses have been a bit in-and-out and driving him mad, so this was great for him. You can't keep a good one down, can you? If I had to be beaten I'm glad it was by Dad.'

Now he concedes that he was disappointed – but only up to a point. 'If someone had told me at the beginning of the year that Broadway Flyer would win two Group races, finish second in a Classic and show so much promise for next year, you'd have taken it, wouldn't you? If Moonax hadn't run Broadway Flyer would have won by three lengths and he would have been a hero.'

He told reporters on that St Leger day: 'I've been second in two Classics, so I should be getting used to it. It was hard because he ran such a great race but I've plenty of time to train a Classic winner.' Sadly for John, who has trained some good Group winners and who can clearly deliver if he has the right class of horse, he has not yet had that compensatory Classic winner.

Moonax's St Leger success came at a crucial time for the family, George Hills recalls. 'My mother, Charlie and I were involved in a fatal car accident only the week before. I got quite badly beaten up (he had fifteen stitches in his head along with other bumps and bangs), Charlie hurt his back and mother was suffering emotionally.'

Mother and son watched the race in the sitting room at home. 'I remember the sense of disbelief as we watched him come from last to first. Family morale was very low after the accident and it was a great uplift.'

Moonax, a son of Caerleon, was the longest-priced winner of the

Leger for 73 years. He had made an inauspicious start to his racing career when unseating Richard Quinn at Doncaster's final meeting the previous year. And he was never a likeable animal. Michael Hills calls him a rogue: 'The safest place was on his back, he couldn't bite you then.'

But there were those who loved him nonetheless. The relationship between a horse and the lad or lass who 'does' him, looking after his needs on a daily basis, can be crucial to a racing career and Barry says that Joyce Wallsgrove, who used to look after Moonax, was brilliant with him.

'He had to be treated with caution,' he says, 'otherwise he would grab you.' Joyce Wallsgrove, who spent eighteen years with Barry, becoming head lad of one of the yards, and who is now a stable manager at Newmarket, used to lead up Moonax on race days in a jockey's body protector and thickly wadded arm guards. Once, at the Curragh, Moonax tried to separate her from her right arm, using his teeth like pliers.

She says Moonax, who was at his most dangerous just after a race when he was excited, was misunderstood and called a lot of names he did not deserve. 'A lot of it was that he had hurt his back. Most of it was pain, though he had his grumpy moments – he and his trainer were well suited. Yes, he was quirky and came across as a big, hard horse, but if he was feeling low he would put his head under your arm to be comforted.'

Others feared the horse but not Joyce, who first started doing him as a spare whom nobody else wanted and then asked to keep him. 'In the box I trusted him. He loved attention and loved to join in. He would take hold of his martingale and carry it around or play with a stick. But he didn't like people getting too close, he liked his own space. He didn't like men very much. He just had a lot of problems, which was why he got as nasty as he did.'

The bond forged between a lad or lass and a horse is often a deep one and can be crucial to a horse's success. Certainly Moonax owed plenty to the unflappable Joyce, who says, like a doting mother in defence of a lager lout, 'It was character, a lot of it, playfulness. But he was a big horse and his idea of play was not always acceptable.'

She even explains away the time that Moonax, who had put a travelling head lad in hospital in Germany, hurt her in Ireland. 'It wasn't his fault. Pat (Eddery) was back in the weighing room, the horse's back was hurting and we couldn't get the girths off. Pat had got done for excessive (use of the whip) and Moonax was lame behind. He was grabbing at everything and unfortunately that included my arm. He made a bit of a mess of it. At first the doctors thought he had bitten right through to the bone. They thought it was broken but it was only badly bruised – from the wrist to the top of my arm.' That sort of stoicism, you cannot help feeling, would have gone down well with Moonax's trainer.

Moonax's St Leger victory was not a flash in the pan. The same autumn he won the French St Leger, the Prix Royal-Oak, at Longchamp, becoming the first horse to double up in that race and the St Leger. He showed the utmost gameness, taking up the lead six out, losing it to Always Earnest but then battling back under Eddery to win by a short neck. Eddery said: 'I thought he was beaten but he kept on fighting. He is a gentleman to ride but when you get off him he'll kick and bite everybody.'

For Barry it was compensation for having to take Moonax out of the Arc, owing to the complicated elimination system and Sheikh Mohammed's desire to run Richard Of York. 'It was probably a blessing in disguise. It's just as well he didn't win the Arc as he would have scattered all the people in the winner's enclosure.'

The next year Moonax won the Yorkshire Cup and was second in both the Ascot Gold Cup (to Double Trigger) and the Irish St Leger, which is not confined to three-year-olds. He should have won the premier French race for stayers, the Prix du Cadran, that year but was beaten a short head by his old rival Always Earnest, who drifted across the track and bumped him, with Double Trigger in fourth. There was a stewards' inquiry and Eddery was confident of getting the race. 'Always Earnest came on to me, he pushed me over,' said the jockey, who added that he had had his whip in the correct hand. But the stewards ruled that the two horses had drifted into each other. Moonax, it has to be said, did not add to his chances by trying to bite Always Earnest in the final furlong.

Moonax was second again in both the Prix Royal-Oak and the Prix du Cadran in 1996 and also won a conditions race at Haydock. Barry was hopeful the son of Caerleon could have become a champion hurdler but his hurdling career amounted to just three races without success. Some horses just don't take to racing over obstacles and he was one of them.

After finishing a disappointing ninth of thirteen in the Ascot Gold Cup in June 1997, Moonax, who won six of his nineteen races on the Flat, amassing a total of £425,777, was retired to stud. The epitaph on his racing career from Sheikh Mohammed's racing manager Anthony Stroud, who paid tribute to a marvellous job done by Barry and by Joyce Wallsgrove, was: 'He was a very tough horse with a great deal of ability. He needed soft ground and ran some very brave races in those conditions but, to some extent, he was always having to battle with himself. On a day-to-day basis he wasn't a cross horse but on race days he was like a raging bull. He got very keyed up and it showed through. All in all, he didn't do badly for a horse who cost £30,000.'

CHAPTER ELEVEN

John Hills: The Making of a Trainer

'If it's important he helps, but if it isn't he says he's got enough problems of his own without worrying about mine. He tells you in his own style and I am sure you know what I mean.'
JOHN HILLS ON HIS FATHER.

John Hills says he and his father sometimes stand and chat to each other on the gallops of a morning like two old farmers at a gate. 'I was with Dad as his assistant for four years and he was a good tutor. He knows what he's doing. He's good with the one-liners when I ask him for advice or something like that. If it's important he helps, but if it isn't he says he's got enough problems of his own without worrying about mine. He tells you in his own style and I am sure you know what I mean.'

Barry admits: 'John is the one of my boys who tends to get the roughest edge of my tongue, simply because he lives the nearest. John's like his father in one respect – a bit stubborn.'

A successful trainer in his own right and one of the best-liked figures on the racing scene, John is the one member of the Hills dynasty who might have broken away from the horsey world. But in the end genes and the lure of stable life – coupled with an interest in a Lambourn girl who ended up married to another trainer – brought him back into racing.

The eldest son of Barry's first marriage to Maureen Newson, John was born in Hurworth Cottage, Newmarket, an abode now owned by William Haggas. John loved Newmarket and was shocked by the idea of going to Lambourn when his father's gamble on Frankincense enabled him to move there and set up as a trainer. He thought it chalk and cheese. 'Newmarket was always busy. Lambourn seemed the quietest back-end place in the world. It might as well have been Mars.'

John, who later nurtured ambitions of becoming a pilot, was more interested in objects with two wings than those with four legs. He remembers watching Concorde's debut on 9 April 1969 on black and white television. 'Then we heard a noise and went outside and looked up and there it was coming over on the first flight. It was the first time I thought: "Lambourn does exist." '

In the early days at South Bank they had a little Palomino pony called Pinkie, who was stabled in what was really a feed shed with a skylight, not a proper box. Snowy Outen, the head lad, used to feed the racehorses and take the buckets back to Pinkie's shed. 'There was a fair bit of grub left, much of which used to find its way into Pinkie.' By Friday night when John came home from school Pinkie was standing on two legs, looking through the skylight, revved up and ready to roll.

'I would get deposited on him on a Saturday morning and be expected to follow the string, but Pinkie had other ideas and tried to pass most of them. He used to run away with me. By the age of 11 I had lost my bottle. I didn't ride again for about three years. I walked away. I used to spend most of my time making models and blowing them up with home-made bombs with my mate Hugh Osmond, later of Pizza Express fame.

John's mother Maureen recalls the very day: 'The pony dumped John and was off towards Wantage. He was angry. He declared, "I just don't want to know about horses," and stalked home to South Bank. Barry used to be very rude to him. "How could any son of mine sit on a horse like a sack of potatoes?" he'd say. He would be working the likes of Our Mirage and Rheingold and John would be watching the passing planes.'

'I was a big disappointment,' says John. 'Father was in despair. About 1972, it must have been, I was up on the gallops with him in his car and he said, "Look, that's Rheingold," and I said, "Look, that's a VC10 up there," and pointed up in the sky. He just rolled his eyes – I can see the expression now.'

Barry says: 'When John started out he wasn't interested at all. In the years of Rheingold he wouldn't even go out to the yard to see a horse and wouldn't know where Rheingold stood.' He did actually – children all have their own way of making a point with parents.

It wasn't easy for the brightest, academically, of the three elder Hills. John remembers: 'Michael and Richard were both destined from birth to be jockeys and they played up to it. People used to say "Little terrors. Of course they'll be jockeys. But what's Big John going to do?"

'I had walked away from the horsey bit. Then about 1975 I took a shine to Kim Allison, now Brian Meehan's wife. I was 14 and very shy. The twins were off riding every day with Kim and her younger sister Jane, who is now managing horses for Paul Roy.

'We had a pony called He'll Do, which used to be Penny's, and he gave me my confidence back. I started going out with the others, though I never got anywhere with Kim. I started hunting at 15 or 16 and got more and more confident. At lunch one day Dad mentioned that I might have a ride in the Newmarket Town Plate on the filly Matinale if I got fit enough. I went back to school, running round the nine-hole golf course to get fit.

'My parents had split up by then and I was living in the village with Mum. I went for lunch with Dad. Hugh Williams and his wife were there and Freddie Maxwell. Then in front of all these people Dad said he didn't think he would run the filly. I got a bit of a flush and he said, "You wouldn't be fit enough anyway." Hugh Williams said, "There is a way of finding out," and made me stand with my back to the wall and my knees and thighs out at 90 degrees, parallel to the floor. But I could do it standing on my head.

'After this Dad's defence had gone, so he ran the filly. She was good – she won the Ascot Stakes the next year – and I won. She was a bit of a good thing, but it was a lovely thing to do, especially in front of my grandfather (Paddy Newson), who died the next year.'

Maureen remembers how they all walked the Newmarket track in the morning, John and her and grandfather Paddy Newson. We walked every blade of grass in the pouring rain.' After the race Paddy sent the twins to tell John to be careful as he jumped off – 'His knees might go.' Wise advice, as this has happened to many an amateur rider, even first-class, experienced eventers.

For John that Newmarket victory was a crucial turning point. 'You can imagine how that spurred on the twins. They were the ones who were going to be jockeys and now this had happened when I couldn't even ride. I don't think until that moment I had ever thought of having a career in racing. But once bitten by the bug I realised that subconsciously I had taken in and learned a lot. Having had it all going on around me since birth I suddenly realised there was quite a lot of stuff I knew. Conversations. The way people reacted. The way horses were. The way people reacted with horses.

'I was leading amateur rider jointly one year with Ray Hutchinson, probably in 1979 or 1980. I won the Moet et Chandon (the 'Amateurs' Derby' at Epsom) and in all I rode twenty-one winners. I wasn't very stylish, I used to look like Liberace on speed when I was riding a finish, but I could steer a good course.' In fact, John Hills and Dermot Weld are the only people to have both trained and ridden a Moet et Chandon winner and John has won it twice.

'I went to Edward O'Grady in Ireland for a winter when I left school, then had two years with Harry Thomson Jones in Newmarket. I had time with John Gosden in the US and with Colin Hayes in Australia. I was away from Lambourn until 1983 – five years away before I started working for Dad.'

It was typical of Barry's tough love with his offspring that when Maureen Hills inquired how John was doing at O'Grady's, she was told: 'Well. But he's very quiet. He spends all his spare time in his room.' It was not surprising. He had to. His father had sent him to Ireland with an old banger and £100 – and told O'Grady not to give him any money.

John says: 'John Gosden is incredibly intelligent. He was young and jolly and incredibly cool to work for, especially having come from somebody old school like Tom Jones. He was so open. With the old fashioned guv'nor in his office or on his hack you don't really talk, you don't really get to ask why they did this or that.

'But working for John Gosden everything was an open book. Every decision you could ask him or he would tell you. With Tom Jones a lot made sense retrospectively. You'd learned it without knowing so. But go out for dinner with Gossie and Rachel (Hood, Gosden's wife) and you suddenly realise there's a whole string of things in the world you've missed. Working with Gosden was the only thing that made me regret not having gone to university. But Mr Grumpy wouldn't agree with that.

'I came back to work for Dad after the Keeneland July Sales in 1983. Robert Sangster had a bet – it was probably over lunch at Wilton's or something like that – that our working together wouldn't last a month. In fact, I worked three and a half years for him and we never had a cross word. I copped a couple of those smart little bollockings but we never fell out. I really enjoyed it.'

John was working with his father when Cormorant Wood won the Champion Stakes and there were other good horses like Desirable, Seismic Wave and Gildoran, who won two Ascot Gold Cups for Robert Sangster. It was in the early days of Sheikh Mohammed's arrival on the British racing scene.

John's career was both advanced and interrupted when his father moved to Manton in 1986. He took over the South Bank yard when his father went to Wiltshire but then had to move out again when Barry returned to Lambourn. John then moved to Hill House, where Paul Cole, these days at Whatcombe, had trained previously. 'Dad's move back probably cost me a year but I ended up buying The Croft (his present yard). I was lucky being able to start at South Bank leasing from Dad.'

There has been plenty of success. 'Wind In Her Hair was a very good filly. She won the Pretty Polly and the Vodafone Fillies' Trial before finishing second to Balanchine in the Oaks and was then fourth in the Irish Oaks. I won a Group One with her as a four-year-old. She won the Aral Pokal in Germany and at stud she was the dam of the fantastic Japanese horse Deep Impact.

'Broadway Flyer won the Chester Vase and the Gordon Stakes before being beaten by Moonax in the St Leger, and Docksider (who won the Hong Kong Mile in December 1999) was the best miler I've had. He won two Group Twos and was beaten only a neck and a head in the Breeders' Cup Mile.

"You could probably say I'm a successful trainer. I've won more than my share of decent races. I've not really trained massive numbers in numerical terms. But I remain someone who could pop up with the real thing. That's what helps me to get up in the morning.'

How does John feel now about the Moonax affair? 'My horse had beaten him in the Chester Vase. Moonax was a savage. Father had intended to run him in the Troy Stakes the day before but left him in the St Leger to take a look and Sheikh Mohammed had other runners in the Troy. My horse was a confirmed front runner. Michael killed anything that tried to race with him. Moonax was told not to compete with him but to stay out the back. We set the race up ourselves, never anticipating that Moonax would run as he did. It was purely the way he was trained by Mr Grumpy.

'It was an emotional time. I took it well. I was 34. I'd had the runner-up in the Oaks with Wind In Her Hair. I thought it was only a matter of time before we got there but horses of her calibre are hard to come by.'

Not every trainer has the budget of a Michael Stoute or Henry Cecil (or, indeed, of Barrington W. Hills). A big Arab owner would help. But the patient John makes the best of the flag-carriers he gets and the enthusiasm is undimmed. Every year, he says, he still fully intends to train the next Sea The Stars.

The family ability is there. But John, a more relaxed figure, does not always keep up the implacable front maintained by his father. He is human enough to admit, as he did over Docksider before a big race at Goodwood, 'My confidence tends to ebb away the nearer I get to a big race. And ten minutes before the start it has usually gone right out of the window.'

John now trains around sixty horses down Uplands Lane. He has a satellite yard near Faringdon Place and uses Barry's gallops twice a week.

'Advice comes in two ways. Sometimes it is short and sharp and hurts briefly. Sometimes it comes over a nice long lunch, when it comes in the form of telling rather than advising. A lot has sunk in over the years, a lot of good advice. It's a matter of knocking corners off and steady advice. He would see it as pure commonsense.'

CHAPTER TWELVE

The Hills Twins: Brothers and Allies

'We are very close. We try to speak every day whatever country either of us is in. I'll be looking out to see what he's riding and vice versa. We're really good mates and we've never been jealous of each other.'

MICHAEL HILLS ON RICHARD HILLS.

Trainers are pretty constantly in the racing public's eye. Drop your strike-rate of winners to runners and comment will soon follow. Have a virus or a bad run of luck and in no time your name is featured on the 'cold list'. But if it is tough for trainers, it is even tougher for jockeys. The all-seeing television camera is rarely absent. Armchair critics, especially those talking through their pockets, are always ready to attribute a horse's failure to pilot error. But Michael and Richard, the Hills twins, never had any hesitation in choosing the jockey's life and both are still in the top flight of riders in their late forties.

The near-identical twins Michael and Richard Hills were born in Newmarket on 22 January 1963, Michael the elder by half an hour. They have been close ever since. Mother Maureen found them confusing because when one had teething pains, the other had the teeth. When one was ill with chickenpox or measles, the other had the spots. Michael says they feel like two halves of the same person. They went to the same school, sitting next to each other in class, did each other's homework and played in the same football teams. Both 5ft 3in and 8st 2lb, they are best friends as well as brothers.

Richard says: 'We've always been very close. We were so bad at school we needed to have an ally. We tended to think alike. It was never that one of us wanted to play football and the other to play tennis. We both wanted to play football or go riding or go to the cinema. Mike's probably my first phone call of the day and vice versa. I trust him and he trusts me. If I ask him about a horse I know I'm going to get a straight answer and a good answer.'

Michael confirms: 'We often ring each other at precisely the same moment, which is a constant nightmare. I ring him and he's engaged because he is trying to ring me. It happens an awful lot. We often turn up with the same clothes on.

'We are very close. We try to speak every day whatever country either of us is in. I'll be looking out to see what he's riding and vice versa. We're really good mates and we've never been jealous of each other. If I'm in a race and I've fallen out, I'm looking up to see if he's still in there. I feel the same when he wins as I do if I've won.'

Employing one of the Hills twins, owners and trainers get two racing brains for the price of one. The pair constantly analyse each other's chances and performances. 'Every day,' says Richard. 'Mike never sat on Nayef (Richard's favourite horse) but he probably felt like he rode him. Any Classic I've ridden, any Group One horse he's ridden, we've been through the races. I've been competing against him in some of them but we'd be talking like, "There'll be pace here, there'll be pace there." Not telling each other what we're going to do but analysing the races as to how we think they're going to be ridden.'

Michael says: 'Richard would ask me about his opposition if I've ridden against them. We've always bounced it off each other since the word go. He'd ring up from Dubai and say, "This horse has done this and that, what do you think? Should I drop this one in, will it stay the trip?" It will be down to him in the end but he likes to hear what

I have to say and I do exactly the same with him. What's the point of having a twin brother if you don't use it?'

That doesn't mean any quarter is given when they are racing. Out of the saddle they will work together to beat the rest. But Richard confirms that when racing there are no family favours, even with his son Patrick now a promising apprentice rider. 'We are totally competitive when we're in a race. You can be competing against your father, your two brothers and now your son, but because I've ridden with Michael and against my father from day one it's never really been an issue. We've got a job to do, we're paid to do it. Brothers, fathers, sons, sisters or whatever, it doesn't come into the agenda. Obviously, when I feel my horse is beat then I'll have a look up to see if Michael's won or Patrick's won. Or if it's one of Father's horses or one of brother John's. I want any of those to win.

'I always have a look up to see where Michael is, but to be honest I've beaten him a short head in the past and not really known until just before the line that it was Michael, so it's never really affected me.

'The only problem would come if I saw something happen to him. We've both been very lucky with falls. We've had breaks and cracks but nothing serious. I saw Michael fall once and it wasn't nice. I got down and got in the ambulance with him.'

Of his son Patrick, Richard says: 'Michael looks out for him. Michael talks to him like his father. Sometimes it's better coming from Michael than from me. I'd probably be a bit softer. Michael would be the B. Hills, a bit blunter, and Patrick would respect that because it needs to be said sometimes, just to put him right. Mike can do it.'

Being nearly identical has had its fun side, and its complications, for the Hills twins. They get accused of ignoring people at the races when mistaken for the other one. They can't be told apart on the phone, both sounding remarkably like their father too. And even he had trouble telling them apart as youngsters. Michael says: 'Dad wouldn't be the best at telling the difference. Nine times out of ten when we saw him we were either on the ponies or riding out, with our helmets on. He would guess but it wasn't important to him which one it was – he would know it was one of us.'

Richard says: 'Mum and brother John could tell us apart, Dad was useless. If one of us did something wrong we both got a kick up the arse because he couldn't tell the difference.'

The difficulties of telling them apart can come in handy. One day a disgruntled punter who had backed a losing horse met them as they left a restaurant in Harrogate. 'Which of you was riding it?' he asked. 'He was,' said Michael and Richard as one, each pointing immediately at the other.

The twins have been known to accept trophies and give interviews for each other. At the end of the 1995 season they were neck and neck in their winner totals. Richard won the last big handicap and Channel 4 were desperate to interview him. Richard was otherwise engaged, so Michael did the necessary. 'I went out and gave them a full interview. They were convinced I was Richard. Until I turned round to go and they spotted my name embroidered on the back of my breeches.'

When Michael won the top French sprint race at Longchamp, the Prix de l'Abbaye, on Handsome Sailor for his father and owner Robert Sangster in 1988, he was rushing to get a flight afterwards. He asked Richard to pretend to be him and accept the prize, which he did. Sangster and his father never knew but when a journalist later relayed the story to Barry the framed group photo of Handsome Sailor's victory quietly disappeared from the trainer's study wall.

'We've done it quite a few times to be honest,' says Richard. 'Sheikh Hamdan spots it every time. He thinks it's really funny. He's always watching because he doesn't trust whether I'm coming out or Michael.' Michael confirms: 'We did it with Sheikh Hamdan one day when Richard was tight for time and said, "Go on mate, run out and get my prize." I went to do so and Sheikh Hamdan looked at me straight away and said, "We have a ringer here." '

On one occasion when they were apprentices working for different Newmarket yards they swapped yards for a night with Jeremy Hindley and Tom Jones. 'We didn't get away with it. Tom Jones was very strict, real old school. Jeremy Hindley was a bit more relaxed and the yard wasn't run like a military camp. When we swapped my horse wasn't done in the way Richard would have done it. Of course Tom copped it right away. So did I.

'If someone says hello thinking I'm Richard, I don't say "I'm Michael". I sort of half blag it because I know his horses pretty well. But you can't get away with it with the Arabs because they pronounce a lot of the horses differently from us. If someone says hello and I don't know who the hell it is, they might know Richard, and so I always say hello because if I blank them they might think what a git Richard is.'

If there is a difference between the twins, say those close to them, then it is the minuscule gap between Michael's front teeth. But in the saddle they can be told apart. Michael rides the British way with his feet right home in the irons, Richard rides US-style with only the toes in. Other items have been ticked off by interviewers over the years. Richard says: 'We look alike and get on so well but character-wise we're totally different. Michael – his car looks like a tip. He's scruffy. He rarely buys clothes. My car is immaculate. I like to wear nice clothes. He always says I run my life a bit like a military operation. I'm organised and Michael's not.'

Mother Maureen says Richard always was the organiser. Michael just 'arrived' at the races and never had anything to do with money. 'Michael,' she says, 'lives on another planet and visits us occasionally.'

When the two lived together it was Richard who organised the nights out – and kept the cashbox. So is he the careful one with money? 'I don't know. We both try to look after it, we've worked bloody hard for it. Michael would probably say I was.'

In the 1980s Michael was telling interviewers that their different approaches to life extended, to a degree, into their riding styles. Richard, he said, wanted to get on with things on a horse. 'He gets hold of a horse and makes it go. I'm more likely just to sit there and let it do the work.'

That said, Michael then preferred sprinters and milers. 'I'm more into speed horses. The big competitive handicaps get me going, the Cambridgeshire or the Stewards' Cup. They give you a chance to test yourself under pressure. Everything's fast – no second helpings. Richard prefers long-distance races which give him more time to settle down and ride a race.'

Richard says: 'Michael's had a lot of success with sprinters. We (meaning the Hamdan Al Maktoum operation for whom he has been the number one rider for thirteen years) don't really have that many sprinters. We generally have horses that we try to stay with for a mile and that revert back to sprinting. I've only won one Group One sprint and that was with Elnadim in the July Cup. It's the type of horses you ride most of the time. I do enjoy riding mile-and-a-quarter or mile-and-a-half horses. Having said that, right since the Tom Jones days I've loved riding two-year-olds, schooling them, teaching them how to do it and how to enjoy doing it.'

Although Michael is the one who has ridden most for their father, Richard is more like him in personal style, according to his brother. 'He's got this very rigid idea of what a jockey should look like, very image-conscious he is, always dresses the part and has a different set of riding gear for each trainer. Our father's like that, very correct. And granddad had about forty pairs of boots, all gleaming.'

In 1989 Richard told *The Sporting Life*: 'Michael thinks I'm tight but he's much, much tighter. He never carries money with him, like royalty. I've known him go to the races with less than £1 in his pocket. If we see anything we want I always have to pay, then he conveniently forgets about it. He's also the scruffiest person I've ever met.'

He agrees that he prefers stayers. 'You can get to know them, form a long-term relationship. Jockeys don't sit on horses for nearly as long as people imagine. A few minutes before a race and a few minutes after. You need to show them what you want very quickly. Michael's more likely to talk to his horses, I tend to get hold of them. He's more open and outgoing, lets his horses run. I tend to concentrate more on tactics.'

Both Michael and Richard married slim blondes, Chrissie and Jaci. Both have one child and both live in elegant thatched houses. Both have bred ornamental ducks. And they have marched in time in their careers. The twins got their apprentice licences the same day, 13 August 1979. Both had their first rides that afternoon for their friend Charlie Nelson, who had spotted their potential early as they came up to ride ponies, and they rode their fiftieth winners within an hour of one another. An article after they had both been jockeys for twenty-two years noted that Michael had ridden 1,368 winners to that point, Richard 1,371. One night in 2003 they both rode winners on Dubai World Cup night.

Good things and bad things tend to happen to them around the same time. On his third ride, at Ripon, Michael came off when the saddle slipped: 'I was so light there must have been three stone of lead in there.' He did not break anything but was bruised and battered. When he came home looking for sympathy it was only to find Richard being fussed over because he had fallen off his bike and broken his arm. (Treating a bicycle as if it were a horse to be driven in a finish is not recommended – Richard had put his whip through the spokes).

The twins have never been seekers of the limelight – one reason, their father says, for their success rate and the longevity of their careers. Nor were they ever academically inclined. Barry says: 'They never really wanted to do anything but racing. They were never really school types. They are basically dyslexic and I think I am too. It's just that we never heard about it in my day.'

In interviews the twins have given over the years they have often caricatured themselves as 'small and thick – the natural material for jockeys'. In fact, one reason why both are still riding in the top echelon in their forties is that both are articulate and thoughtful men. You don't have to talk to them for long to realise that both have much of their father's shrewdness and from the start they shared his relish for the racing life.

Michael explains: 'When we weren't at school we just used to follow the string, every day. We used to have a jockeys' championship. We used to race the ponies like mad. It was great. In the afternoon we used to jump them out of the stalls. They were good ponies but by the time we'd finished with them they were so wired-up they were like racehorses. They were fit as fleas.'

Jockeys around the yard gave them old saddles that the twins mounted on the sofa to watch TV racing. 'Rich and I used to stick the saddles on the sofa arms and watch the TV racing and knock the shit out of the furniture riding finishes. We used to put the saddles on bales in the barns as well. Ernie Johnson, Kipper Lynch and Jimmy Lindley used to come up and show us how to pull a whip through. People looked at us and thought, "They're going to be jockeys." Richard and I never thought about doing anything else. It was just a natural thing.'

Not that it was exactly an easy life at home, for all their father's success.

Richard remembers: 'When we were at school our friends used to say as they were heading off to Spain or wherever, "Where are you going on holiday?" We used to say we hoped we might get a day at Goodwood or the Newmarket July meeting or York. We didn't see a lot of Dad. We were young kids running around with our ponies. Dad was working as hard as he could. John was pretty bright and into aeroplanes and things. There were people coming in and out of the house ... owners, jockeys. You just got on with it. That's part of what made us so close.

'Mike and I were always going to be champion jockeys and that was it. We didn't need anybody to tell us.' Not that there was always that much encouragement. 'I would come home from the gymkhana and say, "Dad, I had three winners," and he would just grunt. He's never really said, "Well done" for anything. Basically he just expected it. His standards are high and that's the way the man is.'

Charlie Nelson says: 'There was no favour for family from Barry. He'd had a tough upbringing and made his way by his own determination, skill and efforts. He expected them to do the same.'

Richard and Michael were riding out racehorses by the age of nine or ten. Michael says: 'On a Sunday morning they just used to walk round the village. Because we weren't at school at the weekends they used to put us on a quiet filly or something. We must have been like little peas on a drum. We probably only weighed about four stone.

'We had all the kit. Not all the lads who rode out had helmets but we did. We used to paint them like Dad's best horse of that year, in the Robert Sangster colours or the colours of a new owner in the yard. We were constantly putting new tape on our whips. Anything trendy, we would have it. If we saw Pat Eddery riding out for Peter Walwyn – he was stable jockey then – if he had a red jacket on we'd be winging down buying red jackets.'

A little later there was help from an international star. When the horses weren't right for a period after Steve Cauthen had come over to ride for Robert Sangster and Barry, the American champion had time on his hands. Richard says: 'We'd take the ponies up to the gallops with Steve and Mike and I would race for three furlongs for a pair of goggles or a helmet cover or a whip. He had come over with a trunk full of gear. For two young 16-year-olds mad on racing it was like Father Christmas. If we didn't beat him racing we'd take him home and play table tennis or golf with him. Steve was a big influence on Mike and me. Over the years I've been quite good from the front as a judge of pace and Steve was a master at it. I used to watch tapes of how he just kept picking up in races from the front and stole a lot of them from the front. We watched all the tapes and I like to think I've stolen a few in my time too. They were really fun times and (Lambourn trainer) Charlie Nelson and Steve helped us a lot.'

Owner Jack Ramsden, Richard recalls, had a horse called Jacket Potato. 'He was big mates with Dad. He came down one Sunday with his son. We were playing football. He was a bit sharp with the football and we gave him a couple of clips. Dad and Jack had seen it, so they put the boxing gloves on us. Mum was going mad and Lynda Ramsden was going mad and Mike and I were kicking the shit out of each other and Dad and Jack were betting on us.'

Soon, however, the three Hills boys had to face up to the trauma of their parents parting. Barry has been a major factor in the twins' racing lives but they do not forget the debt they owe to their mother. Richard says: 'We were young, only about eight years old, when it all started happening. Obviously it had a big impact. We were living next to the horses and we had to move out. We wanted to be jockeys, we wanted to be there. Because you're young you want to be protected through your mother. At the same time we wanted to be near Dad to learn our trade. Michael probably went through a tougher period than I did. He actually stopped riding for four or five months. It really did upset him. I went and rode out on my own.

'But we got used to it. Dad at that period became nicer towards us. He wasn't as sharp and as grumpy. He was certainly easier to talk to. I'm talking about when we were twelve or thirteen. He definitely mellowed. Mum, she basically lived her life for us from then on. We moved to Newmarket when we were sixteen. She moved down two years later and looked after us. She booked our rides for us for the first two years. She drove us to the races and she would pat us on the back when we got beat. We owe everything to Mum. She was there for us. You need your Mum but she would also say, "Listen to your Dad and respect what he says." She has a tremendous respect for

Dad and for what he has done.'

The twins' early life in the saddle reflected another of their father's passions – hunting. Michael says: 'When we were apprentices Dad sent us to Ted Williams for the winter to hunt with the Quorn. He was a horse dealer. He used to put us on horses at the meet and if there was a big hedge he made sure we jumped it in front of everyone on the horses he gave us to ride. Then people would ask, "What are the boys on today?" and he'd sell the horses from there. "Do something flash," he used to say.'

It was Charlie Nelson who set the twins on their way. Michael recalls: 'We left school at sixteen and started riding out for Dad as apprentices and working in the yard. I was about five and a half stone and Richard about five stone. Dad wouldn't give us any rides. He said we were too light. We were big friends with Charlie Nelson and we asked him if he would give us a ride each.

'We winged up to London and got our licences – I don't think Dad knew about it – and Charlie gave Richard a ride at Windsor and me one at Nottingham. I finished up winning my race. Richard finished fourth.

'The day I rode the winner Dad tacked it up and (trainer) Jeremy Hindley was there and asked Dad what he was going to do with me. Dad said he hadn't really sorted it out and Jeremy said, "I'd love to have him in Newmarket," and I went there the next February. John was a pupil assistant at Tom Jones's and Richard went to him. We had been going to Frenchie Nicholson but he didn't have many horses.'

Richard says: 'Charlie was a great supporter and a great friend. We spent a lot of time with him in the holidays learning a lot. He was more of a riding tutor than BH was. Dad was always very busy.

'Dad sat us down that winter and said, "Look boys, you can stay here with me or I can get you each a job in Newmarket." Straightaway we wanted to move to Newmarket. We needed to get away. We'd been at boarding school. We'd had it in our minds to be in Newmarket, at headquarters.' So Richard went to Harry Thomson Jones and Michael to Jeremy Hindley (who had once been a pupil assistant himself with Tom Jones).

CHAPTER THIRTEEN

Richard Hills

Hamdan's long-term Number One

CAREER HIGHLIGHTS
Britain: The 1,000 Guineas with Harayir (1995), Lahan (2000)
and Ghanaati (trained by his father) in 2009, the St Leger with
Mutafaweq (1999) and the 2,000 Guineas in 2004 with Haafhd
(trained by his father).
Abroad: The Dubai World Cup, the richest race in the world, with
Almutawakel (1999), the Woodbine International on Mutamam
(2001), the Dubai Sheema Classic with Nayef (2002) and the Prix du
Moulin with Aqlaam (2009).

In becoming apprenticed to Tom Jones, as he was always known,
Richard had moved from one hard taskmaster to another. 'Tom
Jones's evening stables was a military parade. I've never seen anything
like it. Twisting the straw. Disinfecting the sand. The little bit in the
spring showing the hairs from the curry comb. You had to polish that
horse every night as if you were the Queen's Guard.

'I was never good at cleaning horses or mucking them out when I
was a kid. We just used to jump on them and ride them. The first six
months were hard. He used to kick my arse. I remember one spring
day, I'd spent hours on this horse, polishing and polishing, and I
had it looking like a shiny penny. And he walked in and lifted up its
forelock and there was a bit of dirt under there and he said, "I'll see

you at seven o'clock." After he'd looked at evening stables he went and had his tea and then came back out to see if I'd finished off the job. We even had to polish the brass on the head collars and polish the leather and everything.'

With Richard's brother John there as assistant trainer and jockeys like Ian Watkinson and Steve Smith Eccles around, it was not an unhappy life. 'Those years were just a joy really and I met my wife Jaci there. She was working there too. So I owe my career and my marriage to Tom Jones.'

Although the twins have both been Newmarket-based and even now live close to each other there, they have made their careers in different ways. Richard has spent many years commuting to Dubai. He is closely associated with Arab owners and has long been the number one contracted rider for Sheikh Hamdan Al Maktoum. Michael has ridden the bulk of his winners for his father, although their working relationship went through a painful phase.

For Richard the die was cast early. Tom Jones was the first man to train a Classic winner for the Maktoums and when Richard started with him at Hurworth House in 1980 it was the Old Etonian's second year training for Hamdan Al Maktoum, one of the four brothers who ran Dubai. It was Jones who was chosen to handle Sheikh Hamdan's Ghadeer, then at 625,000gns the highest-priced yearling in the world. He also had horses for Sheikh Maktoum and Sheikh Mohammed. 'I'm not saying he was the founder of their British operation but he had a very close relationship with Sheikh Rashid, the father, and Sheikh Ahmed. From day one he taught me to associate with the Arabs. We used to go into the office on a Sunday and Haj Al Tajir would call and I would pass the phone through to Tom Jones.

'He always used to say, "Make sure you spend five minutes talking to him just so he knows who you are. For example, have you ridden a horse for him or Sheikh Maktoum or Sheikh Hamdan in a gallop or in a race that week?" He put it into my head to build a relationship so that when they walked into the yard they would come and say, "Hello Richard, well done," or "Unlucky" or whatever.

'I think I rode my third winner for Sheikh Hamdan, so pretty early on I'd ridden a winner for the boss. We had Paul Cook in those days. He was first jockey for about three years, then Tony Murray took over. Tony was great. He was very helpful to me, he took time putting me right in an old-fashioned way, taking me off to a corner and giving me a kick up the arse if I'd been hard on one unnecessarily. He was a good schooling man and very good on work at home. He taught me when he was first jockey how he arranged the work, how he wanted it, and he had us all doing what he wanted to do. In later years when I became first jockey it really stood me in good stead. He and Tom Jones taught me to look at the breeding and things I hadn't really thought of.

'Tom Jones watched everything I did. I had to ring him every time I rode a horse not just for him but for anybody. I used to ring him every night. He would watch the races and tell me if I was riding too short or if I was using the whip too much. He would give me a right bollocking. He could give you a bollocking you would never ever forget, but the next morning it would be, "Hello Richard, everything okay?" '

After life with Barrington W. Hills that must have seemed a familiar pattern and Richard says: 'I've worked for tough people. You have to take your bollockings on the chin and move on and get on with the job.'

Jones was impressed enough with his protege to write to the *Racing Post* in May 2004 in response to an item on his stable jockey. 'Richard Hills came to me as an apprentice. Thanks to his background he was a natural and, unnaturally for an apprentice, he could already ride everything in the yard, from my children's dodgy three-day event ponies to the bossiest colt and the bitchiest filly. He was an educated and natural horseman. Furthermore, he was a worker and willing to learn.'

Richard took a key career choice early on. 'I thought to myself there's no way I'm ever going to ride for Dad on a permanent basis, so I've got to find my own way. I looked at the Arabs at that stage as going to be major players. At the age of 20 it was the only thing I wanted to do and I worked damned hard to get it. Dad will admit that he must have told me twenty times to leave Tom Jones and to leave Sheikh Hamdan. He thought I would be a better jockey on my own. Obviously I rode horses the way Sheikh Hamdan likes them ridden and Tom Jones did but basically it has been my career. If I'd left I might have ridden more winners but I wasn't going to listen to that.

'When Tony Murray retired they were looking for a jockey, then Tom Jones told me that Sheikh Hamdan had asked, "Why are you looking for a jockey when you've already got one in the yard?" Tom immediately appointed me first jockey and we were very successful.

'We had about forty horses for Sheikh Hamdan at that time. When racing started in Dubai, Sheikh Hamdan rang me up and asked if I would come out to ride a horse in Abu Dhabi. The horse won and the boss said, "I am going to run him in ten days' time." I said, "Fine," and I ended up staying two and a half months. It was the first year we put lights up at Nad Al Sheba and I would like to think I played quite a good part in building up Dubai racing.'

That was in 1993. Richard is no longer top jockey in Dubai, only going for three months of the year whereas it used to be five, but he remains an integral part of Sheikh Hamdan's operation. 'The Dubai thing brought me independence with the sheikhs. I was first jockey to Tom and then the year after I went to Dubai I was appointed second jockey to Willie Carson and rode everything that he didn't (of Sheikh Hamdan's horses) as well as Tom Jones's horses. A couple of years later (in 1997) after Willie retired I was handed the number one job with Sheikh Hamdan. Instead of waiting on the end of the phone hearing which one Willie was going to ride I was on the end of the phone deciding which one I was going to ride.'

There followed a sticky patch that tested Richard's resolve. 'It was a very big job, big shoes to step into. Willie had been so successful (he rode two Derby winners for Sheikh Hamdan and in one year collected thirteen Group Ones). I didn't ride with a lot of confidence for the first half of that season. I was finding my way and things weren't quite happening. We didn't have a horse, a three-year-old. It was really tough and to be honest I didn't know whether I would last. But then July came. Sheikh Hamdan always comes for the summer for about six weeks. The day he flew in I rode a double at the July meeting. Then I rode a winner the next day and then on the last day I won the July Cup on Elnadim. And then my next seven rides for Sheikh Hamdan all won. I rode twenty-four winners that month for him and I never looked back. Dad had told me not to panic and to wait for the ball to come on to the bat. That's what I did and I stroked a few to the boundary at Newmarket.

'Tom was a great support at that stage because my confidence wasn't great and he said, "This is a loyal man you are working for. You need time to bed in." He gave me the time to do it and I haven't looked back from there on.'

Richard pays tribute to the man he succeeded as 'a fantastic person and a great judge'. 'When I took over Willie backed off a bit at first, left me to it. But when I ride a big winner for Hamdan or a Classic winner, he is the first on the phone. He has only ever tried to help me.'

Riding in Dubai also resulted in a change of style for Richard. 'It was American-based and I started riding with my toe in the iron. I needed to change things. It was the time to do it. I was basically trying to tidy myself up. I spoke with Sheikh Hamdan about it and he was very keen for me to try. He had a few theories about when in a race you gathered a horse and he felt that the American style was the way forward. He encouraged me.'

The man Richard calls 'The Boss', for whom he has ridden since 1982, has something like 300 horses in training with well-known names like

John Dunlop, Mark Johnston, Sir Michael Stoute, Marcus Tregoning, Michael Jarvis, William Haggas … and a certain Barry Hills.

Sheikh Hamdan regularly discusses tactics with his number one rider. 'Oh definitely. Even little things about how you gather up a horse for four or five strides before you give him a crack. I'll never forget the day when I rode the first daughter of Salsabil and he said, "Richard, ride this like you were riding your own daughter." He has fifteen or twenty mares that are precious to him and we like to look after the produce that we have out of those mares.'

Talk to Richard and you sense a man fulfilled, easy with his job and his lifestyle. 'The mornings I love, getting up and riding a two-year-old that's never run. With the job and the position I'm in I could be sitting on next year's Guineas winner. That to me is the best part of my job, nursing those horses along, talking with the trainers, being a part of it. If I sit on a good one I'll ring Sheikh Hamdan the moment I get off that horse. I've got a number for him worldwide and he likes to be involved, he likes to know.'

Hills has enoyed huge success, winning the 1,000 Guineas with Ghanaati, Harayir and Lahan, the 2,000 Guineas with Haafhd and the St Leger with Mutafaweq. One of Richard's greatest triumphs was winning the Dubai World Cup, the richest race in the world, on Almutawakel for the home team. 'He was an outsider. We didn't go into the race thinking we were going to win. It was a first World Cup for Godolphin, a first for Sheikh Hamdan, a great day.' With typical Hills understatement he called it 'a matter of doing my job and repaying Sheikh Hamdan for all the trust he has had in me'.

The best horse he has been associated with, says Richard, is Nayef, who won three Group Ones in Britain – the Champion Stakes, the Juddmonte International and the Prince of Wales's Stakes – and who did even better abroad.

'He was a half-brother to Nashwan. Tom Jones bought Height Of Fashion, the mare, off the Queen for Sheikh Hamdan. He breeds a

Derby winner. Then the last foal, Nayef, comes along and he wins. He was a great two-year-old but he started off bad as a three-year-old. He was weak because he grew, but he finished off by winning the Champion Stakes. I was so disappointed when Sakhee went to Godolphin after I finished second on him in the Derby. But Nayef suddenly took his place and I was praying Godolphin weren't going to take him.

'Two weeks after the Champion he got on a plane to Dubai with me and I rode him out every day for five months. Christmas Day as well. And I really, really enjoyed it. We had three horses: Mubtaker, Nayef and Ekraar. The boss would ring every week and Marcus (the trainer Marcus Tregoning) left it to us. We took this horse over and we built him up and built him up, then we won the Sheema Classic. It was like winning the World Cup. It was five months' preparation. Every day. I was so involved that I could have told you how the horse slept and what he had eaten the night before. Marcus was so fantastic. No one could have trained him better but he really let me dive in. We would discuss everything and I really enjoyed it.

'We did that for two years because next year we went for the World Cup. Those two years with Nayef were probably the closest I've been with Sheikh Hamdan.'

Even after all those successes, for Richard the 2009 season in Britain was a special one. Riding ninety-six winners with a zest and confidence that won him plaudits in all quarters, he finished seventh in the jockeys' table with a remarkable strike-rate of twenty-three per cent wins to rides. Frankie Dettori, with twenty-four per cent, was the only other top jockey to break the twenty per cent barrier. A Classic success on Ghanaati in the 1,000 Guineas and an even more emotional triumph on the filly in the Coronation Stakes at Royal Ascot, on the day father Barry came out of hospital, capped a season in which Richard seemed to be riding big-race winners on every Saturday card, on several occasions cleverly making all the pace to do so. Typical was the Newmarket day he won the opening Group Three Sakhee Oh So Sharp Stakes on Sir Michael Stoute's Tabassum, took the Group One Shadwell Middle Park Stakes on Awzaan for Mark Johnston and rounded off with the concluding Standing For Success Handicap on Michael Jarvis's Alainmaar, all three owned by Hamdan Al Maktoum.

Another highlight was the Prix du Moulin at Longchamp on the William Haggas-trained Aqlaam, which contributed a further £221,903 towards Richard's stakes-winning total of £2.7 million through the season. Not bad for a 46-year-old.

CHAPTER FOURTEEN

Michael Hills

Ups, Downs and a Derby

*'Mike picked himself up, dusted himself off and he rode some
fantastic races. I was really proud of him.'*
RICHARD HILLS ON MICHAEL HILLS.

CAREER HIGHLIGHTS
Britain: The 1996 Derby on Shaamit, the King George VI and Queen
Elizabeth Stakes on Pentire (1996) and the Champion Stakes for his
father on Storming Home (2002).
Abroad: The Irish 1,000 Guineas on Nicer (1993) and Hula Angel
(1999), the Prix de l'Abbaye on Handsome Sailor (1988), the Prix Jean
Prat on Golden Snake (1999) (all of those for his father), the Hong
Kong Cup on First Island (1996) and the Dubai Golden Shaheen on
State City (2003).

Michael Hills's career took off faster than Richard's, partly, he
says, because Richard was riding as second jockey to Willie
Carson for Hamdan Al Maktoum and did not get so many early
chances. Says Richard of Michael: 'His first ride was a winner and he
was flying. I think he had eight winners from his first fifteen rides.
The only reason I rode a winner that year was because Michael broke
his thumb and I got on Border Dawn, a nice filly for Jeremy Hindley
at Doncaster.'

Michael was champion apprentice in 1983 (Richard was runner-up the next year). 'I won the Dewhurst for Jeremy Hindley when I was about 21 and then he made me first jockey.' Richard, he points out, was more restricted in his early days. 'Jeremy Hindley let me ride them any way, but Tom Jones was very strict. Richard had to follow Tom Jones's orders. He couldn't just wing it and hope it would come off, whereas riding for Jeremy Hindley I could. If it came off you were a genius, if it didn't you turned up and said, "Boss, I'm sorry." Richard couldn't get away with that. I've always ridden by instinct, kind of made it up as I go along. Richard has a game plan and sticks to it.'

There were plenty of successes for Michael with Jeremy Hindley and in 1988, when Cash Asmussen pulled out of his contract to ride as first jockey to father Barry at Manton, the young Michael was taken on as his replacement. Although he rode plenty of winners, including Group winners, he was not to the taste of some of the stable's patrons and there followed the kind of setback that could have broken a career. On the urging of Robert Sangster and others, the young jockey was sacked by his own father in July 1990.

That month, on a flight back from the Curragh, where Michael had ridden a stylish race to win on Missionary Ridge, father and son discussed the future and on 18 July Barry confirmed to the *Racing Post* that Michael would lose his position as stable jockey. 'I think the world of Michael. He rides well and he is my son. But some owners felt they wanted a change, they wanted Michael off. With the father-son relationship this has been extremely difficult for both of us.'

Michael, who had ridden thirty-one winners at that point of the season, nineteen of them for his father, took it gracefully, saying: 'I have enjoyed my two and a half years. I have ridden sixteen Group winners during that time and I feel I have learned a lot about racing. The owners put a lot of money into the game and they are entitled to have who they like riding their horses. There are no hard feelings and I wish them the best of luck.'

Now he says: 'I probably did a few things wrong but I don't think I had the right horse to put things right and of course the jock gets the blame. I rode a Group One winner every year that I rode for him – two or three years. There were lots of Group winners but he called me into the office and said, "You'll have to get out and paddle your own canoe." It was hard but then I came back to Newmarket and it was probably the making of me. The following year I had fifty winners by the time of Glorious Goodwood and not one ride from Dad. Then he asked me to ride Further Flight in the Goodwood Cup and he went and won.'

Bouncing back from such a blow, Michael showed an inner steel entirely typical of the family. Richard says: 'That winter we could see that any horse that Mike got beat on he was basically going to get jocked off. So I said he should look for other trainers as a safety net. Mike rang up Michael Bell and asked if he could come and ride work for him. He was an up-and-coming trainer and somebody we could see it was going to happen for. He had good two-year-old winners. From the moment he walked in that yard Mike never stopped riding the man winners. He really didn't. Just at that time I was starting to get a few rides for Geoff Wragg and I was riding a hold-up filly. I was suspended or I had to ride something for Tom Jones and they put Michael on and Michael as usual gave her a beautiful ride and clicked right away with Geoff Wragg. He had the most unbelievable three years of horses. At that stage in his life Michael was very strong, as in strong-willed, something we obviously got from Father, and he was able to withstand the jocking off and his Dad turning round to him and saying that he was sacked.

'It wasn't nice for Dad. It wasn't nice for either of them. But it was business. We were learning that even though we'd got a father in the trade we'd got to go out and do a job and produce. If you didn't, you had to take the consequences. Mike picked himself up, dusted himself off and he rode some fantastic races. I was really proud of him.'

The association with Geoff Wragg certainly brought some spectacular results. Among their victories together were the Ascot Gold Cup with Arcadian Heights, the King George VI and Queen Elizabeth Stakes and Irish Champion Stakes with Pentire, the Sussex Stakes and Hong Kong Cup with First Island, the Queen Anne with Nicolotte and the Cork and Orrery with Owington.

One race in particular reminded the critics what Barry's owners were missing, when Michael won the 1990 Ebor Handicap, Europe's richest race of its kind, on the Hills stable hero Further Flight. A report in the *Daily Express* declared: 'Amid a throng of well-wishers in York's packed winner's enclosure father and son congratulated each other as if there had never been any strain between them. Michael, celebrating the biggest handicap success of his career, said: "I lost the job at Manton because some of the owners were putting pressure on Father. In fact, now that I've turned freelance and ride for Manton as wanted or when available, it's taken the pressure off." '

Richard now takes the silver lining view for his twin: 'It was a difficult time. Dad was under a lot of pressure after moving into Manton and I think it did Michael a lot of good, and Dad too. That's probably one reason why they've lasted so long since. He wanted Michael back desperately. Mike had to make a choice whether to go back or not. Mike's a stronger jockey in mind as well.'

Clearly there is mutual respect born of a long partnership between trainer father and jockey son. Barry does not often give Michael precise riding orders. 'He leaves much of it to me but if he has a strong idea that he wants one to be held up or if he wants me to make the running he would not hold back in telling me. He has a pattern about how he runs his horses and the way he wants them ridden. Until you learn that he wants something specific you basically stick to that pattern and because I've ridden them for so long I know exactly how to address a two-year-old for the first time. I know just from his body language what he wants.'

And what about the renowned bollockings? 'He'll speak his mind. If he's got something on his mind and he wants to tell you he will say it – and then it's said. If it's to me about the way I have ridden a race, it's like, "Don't do it again. If you keep making that mistake you're out." But at least you have been told, things aren't kept from you. It can be hard at the time but you learn to cope with it. If you get off that horse and he's not happy with it he will let you know and he won't hold back. He's certainly quite fond of some old four-letter words.'

Michael won his first major European Classic, the Irish 1,000 Guineas, on his father's grey filly Nicer. With Barry's horses out of form at the time it provided a welcome change of luck when Michael brought the 8-1 shot to take up the running two furlongs out and stay on strongly to beat Goodnight Kiss and Lester Piggott's mount, Danse Royale. For once the emotion of a proud father showed as Barry declared: 'This is the biggest thrill I have had since Rheingold won the Arc for me. To win a Classic with your son riding is unbelievable.'

Michael's biggest success, though, was winning the Derby in 1996 on Shaamit, trained at the old Tom Jones stables by his friend William Haggas. He thus achieved a victory that has so far eluded his father and his brothers. With typical modesty, he told reporters afterwards: 'The people in the weighing room who were really thrilled were the ones like me. It was success in the greatest race, the one everyone wants to win, by a horse from a small yard ridden by someone who is not one of the superstars. I've had ups and downs in my career and got on with it, just like them. And they've realised that if I can do it, so can they. It was a real boost for the middle order.'

Barry, as is his way, made his feelings plain without saying a lot. Michael explained: 'He didn't need to. He knew how I was feeling and I knew that he was so proud that one of us had finally done it.'

In winning the Derby for the popular Haggas, incidentally, Michael was repaying a favour. On his first morning at Hindley's yard he had been in a fluster over his tasks. To help him out, the then assistant trainer mucked out one of his horses for him to get him back on track. That assistant was William Haggas.

Another racing day Michael will never forget is the King George VI and Queen Elizabeth Stakes, which he won in 1996 on one old friend after turning his back on another in one of those painful decisions top jockeys have to face. He chose to ride Pentire, the horse he had ridden through the previous season when the only race they had been beaten in was the King George, going down in a photo-finish to Lammtarra. Together they had won the Sandown Classic Trial, the Dee Stakes, the Great Voltigeur and the Irish Champion Stakes and Michael had promised Geoff Wragg that he would ride him for the rest of his career. Honouring that promise meant getting off Shaamit, the horse who had just given him victory in the most famous race in the world.

In fact, Michael nearly missed the Ascot race through suspension until a two-day riding ban was reduced to one on appeal. Then Pentire looked to have thrown away his chance when stumbling badly coming out of the stalls and losing six lengths. But the little horse was going easily. He had made up the ground by Swinley Bottom and won in great style, beating Classic Cliche and Shaamit with a tremendous burst of speed in the straight.

Will Michael's side of the family produce another rider, as twin Richard has done? There, at last, is a line of separation between the twins. Michael's daughter Samantha, now a trained beauty therapist, won her pony classes and one day asked her father if she might become a jockey. His reply was: 'If you were going to be a successful jockey you'd be telling me, not asking me.' Like father, like son.

CHAPTER FIFTEEN

Charles, George and Patrick Hills

Learning at the foot of the master

'It's one-liners really. He'll tell you when you're doing something wrong. He's not going to sit you down and give you half an hour's tuition.'
CHARLES HILLS ON LEARNING FROM HIS FATHER.

There is no doubt about the most emotional moment in the career of Charles Barrington Hills, Barry's fourth son and the man who shares the duties of assistant trainer at Faringdon Place with the long-serving Kevin Mooney. For five weeks in the run-up to Royal Ascot 2009, as his father fought that desperate illness in Charing Cross Hospital, it was Charlie who had charge of the Royal Ascot preparations, after three years without a Hills victory at the royal meeting.

It was surely his rite of passage that, at the end of the week, as his father emerged from the hospital where he might have died of septicaemia – a form of blood poisoning – it was Charlie who accepted on Barry's behalf the trophy for the leading trainer at the royal meeting after the successes of Ghanaati (Coronation Stakes), Ouqba (Jersey Stakes) and Giganticus (Buckingham Palace Stakes).

Nearly five months before Ascot, with Barry on holiday, I had been up on the gallops with Charlie. As Giganticus went by he declared: 'There they go, that's where the dreams are.' At the time he was referring to the two-year-olds the classy handicapper was leading out rather than dreaming of an Ascot three-timer that reflected every bit as much credit on him as on his father. But that is racing.

Ouqba started the ball rolling in the Jersey Stakes on the Wednesday. The lesser fancied of the two Hamdan Al Maktoum-owned runners from Faringdon Place (in the way these things happen, Hamdan's number one rider Richard Hills had preferred the chance of Infiraad, the highest-rated horse in the race, who found the ground too fast for him) Ouqba picked off the field one by one to provide a first Ascot success for rider Tadhg O'Shea. It was handsome recompense for connections, who had supplemented the Free Handicap winner for the 2,000 Guineas only for him to disappoint at Newmarket.

After Ghanaati's win in the Coronation, also for Sheikh Hamdan, Richard declared it meant more to him than any race he had ever won and that he had been hearing his father's voice as they ran. Certainly it proved her to be the best of the three-year-old female milers. Charlie says: 'She's class and a pleasure to train. I doubt very much if Dad's ever had a better filly,' while her proud owner insisted: 'She is right up there with the best fillies I have had. The trainer has done a very good job and so has the whole stable.'

The 12-1 Giganticus, ridden by Michael Hills, supplied the proverbial icing on the cake, underlining the family nature of the stable's success. The youngest of Barry's sons, George, was over from the USA to see the victory and Charlie's mother, Penny, admitted tears were shed as she and Barry listened to Giganticus's victory in the car on the way back down the M4 to Lambourn (they had watched Ghanaati's success in the Charing Cross Hospital dispensary as they collected his leaving prescriptions).

Afterwards Charlie conceded that a lot had been riding on Ghanaati. It was important that no mistakes were made and he had been nervous beforehand. But he sounded just like his father when he insisted that he had enjoyed the pressure 'because a filly like Ghanaati is the reason we do this job'.

A question frequently asked in racing circles during Barry's determined but painful struggle with illness has been: when will he hand over to Charles? Barry has continued to tease the speculators by saying that, just like another prolific producer of winners, the jumps trainer Martin Pipe, he will suddenly announce his departure one day and that will be it. But Barry has several times given a much clearer hint of what he expects his role to be after that decision day. He loves to tell the story of how, when Brian Clough and Peter Taylor took over at Derby County, they went down to Spurs and made an offer for Dave Mackay.

The Spurs manager admitted surprise at an approach for somebody seeming past his sell-by date. He advised them honestly that Mackay was 'too old and can't run'. Their answer was that it didn't matter he couldn't run: 'We've got nine others who can run around the pitch. We want somebody in midfield to shout at them and tell them what to do.' Charles has been warned. When the day comes, says Barry: 'I'm going to be Dave Mackay. I'm going to stand there, dish out the orders and make sure the job gets done.' That day is yet to come, but Charlie Hills clearly knows what is in store.

Asked for his earliest memories of stable life, Charles replies: 'Being up with the ponies on the gallops at Manton while my father shouted at everyone.' At first it was the saddle that appealed, but from his first ride on his sixteenth birthday it took Charles four years and twenty-four rides to secure the elusive first winner. In all, he partnered five for his father, the first of them being Dancing Feather at Bath in June 2003. He won on his proud mother's Prairie Falcon, whose headstone stands in the copse overlooking the gallops alongside that of Barry's hunter Mick and other family pets. And Charles rode a winner for his brother John on Night Flyer. One problem, he says, was a confusing excess of advice from the family. 'As a family I don't think we're too good at taking advice. We all tend to be a bit stubborn.'

Charlie, a keen golfer and five-a-side footballer with John

Francome's side, won the Bollinger champagne challenge series one year, recording four wins on his way to a title that was stripped from the bogus amateur rider Angel Jacobs (he had previously ridden as a professional). That was in a year when he was in competition with Ian Mongan, who has gone on to be a successful professional jockey riding for the likes of Henry Cecil, and Tom Best. But Charlie's plan was always for a training career.

'I was always a bit heavy to consider seriously a career in the saddle. Weight was not on my side. I never considered a career as a jump jockey either. I have a Flat background and amateurs must be mad to ride over the sticks for nothing. It's too dangerous.'

His riding career brought a total of seven wins, but there were some ups and downs. 'I had a ride up at Haydock on a horse owned by John Grant. I should have won and I finished second. It was one of those where you're in front two strides after the line. I had to ring Dad and I was dreading it. He called me all sorts of names. He said, "You'll have to pay back the travelling costs to the owner," although in the end he did not exact that penalty.'

On another occasion, when he was riding Delightful Dancer in a Redcar sprint, Charlie's saddle slipped and he was unseated. The rider suffered concussion and broke his thumb, which meant that instead of writing his GCSEs he had to dictate his answers to his teachers.

On the training side his preparation included time with Colin Hayes in Australia and two years at Newmarket with James Fanshawe, working with horses like Grandera and Hors La Loi III. Interviewed at the time about his working day there, he said the horses went out in batches of 40. 'I'll watch each and every one as it goes through its paces. Each one is different. Something like rearing up just prior to a race might be a good sign in one horse but might give you concern in another. It's a case of getting to know their characteristics.'

Nowadays he will sometimes ride out in the string and sometimes watch from aboard a hack, his eye, like his father's, constantly looking for the signs of a horse advertising its wellbeing and its readiness to race. Like his father, he is clearly no believer in rushing them: at Faringdon Place they don't go in for precocious two-year-olds, more the kind who will develop later as middle-distance horses.

As a regular around racing stables, I have often been struck by the apparent limitations of the communication process. You see the horses circling in the schooling barn or at the start of the gallops and the trainer has a few words with most of the riders, explaining what he wants them to do, and then asks a few questions afterwards. From the often monosyllablic replies, the body language on both sides and the trainer's few glances at how the animal is walking, breathing and moving at half-speed, crucial decisions are taken about fitness and race planning. It looks casual but in practice it is a far more complicated filtering process, one that few can explain in meaningful detail.

With Barry Hills it looks no different and learning alongside him can be a testing experience, as John Hills discovered in his time. The knowledge is not imparted by formal lecture. Michael Hills, his father's long-time first choice as stable jockey, says: 'Charles is doing great. The trouble with being an assistant trainer at Dad's – and being his son as well, it's the same for me – is that Dad wouldn't stand there on the gallops and say, "I love this horse … this one's going to need six furlongs," or "I think I'll run him at Chepstow." It's all going on up top. Charlie has to try to work out what he's thinking. It's the same for me as a jockey but because I've ridden for him so much I know his body language. I know exactly what he thinks of a horse and where he's headed with a horse because I've been in that paddock in the front line for so long.

'Charlie as assistant trainer has to learn how to get that information out of him because he ain't going to tell you. John had the same thing with him, Peter Chapple-Hyam had the same thing. All those assistant trainers he's had who have gone on to do good things, it was down to them. Dad wasn't going to sit down with them and say, "You should do this and you should do that." He'd say certain things – "That'll win this race" or "This will be a Guineas horse" – but that would probably be all you would get out of him.

'It's harder for Charlie too because (showing the necessary caution after his cancer treatment) Dad won't use his voice too much. He'll only speak when he really wants to say something. He won't talk just for conversation. It's not an easy thing for Charlie, but at least Charlie gets the chance to do a lot of communicating with the owners. And at the end of the day it's the owners who send you horses.'

Charlie agrees that you have to work to learn from the man who leaves him phone messages formally as 'Father' rather than 'Dad'. 'He wouldn't necessarily tell you. He thinks you should just learn from him without him having to tell you. If you want to learn you have to watch what he does.'

Will he explain when asked? 'Oh yes, definitely. He'll explain it well. But you don't want to be asking too many stupid questions. It's quite obvious whether he's in a good mood or a bad mood in the mornings. When he's in a bad mood you just keep at arm's length and keep your head down. It's a pressurised job, isn't it? It's one-liners really. He'll tell you when you're doing something wrong. He's not going to sit you down and give you half an hour's tuition.'

Does his father trade somewhat on that Mr Grumpy image? 'I think he does. But he's definitely mellowed in the last few years. The stories I get from when John was assistant, it seems he was far worse then than he is now.'

Charlie, though, hasn't escaped the bollockings. One day his father, watching the racing on television, saw Charles in the paddock wearing dark glasses. 'He called me up on the mobile and tore me off a strip. "You look like a spiv," he said.'

And what has been the worst experience? 'I've thought of the worst thing I've done in his eyes. I was late for work one morning. This was a few years ago and he caught me in bed with a girl, Philippa, who is now my wife (and the mother of Barry's latest grandchild, James). He woke me up – I've never seen anyone get up so quick and cover herself up – and he made me get up on a walker so I had to ride around the paddock for an hour. I had a ride that afternoon, which happened to win. Barry rang up Robert Cooper, who was doing the commentary, and got him to say on air: "That's not the only winner he's ridden today either," although he did not specify the circumstances.'

The working partnership between father and son has clearly been effective and Charlie is benefiting the yard by establishing lines into a new generation of owners. Even if some of them do wear dark glasses.

Charlie is not, however, going to be the punter his father has been. He is more like a two bets a year man, for the reason, he says, that he is not very good at it. But he did take some of the 33-1 about Ghanaati for the 1,000 Guineas. And he pulled one stroke his father must secretly have admired. Charlie is a good friend of Richard Hannon junior, son of another prolific producer of winners. One year, as their fathers purchased horses at the Newmarket Sales, they splashed out 13,000 guineas themselves on a Pips Pride colt, which was named Light The Rocket. In the bar later Barry turned it down as a training prospect. 'I asked Dad to have it but he said it wasn't good enough and told us to bugger off.'

They had the horse trained by Richard Hannon senior, in return for a quarter share. Light The Rocket won for them at Ascot and Sandown and was placed at Deauville before they sold him on for 44,000gns. The genes are clearly functioning.

Of Barry's five sons, the one who has steered the most independent path so far is George. Like the other boys he remembers having the yard as his playground, and being shouted at on occasions as a consequence. Newspaper profiles of Barry and his horses over the years include occasional references to George push-biking to the yard before 7am to muck out, weighing the popular grey Further Flight and watching his father making the entries.

Not blessed with the frame to consider a riding career, although he did ride out, George has not, so far at least, gone down the training route either. Instead George asked his father if he could go to Ireland and widen his experience there. He did so at the very top, working at the famous Coolmore breeding operation. There he spent three years looking after the mares, foals and yearlings. 'It was an amazing opportunity,' he says, 'not only to work with horses of the top calibre but with the people at Coolmore, who are a lot of very clever, gifted horsemen.' His mentor was John Magnier's righthand man Paul Shanahan, a figure who, says George, 'put a few manners on me' and taught him a lot, although he doesn't miss cleaning Shanahan's car every Saturday morning.

George also worked for Coolmore in the USA, where he was foreman of the maiden mare division and broke in Demi O'Byrne's yearling purchases at the Keeneland Sales. In 2005 he moved to Walmac Farms, an enterprise involving Coolmore, the US owner-breeder Will Farish, who was at one time US Ambassador to Britain, Robert Sangster and Johnny Jones III. George became Director of Bloodstock and Marketing, a role that involved marketing the services of stallions at an enterprise responsible for several million pounds' worth of covers in a year.

Since then, having worked for Coolmore in Australia too, George has broken away to do his own thing with the Sire Brokers company, marketing stallions and brokering nominations. In a partnership with Lynn Jones, he is also involved in all aspects of horse insurance, including mortality, travel and fertility of stallions. In the latest stage of his international equine career George has fallen in love with Argentina, where he spends much of his time. The 2010 Dubai World Cup winner, he is quick to point out, had Argentinian-breeding.

Intriguingly, George shares with John Hills a fascination with aircraft. 'When I was at the races when I was younger,' he says, 'I was more interested in watching the jockeys' and owners' planes –

especially Pat Eddery's – than the horses. Had I not gone down the horse route there is no doubt I would now be involved with aviation in some shape or form.'

Long ago, George set himself the ambition of one day piloting a plane into Newbury racecourse and having, somewhat to his mother's alarm, qualified for a pilot's licence during his days in Kentucky, he has realised that aim. Unfortunately, on the day in 2008 when he was coming in to land, a horse got loose from a starting stalls test and he had to abort the landing and fly in circles until the animal had been caught.

The racing genes, however, were clearly the strongest ones yet again in the youngest of Barry's five boys. George says: 'Dad loved us to go racing and to the sales. He told me that picking horses that can run isn't rocket science. He'd say, "Most people can sit on a park bench and watch others going by, seeing which ones move easily and which ones don't. It's just the same with horses." 'George says the most succinct phrase he heard his father use regularly at the sales was 'meatballs', presumably summing up the future for those that didn't appear to him likely to make the grade.

The other part of his racing heritage for which George will always be grateful is the extended family relationships built up in a yard where Barry and Penny have always kept open house for their owners. Racal boss Sir Ernest Harrison, for example, was like an uncle to Charles and George. Barry always sent him a pork pie at Christmas and the industrialist would always telephone on Christmas Day.

Other major owners like Sir Eric Parker and Paul Locke, George remembers, would bounce ideas off each other and his father, not just to do with racing but covering many other projects too. He may have travelled far, but the family bonds are strong. George's admiration for his father's fortitude is clear, as when he recounts how Barry told his assembled family one December a few years ago that he had a recurrence of his throat cancer. 'There was silence for a few moments and then he declared: "Well, there's f*** all we can do about it for now, so let's have another bottle." '

The latest glimpse of the Hills bloodlines is coming in the shape of Barry's grandson Patrick, Richard Hills's only son, who has been riding as a claiming apprentice since 2006. He was initially based with Mark Tompkins in Newmarket and has since moved to Richard Hannon's yard. He showed a touch of the right stuff to win on his first ride for his grandfather when he brought Namu home at Pontefract on 9 September 2006 in a blanket finish involving four horses.

Patrick, who can ride at 8st, has been given plenty of opportunities by his uncle John and doesn't want for advice from his father, who goes through every race with him, and from uncle Michael.

Patrick, whose tallish frame may lead to weight struggles later on, told reporters that it was probably a disadvantage being the latest member of a racing dynasty – the expectations add to the pressure. But he has been coping. His win for Barry meant that Patrick's grandfather had provided winning rides for his wife, four sons and a grandson.

CHAPTER SIXTEEN

Barry's Jockeys

The riders who have shared
in his success

'He thinks a bit like a jockey. He wanted to be a jockey but I don't think he was very good at it. He kept falling off. I remember that.'
MICHAEL HILLS ON HIS FATHER.

Although the longest and most enduring relationship Barry Hills has had with any jockey is with his son Michael, there have been many other famous names around the three Hills yards over the years. Willie Carson, Steve Cauthen, Ernie Johnson, Edward Hide, Cash Asmussen, Brent Thomson, Darryll Holland, Pat Eddery, Ray Cochrane and Alan Munro are among those who have worked with him for significant periods. There were plenty of rides too for Lester Piggott, whose successes on Rheingold and whose disastrous gallop on Durtal have already been recorded. Barry recalls that in his early days when he was working in the yard on a Sunday morning he would be called to the telephone and be told that it was the success-hungry Lester on the line. 'Wonderful.' he used to think. 'I'm clearly going to have a winner. I wonder which one it is.'

For a man so firm in his ideas about the right way of doing things, Barry is surprisingly democratic when it comes to jockeys. An utter professional himself, he respects professionalism in others. When I asked him one day if Piggott had obeyed his riding orders, Barry replied: 'You didn't give him much by way of orders. You don't really tell top-class jockeys what to do. You let them get on with it. It's instinct.'

It was the same with Steve Cauthen, the American prodigy who became Barry's principal rider when Robert Sangster brought him to Europe. He declared: 'Barry gave me a lot of confidence and told me all the peculiarities of the horses and the courses. It was fantastic riding for Barry because he would give me a plan of the way he thought a race should be ridden but always said that it was basically down to me and I must do what I thought was right. I think that's the best advice you can give a jockey.'

Barry's friend Jimmy Lindley says: 'Barry wouldn't put up with fools but he is not one to blame a jockey for a lost race, though he might sit down and say, "Should we have done this, or that?" '

Barry has had long friendships with a number of jockeys. Willie Carson was a close buddy when trainer and jockey were forging their separate careers at the same time. And Barry had, of course, been a jockey himself for a brief period, riding nine winners. Son Michael, a recipient of a fair few of those famous 'Barry bollockings' over the years, says with a twinkle, 'He thinks a bit like a jockey. He wanted to be a jockey but I don't think he was very good at it. He kept falling off. I remember that.'

Willie Carson recalls with his inimitable chuckle that when Barry was working with John Oxley he had a few rides over hurdles. One Boxing Day they all went to watch him partner a horse called Huguenot at Huntingdon and the money was very much down. 'He was miles clear but he fell at the second last.'

Son John says: 'In general terms he is fairly intolerant of jockeys but over the years he has had fantastic relationships with jockeys. He has called Michael names so often that it is like water off a duck's back but their relationship is very good. He got on well with Ernie Johnson and with Willie Carson and had a real relationship with Edward Hide, who was never stable jockey but rode a lot for Barry on northern tracks.

'Edward Hide was a thinking jockey who would walk the course, who knew everything about the form, unlike someone like Pat Eddery. Pat, who was so talented, wouldn't think about it at all until he got on the horse. He would just ride an instinctive race. Edward would have it all worked out beforehand.

'In the mid-Seventies Edward would telephone on a Sunday morning and say things like, "I'll tell Bill Watts not to run that one there and I'll ride yours. He can run his in that one." They used to piece it together and it resulted in extra winners.'

Bob Street, who spent many years as Barry's second-string jockey, gives a glimpse of how Barry's attention to detail paid off for his jockeys. One day in 1985, he says, Barry asked him to travel with him to Kempton Park.

'The guv'nor drove and when we got there he went past the entrance and round part of the course. At about the three-furlong marker he stopped and led me out on the track. He said, "See that tree there, on the left by the bend? You make a bee line for that and don't worry if the others don't follow." There had been a bit of rain and it was about the third race and nobody had been over there. But I did as I was told and went over there aiming for the tree. I won by a neck.'

That, says Carson, was typical. 'In those days watering systems used to interfere with the ground, covering only half of the track. A lot of that went on. When it rained you knew not to go on the inner. Barry always knew about water tables and that sort of stuff.'

The master of South Bank, Manton and now Faringdon Place has always been good at motivating jockeys too. Carson remembers riding one for Barry at the long-defunct Alexandra Palace. 'We were always worried about the grip at Ally Pally. Horses were always falling over. He said to me, "Don't worry, I've told the farrier to leave the heads up on the shoes. You'll be all right." Whether he had done so or not, he was giving me the confidence to be brave.'

Although Barry's own career as a jockey was short, he had knowledge to impart. Bob Street recalls: 'Every time I had a ride for him he would say, "Jump out of the stalls, sit on him, let him find his legs to halfway, then gradually close as best you can without knocking him about." By doing that when I was riding regularly he taught me how to read and ride a race. You'd sit there and think, "They're going a bit quick, they can't keep it up, they'll come back to me." When you've been out the back they'll stop and you'll come through sometimes. I've certainly won races like that. He likes his jockeys to ride his horses like that.'

WILLIE CARSON

Willie Carson has always been one of Barry's true friends 'He was focused on training, I was focused on riding, but we grew up together in racing. I always think the horse that made Barry was one owned by Lord St Germans called Fred Babu. Barry's plan was to have all the owners along and win the nursery at Newmarket when the sales were on so that they would all buy horses for the following year. Fred Babu duly won the Tattersalls Nursery Handicap at 3-1, by a neck, having won previously at Lingfield for Eric Eldin. The money was down and the owners were all on.'

Of the others, Carson says: 'I got Ernie Johnson the job. I put my own nose out of joint. But I still rode work for Barry and I was still about when Steve Cauthen came. Cash Asmussen and Barry didn't hit it off, but he liked Brent Thomson, who was a drinking pal of Robert Sangster's.'

Carson was a wonderful man to have riding out for you. Fellow jockey Ray Cochrane, who learned his trade as an apprentice in Barry's yard, recalls watching him. 'Willie Carson was always fantastic to ride work with. I learned a lot. He wouldn't tell you anything. If you wanted to learn you just had to watch what he was doing. You needed to watch the way he changed his hands, how he used his feet. He'd be Tck, Tck, Tck, clicking at horses, giving them a little tap down the shoulder. That's how I learned all my pushing, getting hold of horses, all that kind of thing. You learned to get hold of a horse.

'Willie didn't stop, like some, to ask: "Does this jog, does it whip round, does it kick?" It was just, "Give it to me. It's a horse. I'll guide it." Full stop. He didn't fuss if there were cows or sheep in the field (as there sometimes were in Barry's early days). He didn't care. If necessary, Willie would ride it on the verge up the side of the road.'

Carson used to go hunting with Barry and Penny's family, the Woodhouses, in Leicestershire. They rode with the Quorn and the Cottesmore. Carson still has on his wall a picture of a hunter, called Owen, given to him by the trainer. 'Barry said to me one year, "If you win the Gimcrack on Stand To Reason I will give you a hunter." I didn't win, I finished second, but he still gave me the horse.' Prominent among the elegant portraits of the winners Barry has trained, there is in his house too a portrait of his old hunter Mick.

Carson's wife Elaine says: 'Barry and Penny were the first people we rang up when we got engaged. We used to stay with them at York and we went on holiday with them to South Africa and to Woodlands in Barbados.'

In some ways it is surprising that Carson never became his friend's stable jockey. On a couple of occasions it nearly happened. In the autumn of 1973 Barry approached Carson with an offer of more than he was getting from his then employer Bernard van Cutsem. Carson, who was buying houses in Newmarket, turned him down, partly out of loyalty to Van Cutsem, who was ill, and partly because he dreamed of winning a Derby in the famous black Derby silks.

Two years later, when Van Cutsem died, it once again looked as though Carson might be heading for South Bank. He was riding plenty of the Hills horses. But then he rode a horse for Robert Sangster called Solitary Hail. They won at Ascot but then got beaten by Henry Cecil's Wollow (who was unbeaten in four races as a two-year-old and went on to win the 2,000 Guineas) in the Laurent Perrier Champagne Stakes at Doncaster. On Solitary Hail's next run, in the Observer Gold Cup at Doncaster, the ride was given to Lester Piggott. Barry explained: 'Robert Sangster asked me to engage Lester if he was available and that's exactly what happened. Willie has never done anything wrong on the colt and I loathe having to do it. But to say we have had a row is a load of rubbish.'

Carson basically refused to ride for Robert Sangster after that episode and the only tension between him and Barry came because of the Sangster factor. There was a minor fracas when Barry put him up on a Sangster horse at Nottingham one day. The horse was withdrawn, in fact for veterinary reasons, but Barry, who was not at the track, was fulminating. Carson reckons it was a case of the trainer believing, erroneously, 'that little bugger has refused to ride because it's one of Robert's'.

Row or not, the jocking off was the point, friends say, when Carson decided against a formal link with Barry. He was not prepared to have another Solitary Hail situation with Sangster. Solitary Hail, incidentally, though backed down to 7-4 favourite, finished unplaced at Doncaster and never ran at three.

Barry says: 'Willie should have been first jockey to me. Unfortunately it was the year Robert Sangster was out of the country for tax reasons and a lot of other people were advising him. They were betting and talking through their pockets really. Willie got beat and people told Robert he should have won, so he went and got the job with Dick Hern.'

But the friendship between Barry and Carson has endured, and Carson doesn't forget the support he received in harder times. 'In 1967 I got smashed up in a car crash at the back end of the season. I was in Ilkley Moor Hospital for three months and I remember Barry turning up with a case of half bottles of champagne.' A practical, restrained man but one always ready for a party too.

The Sangster colours at Cheltenham – Nomadic Way (far side) won the Stayers Hurdle and was second in two Champion Hurdles

In the hunting field, for so long Barry's favourite pursuit

Steve Cauthen, brought to England by Robert Sangster and Barry Hills, had to battle with his weight

Darryll Holland, one of the jockey talents discovered and developed by Barry

Robert Sangster with Barry and Penny Hills at Chester in May 1990

Ghanaati with her owner and trainer after winning the 2009 1000 Guineas

Distant Music (Michael Hills) wins the Champagne Stakes from Rossini in 1999

Distant Relative (Willie Carson) takes the Sussex Stakes at Goodwood 1990

Moonax and Pat Eddery win the St Leger in 1994 (Martin Lynch)

The crowd pleaser: Further Flight (Michael Hills) scores one of his 24 victories at Chester in 1997 (Dan Abraham)

A Hills Derby victory: jockey son Michael returns to the winner's enclosure after winning the 1996 Epsom Derby on Shaamit (Tony Edenden)

A trio of Irish Classics. Top: Hula Angel (Michael Hills) wins the Irish 1,000 Guineas from Golden Silca in 1999 (Ed Byrne). **Middle:** *Bolas (Pat Eddery) takes the Irish Oaks in 1994 (John Crofts).* **Bottom:** *"Well done, Son" Barry greets the grey Nicer (Michael Hills) after her win in the Irish 1,000 Guineas in 1993*

Barry Hills and Haafhd after Hamdan al Maktoum's colt won the 2,000 Guineas in 2004

Maids Causeway (Michael Hills, orange colours) gets the better of Karen's Caper to win the Coronation Stakes, Ascot at York 2005 (Julian Herbert)

Something to think about: Assistant Charlie Hills and his father in contemplative mood after Etlaala wins a Newbury maiden in 2004

Three Fast Horses for Michael Hills: Top: *Red Clubs wins the Haydock Sprint from French hotpot Marchand d'Or in 2007.* Middle: *Royal Applause wins at Ascot in June 1997.* Bottom: *Handsome Sailor collects the William Hill Sprint at Haydock in 1988. All three were ridden by the trainer's son and stable jockey Michael (Mark Cranham)*

The Master Builder: Faringdon Place Stables taking shape in 2001

Richard (left) and Michael Hills help their father celebrate his 300th Newmarket winner in 2010

Another Group One: the celebrations after Equiano takes the King's Stand Stakes at Royal Ascot in 2010 ridden by Michael Hills

The horse who began it all: Barry with a portrait of 1968 Lincoln winner Frankincense

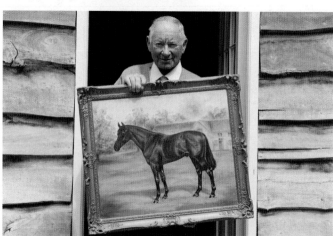

STEVE CAUTHEN

At the age of seventeen, in 1977, Steve Cauthen rode 487 winners in America, more than any other jockey had ever done. The next year, when he was still only eighteen, he won the Triple Crown on Affirmed and had his first biography written. That year he became known as the Six Million Dollar Kid for the sum amassed by his victories.

J. T. Lundy, President of Calumet Farm, where Affirmed was bred, once asserted: 'That boy could ride a swamp hog naked through the Louisiana bayous and still win twenty-five lengths.'

But fame and fortune can be fickle. Between New Year's Day and 8 February 1979 Steve hit an extended losing streak, riding 110 consecutive losers. Suddenly he was under the spotlight for the wrong reasons. At that point the canny Robert Sangster saw his chance and he and Barry Hills made an offer that would enable Cauthen to test his skills against the best in Europe. One key factor was that Cauthen was going through a growth spurt at the time and on average he would be able to ride some five pounds heavier in Britain, where racing weights were higher.

Former top jockey Jimmy Lindley remembers Sangster saying to Barry over dinner at an Italian restaurant in Newbury: 'You could do with a really top jockey.' 'Where am I going to get one?' replied Barry. 'All the top ones are booked.' 'You ought to get hold of this Kid in America.' 'If he's that good he'll stay in America.' 'Not necessarily, because he's getting a bit heavy for over there.'

Lindley says: 'I could see Barry was going, "Boing, Boing, Boing." The next thing he said was, "Go and get on an effing plane and get him." Sangster and Barry paid for me to go to America and see Steve and his parents. I had never met him and I went to this hotel in Kentucky. The Kid walked in in a pair of jeans and sneakers and that was it. Wham! I thought it was bloody Frank Sinatra. Everyone was going mad. Women were rushing up and saying, "Can I have an autograph for my daughter?" '

Jimmy met Steve's parents and arranged for him to come to Britain. He then continued the association. The two of them walked every track in the country together. 'The first day the Kid walked in he asked for a glass of sweet red wine – that really threw us. He stood in front of the fire in a pair of terylene trousers: he could have melted. But he adapted like nobody I've ever seen. When he first came he had a problem keeping horses straight but every time he went out to ride he improved by pounds. He changed the style of our boys – they're all based on him now.'

Snapping up Cauthen, says Jimmy, was typical of Barry. 'When other people are starting to think about things Barry is already past the winning post. That's him.'

Journalist Charles Benson, Sangster's drinking and gambling chum, called the Cauthen deal the 'largest annual contract ever offered to a jockey in England'. Cauthen responded: 'I hear some reports have suggested (a guarantee of) £200,000 or more. Well, that is rubbish. The guarantee is less than half that. But it is only a guarantee and I certainly hope to prove my worth by earning a great deal more than that.'

Barry still has in his files a copy of one proposed offer to Cauthen, which included a £100,000 retainer including an accommodation allowance, a one-fortieth share in colts that won a Pattern race, an additional seven and a half per cent of the prize-money for colts he rode into first, second or third in a Pattern race. That rose to fifteen per cent extra for fillies, although the money in their case would not be paid for two years and only then if the retainer was still in force. Shares in the proposed retainer (which was not the one finally agreed) were to be split proportionately between Sangster, Sheikh Mohammed, Khalid Abdullah, Gerald Leigh, Sir Ernest Harrison, Tony Shead and Alan Clore.

With Sangster insisting there was no pressure, Cauthen was taken in by Barry and Penny virtually as a member of the family. Steve says: 'Barry treated me like a son. I lived with them for a while. It felt like we were on an even par but also that he was always looking out for me. Penny was like a mother hen. They were always trying to make sure I knew what I was dealing with.'

After his rapid rise to fame in America, the courteous American admits he had been to some extent going through the motions. 'Barry's attitude of "let's go fricking win something good" got me revved up and wanting to be a champion. I understood how Barry wanted his horses ridden and he understood that I understood. We hardly had to talk. We had a great connection. I credit him with helping to remotivate me.'

There was one small bump in Cauthen's learning curve. 'I had been in England two or three weeks and we were due to race at Nottingham. Penny usually drove the Mercedes. I would sit in front. Barry would be in the back reading the *Sporting Life*, doing the entries, smoking a cigar.

'But the night before there had been a big party to introduce me to people. Sir Gordon Richards was there, Peter Walwyn, Nicky Henderson. It was a late night and there'd been plenty of champagne. Penny felt a little tired and asked me to drive. I'd been dying to. But I had very little experience of smaller English roads. I kept pulling out to get by trucks and swerving back in again. I didn't quite understand how to kick the Merc in the belly.

'After a few of these manoeuvres Penny started looking nervously for the reaction in the back, but there wasn't a word from Barry, who went on with his work. The comment was saved for when we got to the track. B. Hills climbed out and said to me: "I hope you give my horses a better f****** ride than you've just given me." '

The young American made his debut a winning one over the unfamiliar straight mile at Salisbury in the Grand Foods Stakes on 7 April 1979, riding the Barry Hills-trained Marquee Universal for Keith Hsu. Despite the inclement weather, Salisbury had its biggest crowd for a decade.

At the furlong marker, as he picked up his stick, it was clear that Cauthen would win and the crowd began yelling, 'Come on Steve,' an echo of the traditional yells of older times when Steve Donoghue was Britain's champion jockey from 1914 to 1923. Cauthen did not need to use the whip and rode out Marquee Universal for a hands-and-heels victory by one and a half lengths.

On the same day he rode Ring Lady in the 1,000 Guineas trial and Tap On Wood, who was fourth in the 2,000 Guineas trial. In the process he showed himself to be not just a stylist but a thinking jockey, too, in the way he treated potential Classic horses.

Steve explained that he had not wanted to punish Tap On Wood and give him a hard race in the soft ground. 'I wouldn't have wanted to do that. It's a long season and I like him.' It proved to be a kindness repaid.

Eleven days later Cauthen won his first Group race on Hawaiian Sound in the Earl of Sefton Stakes at Newmarket. Within six weeks he had won five more Group races, including the 2,000 Guineas on Tap On Wood. After the Guineas victory Steve reflected: 'The cheers weren't just for winning. I know they were a sort of welcome as if to say, "Glad to have you here." '

Although Cauthen was to go on to ride for trainers up and down the land, the connection with Barry Hills was a deep one. In 1984, the first year that Cauthen was Britain's champion jockey (he also took the title in 1985 and 1987), Barry provided thirty-six of his 130 winners. The only other trainer with a double-figure contribution was Fulke Johnson Houghton.

Few British racegoers will ever forget Cauthen's epic battle with Pat Eddery for the jockeys' title in the last of those years, a battle that Cauthen won 197-195. Next year he broke his neck, his weight problems increased and in 1993, at the age of only 33, he retired. He had ridden 2,794 winners and earned more than $23 million in prize-money. He was the only jockey ever to ride the winners of the English, French, Irish and Kentucky Derbies.

In a career shortened by his weight problems, Cauthen not only won ten British Classics, he was an exemplar to young jockeys of the American style and he proved hugely influential in British racing. As a result of his arrival a number of British jockeys began riding with just the ball of their foot in the stirrup, not with their feet right in the irons. Following Cauthen's example they also became less afraid of riding races from the front, improving their judgement of pace.

Steered by Barry in many aspects of life, Cauthen did a lot for the image of racing. He was polite, articulate and good-looking. He was also something of a weighing-room diplomat. There were stories in the early days of British jockeys ganging up on the young American but when he was questioned by pressmen after a rough race at Chester one day, Cauthen replied: 'I don't think the other jocks were going for me in particular. Five furlongs at Chester is pretty tricky and everyone wants the fence. I just got the worst of that particular tussle.'

Cauthen found in Barry a trainer always responsive to new ways of doing things and he relished the organisation of his yard. 'Groups of horses arrive at the gallops at five-minute intervals .The work riders are ferried to the bottom of the gallops by car after each lot. That way I was getting a feel of perhaps half a dozen horses in quick succession – so efficient.'

He didn't much enjoy the travelling. 'In America we don't "go racing", we're there for weeks on end.' But if he found it onerous not doing his racing in a single locality Cauthen relished the chance to test his skills on a range of different courses and to ride some 'hold-up' horses as well as racing gate to wire in the American style.

There was disappointment for Barry when the talent he had nurtured was tempted elsewhere as part of a merry-go-round of jockeys' contracts in 1984. The short-fused French owner Daniel Wildenstein refused that year to have his horses ridden by Newmarket trainer Henry Cecil's stable jockey Lester Piggott. Cecil and Piggott parted in June and Cecil said Cauthen had agreed to be his stable jockey the next season.

The appeal of Cecil's offer was probably as much to do with winning the jockeys' championship as it was to do with retainers. Willie Carson was sidelined through injury, Piggott had three injury breaks and was not riding the Wildenstein horses and Pat Eddery was spending many weekends in Ireland as Piggott's replacement with Vincent O'Brien. With a stable like Cecil's behind him, the way was open for Cauthen to win his first jockeys' championship.

The American insisted it was the new challenge, not money, that drew him to Newmarket, telling reporters: 'I think the world of Barry and it wasn't easy for me to leave. I'm glad I'm still able to ride for him. He's a first-class professional in everything he does and has been a very good friend to me.' He added: 'Barry is one of my best friends and I've given him six of the best years of my life since I came to Britain. I'll always ride for him if available.'

Although they went on working together his mentor's disappointment was plain for all to see. Barry said: 'Of course I am unhappy about Steve leaving me. It's a question of loyalty. I launched him and stood by him over the years. I won't groom another jockey to ride for another top stable. I will not have a stable jockey this season, although Brent Thomson will ride the Sangster horses in my yard.'

Steve Cauthen says today of their split: 'It was one of the toughest decisions in my life. I'm a loyal person. They'd done so much for me. But I knew I'd only got so long to ride and Henry Cecil had a yard full of potential Classic winners. I won four Classics for him in the first year.

'It went better than I had anticipated with Barry because he is that kind of guy. Barry let me know that it sucked and I was sad. But we carried on working together, that's what makes him such a special guy.'

ERNIE JOHNSON

When Steve Cauthen came over and began riding for him, Barry stressed he would also still be employing Ernie Johnson, his first full-time stable jockey, who had been aware he might sign up a big name. 'Ernie has done us proud in the past and he will still get plenty of rides.'

As the rumours flew the trainer insisted: 'Ernie Johnson will be my stable jockey this season, next season and the one after and he will certainly ride as many winners as he has done in previous years.' Ernie, he told pressmen, was 'a good judge, a kind rider and has a brain'.

Johnson, who rode Blakeney to win the 1969 Derby for Arthur Budgett, was one of the few jockeys who didn't have to starve to make the weight. He was apprenticed to Sam Hall at Malton and could have moved south after his Derby win but went back north, reckoning he lacked the experience to ride continually against the top jockeys. When Barry took him on, at a retainer said to have been £10,000 a year, it was his breakthrough into the big time.

There was a mutual respect between Barry and Johnson, but that did not mean there were no ructions. The jockey 'quit' for the first time when the owners insisted on putting up Yves Saint-Martin on Rheingold on his first run after his tantalisingly close Derby second with Johnson aboard. These things happen in racing, where confidence is crucial, and although Ernie had ended his retainer he was soon back riding for Barry and the contract was renewed.

In the late 1970s Johnson was out of the saddle for a while after breaking his left leg badly when Courjet ran out with him at Newmarket. He came back to ride for Barry but once again quit to ride as a freelance when Steve Cauthen was given the 1979 2,000 Guineas ride on Tony Shead's Tap On Wood, a horse Ernie had ridden to six successes the previous season.

Barry said at the time: 'Ernie was understandably upset. He has ridden 200 winners for me and I have always had the highest regard for his integrity and his talent. But the wishes of the owners must come first. Cauthen is world class and owners want him on their horses in the big races. I think Ernie has acted too hastily. I have 119 horses in my yard and as second jockey he would probably ride fifty winners. I fear his decision may have blown his chance in the Derby because I have four candidates and Cauthen is not certain to pick the right one.

'I hope at this late stage it will be possible to patch up our differences. I would welcome Johnson back because we have always worked closely together and he has never once let me down.'

Johnson responded: 'There is no aggravation with Barry Hills and I will continue to ride for him if asked.' It was agreed that he would in future be a freelance but would have the pick of the stable's spare rides.

Johnson spent 1984 riding in Ireland for Edward O'Grady and most of the next two years in Singapore. But to this day he rides work regularly for Barry and the two remain firm friends.

The rider says of his long-time employer: 'He's very straightforward. Forthright. You can say what you feel. You don't have to sugar coat it. You just work together. He's up front and you're up front and that's the short way to finding out the truth.'

And did Barry listen to his advice? 'There were times when he did and times when he didn't. But he's been right more times than anybody.'

CASH ASMUSSEN

Steve Cauthen was not the only American rider to work for Barry. For a period in the late 1980s, so did Cash Asmussen, the US rider with the low-crouching Cossack style who enjoyed considerable success in France.

Again it was thanks to the Sangster connection. Asmussen rode for the Ballydoyle team, of which in those days Sangster was a partner, and it was mostly Sangster's horses that Asmussen rode for Barry, who was not his greatest fan.

Sangster flew in for a look at Manton one day in 1987 and Barry gave him a double at Bath in the afternoon with Fatal Charm and Schaufuss, both ridden by Pat Eddery. Cash had asked for a couple of days off to ride in France and Barry agreed. 'Nobody's indispensable in this job. There's a strong nucleus of jockeys to choose from.'

He felt the American's approach was wrong. After Asmussen had finished second on two Sangster-owned horses at Nottingham, Strike Force and Obeah, Barry declared: 'He is riding as he did in Paris and he has got to change his style. They don't fall away here.'

In an interview on his lifestyle, Asmussen said: 'Some of the Press seem to want to get something started but the fact is Barry Hills and I get on fine. He's a good man to ride for and he tells you everything he knows about each horse but then lets you do the job.'

After he won Waterford Candelabra Stakes at Goodwood on Obeah at 16-1, coming from last to first, Cash disclosed that his orders from Barry were: 'Do what you want but don't mess it up.'

Certainly Asmussen was a man with a mind of his own. Peter Chapple-Hyam, who at that time was an assistant to Barry Hills at Manton, says with a rich chuckle: 'He cost us a lot of money on occasions. If Cash wasn't happy with a horse going down to the start he would give it a quiet race. But he was some horseman. One day when the sprinter Gallic League was playing up he backed it into the stalls. But he was too clever for his own good. He did better in France with the soft going there.'

When Asmussen announced he would be ending his arrangement with Ballydoyle, finding that riding in three countries was too much, the expectation was that he would concentrate on riding for Sangster and Barry Hills. But then André Fabre expressed an interest and so did Daniel Wildenstein and the American resumed his career in France.

Asmussen was not one for underestimating his own worth, and he lived up to his name. Once he is alleged to have demanded £2,000 for riding a horse in the Derby. 'No problem,' he was told. 'X, in whose name he runs, owns half of Berkshire.' 'If I had known that,' he responded, 'I would have asked for £4,000. I own half of Kentucky but I want to own the other half.'

Barry chuckles at that and adds of the American: 'Cash is my name, cash is my nature.'

BRENT THOMSON

Another Sangster import was the popular New Zealander Brent Thomson. He was brought to Britain in 1984 by the pools millionaire, who had many horses in training with his employer Colin Hayes in Australia. Thomson was a great favourite with the Hills family. John Hills recalls: 'There were a lot of bollockings but we all loved him as a person. He was a star to work with.'

The outgoing Thomson got on well with his fellow jockeys and the racecourse crowds liked him too. But at first he found it strange not being top dog as he had been at home. 'You're starting all over again and you've got to work pretty hard. But I don't think it does you much harm being brought back to reality. The other day I drove to Beverley from Lambourn for a couple of rides – at home I wouldn't drive that far to go on holiday, let alone ride.'

One of Thomson's finest efforts in the saddle in his own estimation was on Gildoran, the stayer whom he partnered to his second Ascot Gold Cup in 1985, following Steve Cauthen's success on the same animal the year before. Boldly, Thomson, left to choose his own tactics, decided to make it all on Gildoran in the ultimate test of stamina.

Thomson says: 'He was a horse who used to pull a bit. I'd been in England long enough to know that without me going on and leading he would pull because there wouldn't be anything going fast enough for him. I walked out of the yard with the fixation that I was going to lead but I can tell you that for two and a half miles that is a very lonely place to be. It's one of those things that if you carry it off you get a slap on the back and people say well done. If you don't ...'

Thomson gives the impression that his two years plus in England were a highlight of his career. He enjoyed not just the riding but the socialising with Sangster and Barry and other owners like Bobby McAlpine and Bill Gredley. In a Dubai bar at World Cup time, he recalled the flavour of the times: 'Barry liked playing golf. There was the Brian Taylor memorial event on the eve of Royal Ascot in 1986 and he said, "Come with me." He'd got a driver. I thought, "Good, I'm with the guv'nor and we can't get in any trouble here." We went to Sunningdale – I think I played with Eamonn Darcy – and afterwards we went into the clubhouse and had a couple of Pimms. I was thinking, "Fine, we'll be heading off shortly," and then Robert Sangster came in. We ended up in Reading or somewhere for dinner and Barry and I finally knocked up in Lambourn at about two o'clock the next morning with me thinking, "This isn't quite the way I'd planned it."

'Of course, I was up to ride work in the morning at seven o'clock and not feeling too flash – Barry and I were both a bit green – but anyway we went to Ascot and won the St James's Palace Stakes with Sure Blade. It was one of those times when he didn't say anything and I didn't say anything. But the wives weren't happy.' Not, perhaps, the perfect preparation for an important day at Ascot, and just as well that in those days jockeys were not tested for alcohol levels.

Then there was Robert Sangster's fiftieth birthday party. 'There was some comment at the time about my strength in the finish. We were on the Isle of Man staying with Robert. I remember jumping on Barry's bed on top of him and taking my stick out and saying, "Is this strong enough for you now?" He threw me out of the bedroom.'

Thomson joined Barry at a difficult time, after the wounding departure of Steve Cauthen. He rode two seasons but part of the way through the third, when Barry's horses had been having a disappointing time, the former Australian champion received a big shock. Over breakfast one morning he was told his contract would not be renewed the next season.

He felt, he says, as if the carpet had been pulled from under him but there was no animosity. He rode through the rest of the season, ironically with the horses coming back to winning form.

'I didn't really want to leave England but I had a family and had to sort things out. I remained very good friends with Barry and I always wondered if it may well have been that Michael and Richard were coming through and blood is thicker than water. There was no animosity. Michael was coming through and that was the way it had to be.'

In March 1988 Barry told the *Racing Post*: 'I found Brent Thomson a very likeable man but I just wasn't satisfied with the quality of his riding. I told him as early as possible in the season so that he could make up his mind whether to go back to Australia.'

Barry's greatest achievement in his time, Brent believes, was his training of Sure Blade to win Ascot's Queen Elizabeth II Stakes in 1986 after a three month lay-off through injury. .

'He was up against that old warhorse Teleprompter. Joe Mercer was my agent and was driving me to Ascot while I was trying to work out how to win the race. In with a horse like Teleprompter it was going to be hard to bury him. We were nearly at the course when I said to Joe, "I've just worked out how to win this race. I'm going to head straight towards the middle of the course. When I get to Teleprompter I'll be running out of gas." Teleprompter wore blinkers. In the end I beat him half a length. He was worrying us out of it. That was one of Barry's greatest achievements in my time and one of my greatest rides.'

DARRYLL HOLLAND

One of Barry's discoveries was the precociously talented Darryll Holland. When the young apprentice, aged only nineteen, rode his second double in a week to reduce his allowance to three pounds,

Barry declared he was 'a bit of magic'.

He added: 'I've only known three natural jockeys in my life. One was Manny Mercer, he was like electricity on a horse. Steve Cauthen, already a beautiful rider when he came here, was obviously a natural from the beginning. And you could spot that with this boy from very early on. When he came to me we had him booked to go to the British Racing School, but he advanced so quickly it would have been a waste of time sending him. He gives a horse a good ride from the gate, there's none of this shunting up and down. He gets a horse into its rhythm straight away. He's got a great future if he can keep his feet on the ground.'

Under Barry's guidance, Holland achieved a new record total of winners for an apprentice with eighty-three winners in a season. To give that some perspective, the previous record of seventy-five had been shared by Edward Hide and Frankie Dettori. In May 1991 a *Sporting Life* profile of Holland declared: 'If they opened a book on the first champion jockey of the next century he would be among the favourites.' That was just three years after the Manchester schoolboy, whose only racing experience had been an occasional visit to Chester, had sat on a horse for the first time.

It was Barry's high strike-rate at Chester that made Holland include him on the list with Henry Cecil and Luca Cumani when, after taking his O levels, he wrote to three trainers seeking an opening in racing. He went to Manton for a two-week trial and was taken on.

At first he did not feel a natural. The first horse he was put on, Roupala, supposedly the quietest in the yard, played up with him. So did the filly Rambushka on his first canter. And Budapest, on his first public ride at Newbury: 'First it took off with me, then it stopped dead when I started pushing and kicking. I was so tired I nearly fell off when I came back in.'

Nevertheless he progressed to end his first season with twenty-seven wins against professionals and four in apprentice races. Barry then sent him to spend three months with Gary Jones in California through the winter. 'I thought I looked pretty neat on a horse but when I was in America I realised there was still a lot of room for improvement. Their jockeys sit so tight into a horse, whereas in Britain the style is much more vigorous.

'While I was there I got important experience in how to make the pace. I felt very confident when I came back. I think I matured into a better person as well as a better jockey. I wasn't good enough to get a ride over there, so it made me appreciate what I had got here.'

Other talented apprentices like Alan Munro and Ray Cochrane had been with Barry and Holland benefited from their experience. Barry told reporters as the youngster's career took off: 'When Alan was with me we did not have a lot of ammunition for the kids to ride but three of my owners and I put in £10,000 each to buy four horses and it has helped Darryll and the other lads.'

Holland says: 'They claimed a couple, one I think from Reg Hollinshead. Monteros Boy won four on the trot for me and I won three times on Fallow Deer. Everything won that we claimed, it was just a bit of fun for the apprentices. They were like my horses. It was like being stable jockey, it was a good feeling.'

One of the owners who chipped in was Ken Knox, a Swindon businessman, who recalls: 'Barry said, "This lad can really ride," and that if we bought the four horses he wouldn't charge us anything for training them if we let Darryll ride.'

It proved to be a very good deal. 'They ran in my name and that of my partner Barry Wilsdon. In the first year we had six winners. Darryll rode his first winner in my colours, his last as an apprentice at Brighton and his first as a fully fledged jockey.'

Barry's tutoring was a real benefit. Holland said at the time: 'The guv'nor picks out the things I've done wrong rather than the things I've done right, but that's good because I am a perfectionist and getting better is what motivates me.' After winning a Catterick apprentices' race by half a length with a well-timed challenge on Mrs Barton, Holland revealed: "The guv'nor told me that if I hit this filly more than three times I was in trouble. He said I was to try to change my hands to shake her up rather than use my whip, even though she is a lazy filly.'

The trainer watched his protege's diet too, helping the one-time six-stone boxer settle into doing a regular 7st 10lb. Darryll had felt dizzy one day at Brighton and had to be sent home, missing four fancied rides. He revealed: 'Barry Hills was annoyed with me but he was also very concerned for me. He is like a father figure. He makes sure that I go to his house every morning for breakfast.' Although he added: 'The rest of the time I still live on lettuce.'

Eventually Barry and Holland went their separate ways. But he is still pleased to get the opportunity of riding for his early mentor and when asked in a racecard interview who had had the most influence on his career he named his mother 'and also Barry Hills, who put me on the road and has been like a father figure, keeping me on the right track, not just on the racecourse but also showing me how to conduct myself in public. I owe him a lot.'

Barry was frustrated at one stage that Holland did not always make the best use of his talent. He said in 1998: 'I thought right from the start that Darryll was going to be a good jockey. The trouble was that he tended to be like one of those Scalextric racing cars – he'd do three laps and then crash off. Now he has matured and become more positive I am sure he has a great future.'

The jockey always remembers winning the Group Three Rockfel Stakes on Yawl in 1992. 'I was only twenty and it was a huge thrill, especially being for the guv'nor.' He was also indirectly responsible for the trainer's son Michael winning his first European Classic, the Irish 1,000 Guineas, on Nicer. It was to have been Holland's ride, but he missed it through suspension. The trainer said: 'I feel sorry for Darryll. But being suspended for excessive use (of the whip) on a horse who finishes only thirteenth of fifteen is a lesson for him to learn.'

Barry's teaching methods could be old-fashioned. Holland says: 'I was a raw lad from Manchester. I was fifteen. I had discipline at home but not to the extent I found when I came to the yard. He wanted things done right. If it wasn't done right he told you. Claiming seven pounds I rode him a winner at Doncaster, won a short head and I got done for the whip. I got three days' suspension. I went to an evening meeting at Sandown and I rode another winner there and I got banned on that. The next morning I went into the yard and he got the Long Tom and whipped me right on the back of the legs. I turned round and said, "What was that for?" and he said, "Now you know how those effing horses felt."

'I stormed off and was going to quit. But he rang me up at the house and said, "Are you coming in for second lot? Your horse is tacked up." So I came in and that was that.' Holland's father called Barry to complain about him hitting his son. Barry replied: 'I wouldn't have bothered to do it if I hadn't cared about him,' and the matter ended there.

A *Sporting Life* news clipping in Barry's scrapbooks adds another story. The joint report on the Stable Lads Boxing Championships by Neil Morrice and Simon Crisford, for many years now a kingpin of the Godolphin operation, detailed how Holland, the 'Manton Mauler', stopped his opponent in the first round in the 6st junior class. It seems to have been a profitable evening for all concerned, the realisation of another Hills-Sangster coup.

Holland remembers: 'Sangster and co had all backed me. There was big betting on it at the Hilton Hotel. They had put me in training in Swindon and I trained very hard for for half the year. I was in tip-top shape and it was all over very quickly. The fight got stopped straight away. I remember coming round with the trophy. The boss said, "Well done," and gave me a hug. They all started putting tenners and twenties into the trophy, which was equally nice, especially when you're only on £45 a week. I must have got a month's wages.'

RAY COCHRANE

Another leading jockey who spent a formative period with Barry was Ray Cochrane, who joined him straight from school in 1972, working alongside Geoff Snook and long-time assistant trainer Kevin Mooney, who are both still key figures in the yard.

Ray went on to make his name as Luca Cumani's stable jockey and as the man who rescued his friend Frankie Dettori from a burning plane. But the joy of his time with Barry was the flying filly Nagwa, who set a record by winning thirteen races as a two-year-old in 1975.

As an apprentice Ray was getting disillusioned with his lack of rides and decided to confront his boss. 'I didn't want to be a stable lad, I wanted to be a jockey. One Sunday morning I got changed, walked up to the yard, and then walked round half a dozen times. He wasn't the sort of man you readily approached, like a bull terrier sitting in the office.'

After nearly losing his nerve and heading down the drive, Ray decided he had to go through with it and hammered on the door. 'I gave him my story. He looked at me and said, "You'll do what you're f****** told, when you are told. Get out."

'I was going on holiday and I said, "If I'm not going to get a chance I will have to go somewhere else." He repeated: "You'll do what you're told when you're told. Out." But clearly boldness had been respected.

'The next day he trotted upsides me in the morning and he said: "When you come back off holiday you can have a ride on Nagwa." I rode her ten times and won nine. With a few other chances I think I had twenty-two rides and rode eleven winners from August onwards.'

And what was Nagwa like? 'She was an unbelievable little filly, very athletic. After she ran her first four races Barry never really trained her. She would just trot up to the gallop and come home. I remember the head lad getting a severe bollocking because he gave her a canter, letting her go up with the rest of the horses. Barry turned round and said, "What's she doing up here?"

'In her races she just jumped out. It seemed to me that whatever the distance you cantered down (to the start) she knew how far it was to come back. If it was a seven-furlong race she'd take her time, if it was a five-furlong race she'd be gone. She was an unbelievable little animal. Every time you pressed the button she just picked up, picked up, picked up. She was fantastic to ride. Absolutely brilliant.'

But how did she take so many races? 'She was hard as nails, but the kindest little thing you'd ever come across. Most of the time I was with her, I knew what she was like because I always travelled in the horsebox with her. I didn't have a car. I'd be leading up another horse.'

Ray says the stable staff in those days were true professionals. 'I wasn't trusted with too many of the good ones. We were all proper lads who could ride a bit, who could get on anything and ride anything. Whenever I progressed I was thrown on some of the lunatics. There was one filly, No Axe To Grind, I think she was called, whose party piece was to rear over backwards or back herself into a hedge. Everyone was frightened to death of her. It was a great cure for constipation when you saw your name down next to that one. I eventually got her going. She turned out to be a decent little filly, she won four races.'

The season after Nagwa's winning streak, Cochrane had an accident in the practice starting stalls, breaking his pelvis. During his recovery he grew too heavy. After a row on the gallops with Barry one morning Cochrane left and went jumping for a while with Fulke Walwyn and Kim Bailey and then worked with Ron Sheather in Newmarket. He got kicked in the head and broke his skull, and this time while he was recovering the weight fell away. Back on the Flat he had soon ridden fifty winners as a freelance and became Luca Cumani's stable jockey.

Fences were mended with Barry long ago and he rode winners for him too, notably an awkward sprinter called Cadeaux Cher. 'It scooted up at Leicester one evening. Next time out Michael Hills was in the car with Barry on the morning of the race and said, "This will win, won't it Dad?" Barry replied: "Nah. No chance. Only won a tinpot race the other day." '

Michael asked Ray what he thought and he replied, 'I think it's got a hell of a chance,' and he duly won on it again. 'The change of hands and the way I rode him obviously suited the little horse. I went on to win the Portland on him at Doncaster.'

In Cochrane's time Michael Blanshard, now a trainer in Lambourn, was working in Barry's yard and he was responsible for the most expensive horse in the yard. 'It was a great big goofy thing owned by Robert Sangster that had a habit of whipping around. One day, up the Baydon Road, it whipped round and got its foot stuck between a car body and bumper and stood there. Everybody was saying, "We'll have to end up shooting it, it will pull its leg off." I saw Barry go four different shades of green.' The horse proved cute enough to extricate himself delicately from the car but that did not, says Cochrane, spare Blanshard one of Barry's more memorable bollockings.

He hasn't forgotten one he endured himself. The young Hills twins, then 'three stone sopping wet', as he puts it, used to ride out with the string. 'I was coming up the gallop the right side of Faringdon Road with Michael and I was worried that my tack was not secure. I saw a horse take off with Michael. And the further we went the more you could see it wasn't going to stop. At the end there was a big barbed wire fence that wasn't usually there. Michael called out, "Ray, I can't stop it." I drove mine upsides him, got a hold of its head, got a hold of Mike's reins, and thought, 'That's it." I got both of them easing down and then my tack went. Both horses galloped over me. My horse galloped off, Mike's pulled up on seeing the other horses. My horse went on to knock over old Major Nelson (the Derby-winning trainer of Snow Knight). It bowled over a couple of his lads and went on down to Peter Walwyn's. I think they caught him in Upper Lambourn about a day and a half later.'

Barry hadn't seen the earlier incident and Ray got an earful before Michael came up and told his father what had happened.

ROBERT WINSTON

One of the more recent additions to Barry's roster of jockeys has been Robert Winston, whose career demonstrates the perils and pitfalls of a rider's life. In 2005 he was leading the jockeys' championship with 124 winners and getting rides for the likes of Sir Michael Stoute when he broke his jaw in a fall at Ayr, putting an end to his challenge. Later that year he admitted to finding himself in 'a big black hole' with chronic alcoholism, a family affliction, and booked himself into an addiction centre. That challenge confronted and surmounted, in February 2007 Winston was suspended from riding for a year for passing information for reward. Since he completed his sentence he has moved to East Ilsley and concentrated on rebuilding trust with owners and trainers to get his career back on track.

That operation has been a success, and one of those who has begun making use of Winston's services is Barry Hills. Winston now rides work at Faringdon Place a couple of days a week and has been rewarded with some useful mounts. He repaid the compliment in 2009, winning the Group Three Prestige Stakes at Goodwood in August on Sent From Heaven. Setting a blistering pace, which few thought the filly would be able to sustain, Winston managed to hold on until the line, even though he told Charlie Hills afterwards that Sent From Heaven didn't really handle the downland track.

In 2010 there came another Group success on a horse who has tested even Barry's famous patience – Prime Defender. The yard never lost faith in Prime Defender's ability, running him regularly in top sprint races at home and abroad. He had secured a couple of Listed successes but when in May 2010 Prime Defender ran in the Duke of York Stakes at York, it was his twentieth race in Group company and there hadn't been a single victory at that level. That day, ridden by Winston, he beat the useful Showcasing by half a length for the Group Two prize.

Winston had ridden Prime Defender once before, getting beaten half a length in the Cammidge Trophy at Doncaster. He recalled: 'He came to win his race and when I hit him I felt he curled up with me. I said to Barry afterwards that, although he was game enough, he didn't like being hit.' Apart from one brief flick, the jockey rode out Prime Defender at York with hands and heels to give Barry his seventh victory in the race. Charlie Hills said afterwards: 'He's always been a good horse. He just needs things to go right for him.' Winston commented: 'These are the sort of races you want to be winning. All credit to Barry for giving me such good support.'

Undeterred by Winston's past problems, Barry says: 'You can only help those who help themselves. Hopefully he's here for the long haul. He may not be the tidiest in a finish but he's strong and effective.'

TONY CULHANE

If Barry is demanding of his jockeys, he can be forgiving too. In July 2002 Tony Culhane, who used to ride some of Barry's runners in the north, was guilty of a major pilot error on True Courage, an odds-on favourite, at Pontefract. He had held an eight-length lead but stopped riding, began to ease down and took time to pull his mount's ears and pat him down the neck. Ted Durcan, on the John Dunlop-trained Kahalah, saw what was happening, galvanised his mount for another effort and by the time Culhane realised it was too late. He was passed and beaten a length, having committed the cardinal sin of dropping his hands inside the final furlong. He was given the 21-day maximum suspension and needed a police escort away from the track to avoid punters' anger after being chased into the weighing room.

Culhane was devastated by his mistake. 'I messed up in a major way and I can't blame punters for reacting the way they did. The horse was a bit difficult going to the start. He is a bit nervous and I was trying to give him confidence by winning as easy as I could on him, so that he would progress from the race, but, as I say, I messed it up. I have seen other jockeys do it and I have always said to myself that it would never happen to me, but I have gone and done it and I have let the owner, the trainer and the punters down. I can only apologise to them.'

Barry, who was at Newmarket, said: 'It's so unnecessary and so unprofessional. Tony's been riding well and rode me a few winners last year but this won't do.' As headlines continued over the incident, the Jockey Club pointed out that Culhane would lose thousands while he was stood down and trainer Mark Johnston argued that the hideous error was a result of the handicapping system because jockeys are thereby steeped in the culture of never winning by too much and get chastised by owners and trainers if they do. According to some stories, Barry sympathised with calls for a ban of three months or more for similar offences.

In a letter to the *Racing Post*, trainer John Berry pointed out that Culhane had ridden 382 good races before the bad one. He quoted Australian trainer Bart Cummings, who, having been asked by a journalist if he would be changing his horse's pilot after a jockey error, said: 'They don't sack you blokes for one bad story.' Barry clearly had some sympathy with that view too.

When Culhane returned from his enforced 21-day holiday from the saddle, one of the trainers who put him up on the very first day was B.W. Hills, who gave him a ride on Khalid Abdullah's Sight Screen. Culhane said: 'I take my hat off to Mr Hills. He is an absolute gentleman to do that for me and I just hope I can repay him with a good performance.'

CHAPTER SEVENTEEN

Barry's Owners

Some of those who have played
their part in the story

Training racehorses isn't just about buying decent horses and getting them fit. A crucial part of the job is finding good owners and keeping them. Barry, who started off with a small band of eager gambling owners, has always had an eye for quality in that department. He has always looked the part as well as playing it.

'Buy a suit off the peg,' he says, 'and it is just a suit. Get one made and you have something that has been built. When I was young and had half a crown in my pocket I always went and had a gin and tonic in the good bar rather than a beer in the spit and sawdust. You might meet someone in the smart bar that you wouldn't in the other one.'

His friend Jimmy Lindley says: 'Barry's drive comes from within himself. He's a self-taught man. But he took advice from George Colling in the old days and George Colling was immaculate. If you ever see B.W. Hills in an unpressed shirt or a dirty pair of shoes I will give you a million quid. He's a fashion icon. Colling taught him how to be with people. Everything's got to be perfect or he won't do it.'

It would not have happened without the results, of course, but Barry knew from early on that he wanted to be training for the likes of Robert Sangster and Sheikh Mohammed, for Sheikh Hamdan Al Maktoum and Prince Khalid Abdullah, for old-school breeders like Dick Hollingsworth and for international horsemen like Dick Bonnycastle.

Sheikh Hamdan continues to have more horses in Barry's Faringdon Place yard than any other owner and has for many years retained Richard Hills as his first jockey. Neither he nor Prince Khalid Abdullah court publicity. Barry says Prince Khalid joined him as an owner in about 1982 when Alan Clore, a regular Hills patron with five or six horses, who lived in Paris and gave him a cheque every six months, sold a filly, Slightly Dangerous, to the Prince.

Slightly Dangerous was left in training with Barry. He says: 'She was second in the Oaks and had a beautiful pedigree. She was probably one of the cheapest he ever bought. He has had horses with me ever since and is a very good, loyal owner. We have had lots of success together.

'He's a quiet, unassuming person but he fires a few shots from the back of the pitch. Sheikh Hamdan knows the horses. Prince Khalid is a bit like Robert Sangster. Robert would come and say, "Show me the best of what I've got, the five best horses," and he wouldn't want to see the rest. But he'd know the pedigrees inside out and the matings. So does Prince Khalid, that's his passion. He doesn't miss anything. The Prince doesn't come down here very often but he follows it all closely.'

Barry has provided huge success, too, for Sheikh Hamdan, not least with the two Classic winners Haafhd and Ghanaati. 'Sheikh Hamdan comes down at least twice a year and he has a wonderful memory for pedigrees. He's seen them all as foals and he still recognises them the next year. He is fair with all his trainers and he sends us fifteen yearlings every year. They are both great ambassadors for the whole sport – and graceful in defeat too.'

Some of the owners who helped Barry's rise to prominence, including several of the Rheingold syndicate, have passed on and there is no doubt whom Barry misses the most. Robert Sangster, the man who demonstrated that racing and breeding could simultaneously be good business and good fun, was both patron and playmate. Surrounded by good-looking women, well-chilled champagne and court jesters like Charles Benson, Sangster, says Barry, always turned a day at the races into a day out.

They met one day at Haydock Park. 'He asked me to stay and I went to see two yearlings at his Swettenham Stud that were in the sale at Doncaster. I offered him £3,000 for a grey filly but he said that because it was in the sale next month he couldn't possibly sell it. I went to Doncaster and bought her for £4,100 and she turned out to be Lovelight, who won five races. He then bought the filly back for his stud, sent her to America and she became the dam of Motavato. It went from there to Dibidale.'

Robert Sangster died of pancreatic cancer on 8 April 2004 at the age of 67, leaving six children from three marriages. He had homes in the Isle of Man, London, Barbados and Australia. Horses bearing his famous blue, emerald green and white colours flashed past the post in first place often enough to make him champion owner in Britain five times and he was the last native Englishman to hold that title.

Instrumental in his first owners' championship was The Minstrel, trained by Vincent O'Brien. Bought at Keeneland by 'Sangster's gangsters' for $200,000, The Minstrel amassed winnings of £333,000 and was sold to an American syndicate for nine million dollars. Alleged, bought for $175,000 and also trained by O'Brien, was sold for $16m after winning two Arcs.

Sangster founded the Swettenham Stud in Cheshire (it was later absorbed into the Manton complex) and became a leading breeder, instrumental in changing the face of international bloodstock practices. Sadler's Wells, whom he bred and owned, became the pre-eminent European stallion of modern times.

Sangster joined forces with O'Brien and John Magnier at Coolmore in raids on the American sales rings, looking for yearlings with the potential to become champion sires. Their concentrated efforts to corner the market in the best blood from the Northern Dancer sireline paid off. Sangster, who also developed the Collingrove Stud in Australia, was one of the first advocates of the 'shuttle sires' who spend six months alternately covering mares in the northern and southern hemispheres, in Europe and in Australia.

Seeing horseflesh as an international currency and breeding as a commercial business, Sangster and his associates had up to 1,000 horses in training worldwide. When an Australian journalist once asked Sangster how many horses he had, the response was: 'Do you ask a stamp collector how many stamps he has got?'

The Sangster team dominated the bloodstock market until the arrival of the Maktoum family with wealth they could not match and a less commercial imperative. An Arab owner told *The Daily Telegraph* on a visit to Britain: 'I was surprised to read in your paper that Mr Sangster is regarded over here as a rich man.'

On Sangster's death, Barry told the *Racing Post*: 'Robert won every race in the book around the globe and he was a legend because of the way he promoted racing. In my lifetime he was one of the sport's most influential characters. He introduced a fresh dimension and was a major player at the sales for many years. Without him we would not have seen Steve Cauthen, Brent Thomson and Willie Shoemaker in Britain.'

The other element appreciated by the man who trained more Group winners for Sangster in Britain than anyone else was that Sangster was the ultimate sportsman. 'We celebrated when we won and usually celebrated when we lost. There was never an inquest into what went wrong. He would never take a horse away from a trainer and he loved a bet. The only time he'd become upset was when his horse won and the trainer hadn't told him it had a chance.' Sangster prided himself on not interfering, arguing: 'When the passengers want to fly the plane it's time to get off.'

A photograph of Sangster still sits behind Barry's desk. Michael Hills says: 'He will sometimes sit there now and someone will mention Robert and say, "Do you think of him?" and he'll say, "Every day." He was with him from the start and he really did miss him when he went.'

It was Sangster's zest for life that appealed to Barry. 'He knew how to live and he lived well. He liked to bet, he liked his horses and he liked the people who went with it all.' At Sangster's memorial service Colin Ingleby-Mackenzie put it this way: 'It is now, sadly, the end of a chapter of delightful scams and tasteful skulduggery and generosity – Robert was always ready to answer calls of any charitable requests – of great kindness and too many cocktails and endless fantasies of the fairer sex.'

Another owner, their mutual friend Bobby McAlpine, recalls bloodstock agent Pat Hogan coming in at the sales to see Sangster. 'He was at the end of the second or third "last bottle" of champagne. A rather distressed Hogan said, "I thought you were going to be there with me. I've just bought this horse for you for £15,000 more than I was meant to pay." Sangster said, "You ought to know by now that I don't know one end of a bloody horse from another. I rely on you to tell me all about conformation. If it's all right with you, it's all right for me," and he poured himself another glass.

There is a famous story of Vincent O'Brien putting a consoling arm round Sangster's shoulder after they have lost out to the Sheikhs at Keeneland for a $13m horse and saying: 'It's all over.' McAlpine's version was that the Sangster gang had decided to bid up the Maktoums to $11m and had no intention of buying the horse. And the consoling arm round the shoulder? 'The problem was that Vincent O'Brien got carried away and kept on bidding. Finally Sangster and Magnier had to grab an arm each and pull him down to stop him.'

Sangster liked to be kept amused and one reason why his Manton experiment with Michael Dickinson failed was that the talented

Dickinson, an obsessive workaholic, was no party companion for his owner. Barry and Penny lived much more comfortably with Sangster's style and with his friends like Charles Benson and Billy McDonald, a super-salesman who, says Barry, 'could get on any plane and get off the other end with the richest man on board,' and who bought and sold horses for Sangster in California.

The socialite Benson had fixed up in advance a big party for forty people at Annabel's nightclub when Blushing Groom was expected to win the 1977 Derby for the Aga Khan. Flowers were ordered for the tables in his red and green colours. Then Robert Sangster won the race with The Minstrel. Benson called Annabel's. The distraught manager said: 'I suppose you are going to cancel the party?' 'No,' replied Benson, 'just change the flowers to Sangster's colours.'

John Hills says: 'Sangster wasn't the kind of person who wanted to be pals with everybody in the room. He surrounded himself with a small, protective group of people whom he liked.' Certainly the pools millionaire and Barry gelled from the first, and both loved a bet.

Tales of some of the successful gambles Barry and Sangster launched together are in another chapter of this book. But an example deserves a place here. Both had backed Nomadic Way, the horse Barry also trained to be a Cheltenham Festival winner over hurdles, when he won the 1988 Cesarewitch. They started with the ante-post 20-1 and continued through to the 7-1 available on the day. At one stage in the race Nomadic Way, who went on to be placed in the Champion Hurdle and to win the Irish equivalent, looked beaten. But they had the tireless Willie Carson on board. He kept driving and niggling in his inimitable style and Nomadic Way got up to win what was his fifth race of the season on five different courses. A delighted Sangster said: 'I would say this success was eighty per cent down to Barry and twenty-five per cent down to Willie. Mathematics was never my strong point.'

Nomadic Way, of course, was one of the horses who has helped to stump a few racing 'experts' in pub quizzes when they have been asked to name the two Cheltenham Festival winners trained by B.W. Hills.

Barry has always loved the Cheltenham Festival and goes for a day or two most years. But his is almost exclusively a Flat yard. He has not trained many jumps horses because his owners have not asked him to. These days if Flat trainers have a horse in the yard who looks capable of winning over jumps it will often be sold on at a profit to the owner and passed to the likes of Paul Nicholls, Nicky Henderson or David Pipe.

The Sangster-owned Nomadic Way was an exception. After winning his Cesarewitch he made a winning debut over hurdles at Sandown Park and became winter favourite for the Triumph Hurdle. Barry also had the useful hurdler Sudden Victory at the time and the experienced Kevin Mooney to help with their schooling. Nomadic Way won the Irish Champion Hurdle en route to the 1990 Champion Hurdle at Cheltenham, where Sudden Victory acted as a pacemaker for Nomadic Way, blazing away in the lead.

The furious pace continued with Nomadic Way and Past Glories scuttling round the final turn like greyhounds. Kribensis had a nice run through behind them and Beech Road was poised to challenge. With four of them almost in a line approaching the last, Kribensis jumped high and Nomadic Way got first run up the hill. But then Richard Dunwoody called on Kribensis's superior Flat speed and he drew clear to win by three lengths from Nomadic Way in a record time with Past Glories three-quarters of a length away in third.

Nomadic Way was second again in the 1991 Champion Hurdle but he finally got to the Festival winner's enclosure in 1992 when he won the Stayers' Hurdle, beating Trapper John (who was disqualified because his jockey weighed out 3lb light), Ubu III and Crystal Spirit. Jamie Osborne, who was on his third winner of the day, had discussed tactics with Willie Carson, the man who had been on board for the Cesarewitch success.

Barry declared: 'I've waited a long time to get a winner at this meeting. In fact, Nicky Henderson rode one for me the day Midnight Court won the Gold Cup in 1978, but that was when it was run in April.'

DICK BONNYCASTLE

Some early owners, including Henry Zeisel and Tony Shead, appear in the chapter on Rheingold. The convivial Bobby McAlpine features alongside his Champion Stakes winner Cormorant Wood. Another long-time associate of the Hills yards has been the Canadian Dick Bonnycastle, for whom Barry won the 1,000 Guineas in 1978 with Enstone Spark.

Barry says: 'Dick Bonnycastle came through Robert Hastings. He wanted to have some horses with Peter Walwyn, who was full and couldn't take them. Robert then said, "There's a young fellow down the road who's just come to Lambourn," and recommended me to have them. That's how it started off, in 1970 I suppose, and we've been stuck together ever since.' The pair enjoy shooting together as well as their successful racing partnership.

Bonnycastle, a major figure in the Canadian Jockey Club who is based in Calgary, is a venture capitalist, a publisher and a breeder who also races horses in North America. He said after his horse Cheap Seats won a nice race at Ayr one day: 'Racing here gives the young horses more time than in my country. But when they mature it is better to switch them to North America where the prize-money is better.'

Barry says: 'He's got a few horses at Woodbine. He doesn't like the prize-money over here. He still wants to win the Derby, but I don't suppose he would have any horses here apart from the fact that he's a great friend with me. That keeps it going.'

Bonnycastle had a share in Mr Combustible, who was fourth in the 2001 Derby, and in Hawaiian Sound, who was second in 1978. He also had forty per cent of The Last Drop, who finished second in the 2006 St Leger.

Another Dick was also an associate from early days. Dick Hollingsworth, who died at the age of eighty-two in 2001, ran the Arches Stud in Hertfordshire, which he had inherited from his father in 1953. Barry said at the time of his death: 'For half a century he was one of the true English breeders who bred horses to race and not to sell. He was very rare in that all the family came from the same dam. I had known him since 1952 and knew all his good horses. I was privileged to train for him and he will be sadly missed. He was a true gentleman in every sense of the word.'

The *Racing Post* obituary noted that Hollingsworth, a retired stockbroker who bred and owned the 1980 Oaks winner Bireme, had kept to the principle of trying to breed a Derby winner who would take the Ascot Gold Cup the next year. He had many good horses descended from Ark Royal trained by Barry's mentor George Colling, including the fillies Cutter and Kyak, and then had horses with John Oxley and Dick Hern.

BILL GREDLEY
The Newmarket-based property man and art collector Bill Gredley, owner of the Stetchworth Stud, is another long-time Hills owner and friend. Like many of the Hills owners, he has remained a friend even when he has not had horses in the yard.

In August 1997 he announced when Barry had given him his first winner of the season with Cybertechnology, after thirty-five starts by horses in the hands of various trainers, that he was concentrating his racing operations on Barry.

After twenty years of ownership with various trainers, Gredley said: 'Nearly all of my horses will be trained by Barry Hills from now on. Barry and I have come to an understanding. We will put them all under one roof and he has a brief to cull them where necessary. I haven't fallen out with my trainers but I believe this is the best policy.' He said he would be keeping a spelling station in Newmarket but flying over once a week to see his horses in Lambourn.

On Cybertechnology, Gredley said: 'We have been going wrong with him running over a mile and a quarter and a mile and a half. Barry saw a bit of speed on the gallops and he showed that in the race.'

Gredley's yellow and black colours were made familiar by User Friendly, who in 1992 won the Oaks, the Irish Oaks, the Yorkshire Oaks and the St Leger before narrowly failing to hold off Subotica in the Prix de l'Arc de Triomphe. Memorably, he once declared: 'At least in racing people share your disappointments. In business if you fall flat on your face people seem to enjoy it.'

Gredley was one of four partners who shared Chancellor, a Derby runner in 2001, the others being Sir Ernest Harrison, Guy Snowden and Seymour Cohn. 'We instructed John Warren to buy four horses for us. We then drew lots. Each of us could send the horse we drew to whichever trainer we wanted and run it in our name and colours.' Gredley drew Chancellor, a 190,000 guineas yearling, and sent him to Barry. Why choose him? 'Barry puts so much mental energy into the job. He is always examining everything, debating and challenging. He has a very alert mind.'

MRS CATHERINE CORBETT

Two of Barry's owners whose interests have happily coincided are Chrysalis Records chairman Chris Wright and Mrs Catherine Corbett, who together owned 1993 Irish 1,000 Guineas winner Nicer. She has been successful with the greys she likes to buy and he wanted to go into partnership with her. Barry was looking for a filly for Mrs Corbett and every time he looked at one he found himself bumping into bloodstock agent Charlie Gordon-Watson looking at the same filly on behalf of Wright. Since the Corbetts and the Wrights were friends, with Chris Wright regularly playing tennis with Joe Corbett, they decided that rather than bidding against each other it made sense for them to go into partnership and they bought Nicer together for 27,000 guineas.

Barry says: 'Before she won the Irish 1,000 Guineas she completely demoralised her galloping companions. We thought the gallop wasn't quite right. It wasn't until we worked her partner again that we knew she had worked exceptionally well.'

The Hon Catherine Corbett (nee Lyon-Dalberg-Acton), whose brother Robert Acton manages the Dalham Hall Stud and whose husband Joe's brother Atty trained both Flat and National Hunt horses, took up ownership for a second time after her children had been educated. She first asked Barry to buy her a cheap grey filly, the only proviso being that the dam and grand-dam should have been winners. The result was the purchase of Desirable, winner of the Group One Cheveley Park Stakes in 1983 and third to Pebbles in the 1,000 Guineas the following year. She cost 7,000 Irish guineas at Goffs. Mrs Corbett only took a half-share and originally Penny Hills took the other half. Sadly she sold it on to Robert Sangster before the filly won the Cheveley Park Stakes as a two-year-old. Mrs Corbett kept her half-share and when the filly went to auction at the end of her racing career Sangster purchased her for more than £1 million. The deal, he pointed out, netted him 'a tax-free £500,000'.

Mrs Corbett was originally going to send a horse to Jeremy Tree. 'But he said he was full up. We went to Barbados and met Barry at a dinner party and since then we have never looked back.' She will never forget Desirable's close victory in the Cheveley Park, turning to Penny Hills for confirmation they really had won a nail-biting contest. 'We had had horses with Joe's brother Atty Corbett,' she says, 'but those ran in smaller events. I had never dreamed of winning such a grand race.' She pays tribute to Barry's incredible work-rate and to his and Penny's warm hospitality for their owners, adding: 'It is quite extraordinary for someone like me to have had three Group One winners.'

Interestingly, Desirable is one of the Hills winners whose portrait has wall space in Barry and Penny's elegant, airy drawing room at

Wetherdown House. The other horses accorded that honour are Cormorant Wood, Further Flight, Distant Relative and, of course, the great Rheingold.

Greys carrying Mrs Corbett's blue and silver silks have included Nicer, who was sold on to Fahd Salman for 270,000 guineas – ten times her original purchase price – after her Irish 1,000 Guineas success, and Negligent, who was third in the 1,000 Guineas in 1990 and later sold to Sheikh Mohammed for a nice profit on her 38,000 guineas purchase price. Mrs Corbett has also had two Derby runners with Barry, The Fly and The Glow-Worm, who finished fifth and sixth. The Fly was purchased as a yearling at auction in partnership with Jack Hanson for 10,000 guineas.

'I had a very bad filly that Barry had managed to sell very well, so he said, "Now Catherine, you must buy this," ' she told the media. But at that time she needed persuading because he was a colt. 'Fillies have better salvage value, you see.'

The Corbett/Wright partnership also prospered with Dark Angel, a 61,000 guineas purchase. The impressive two-year-old had been entered in the Group Two Gimcrack Stakes at York, a traditional target for two-year-olds at the Ebor meeting. But a trainer who looks after his owners thinks of hard cash as well as prestige. Instead Dark Angel was targeted at the £300,000 St Leger Yearling Stakes at Doncaster, the richest race for juveniles in Europe, which Barry had taken the year before with Prime Defender. After winning there, despite a spread plate and a sore foot in the run-up to the race, Dark Angel was sold on for a seven-figure sum. Following such a success, said Barry, he would have been very difficult to place the next year. 'While he was a very good horse he wasn't going to get much more than six furlongs.'

There are moments of profit in his relationships with his owners and moments of humour too. One news cutting in Barry's scrapbooks records that one day, when Barry and the revered Timeform founder Phil Bull had a game of snooker, Bull sent his plane to Halifax (where

Timeform was based) to fetch his cue, only to discover when it arrived that Barry had a half-size snooker table. A note emphasises, 'But everything else is full size.'

Jimmy Lindley confirms the tale of film mogul Sonny Enfield, who had a horse with Barry called Natsun. The animal was due to run in a four-horse race at Newbury. Noting that there was prize-money for all four places, Sonny Enfield exulted: 'Never in my life have I got something for nothing, but today I will.' Unfortunately he didn't. With his owner watching with incredulity, Natsun refused to enter the stalls and was withdrawn.

GUY REED

One long-term owner with whom Barry fell out was the Yorkshire-based Guy Reed, for whom he trained La Cucaracha to win the Nunthorpe Stakes – the owner's first Group One success. He also trained Pablo to win the Lincoln Handicap in Reed's familiar black and gold check with pink sleeves, but in the *Racing Post* of 23 January 2007 Reed confirmed that he had removed all but one of his seventeen horses from Barry's yard. Losing so many horses at a stroke of the pen was undoubtedly a blow for Barry after a season in which he had finished third in the trainers' table to Sir Michael Stoute and Mark Johnston, but it was a case of an unresolvable standoff between two proud and determined characters.

Reed offered only a veiled explanation for his decision to remove his horses from Lambourn. He said: 'I suppose we agree to disagree – obviously the numbers indicate that – but I don't want to say any more than that. It is nothing to do with one horse in particular. Barry has had success for me, but don't forget I've supplied the horses and there are two people in this game, him and me. But we shall continue in life on a friendly basis. End of story.'

When I asked Barry for his end of the story he, too, was reluctant to go into detail. But he said: 'We had a disagreement over money and I asked him to take the horses away. He wouldn't pay me a commission on the sale of a horse.'

When I pressed him for detail, he said: 'Some people put five per cent on the training agreement. I don't charge commission for buying them. But if they make a good profit I expect five per cent. If you got a horse for £50,000 and you spent another £50,000 on a couple of years' keep and it only made £150,000 I wouldn't expect anything. If you got a quarter of a million I'd expect five per cent.' It is the value-added principle.

Barry was clearly sorry to see La Cucaracha go. He says: 'She was a lot better than she ever did. She was a very big filly, a strong masculine filly, but she had a series of injuries. I remember Richard Hannon asking me one day in the paddock at Newbury: "Is that a three-year-old?" In April as a two-year-old she looked just like a three-year-old. When she won her first race at Leicester by about eight lengths the jockey who rode her couldn't believe it – he thought she was the strongest filly he'd ever ridden. But she had quite a lot of surgery, three operations in Newmarket. If she'd had a straightforward career she could have been a lot better.'

One thing Barry's owners can be sure of is that there will be no tales out of school. He is always polite to the media, recognising they have a job to do. But he is happy to resist the clamour for more and more information to be given to the racing media and, through them, the betting public. He puts it this way: 'I'm forthright and honest, but why should I tell everything to everyone about my horses? Dick Hern never did. The punters don't own the horses. I'm paid by owners to train their horses; therefore my first duty must be to them. What is the point of getting up at 6.30am every day for a lot of aggravation and then telling every detail of what happened to all who ask?'

Owners might also appreciate Barry's definition of what is needed for that role: 'You need true patience and plenty of money – plus a trainer who tells you when a horse is no good and to get rid of it.'

CHAPTER EIGHTEEN

Man and Methods

How Mr Combustible does it

'I never ask my horses much at home. The secret is to get them to peak fitness without really testing them.'
BARRY HILLS.

A s much a fixture in Barry Hills's life as Chester in May or Newmarket in July is the Chelsea Flower Show. In his study there are nearly as many books about horticulture as there are about horseracing and he and Penny have landscaped a glorious garden around Wetherdown House with trees, shrubs, pools and sculpture. Appropriately he is fond of saying that horses are like flowers: 'They bloom when they are ready, you cannot force them.' When he patiently brought back the top sprinter Equiano after a lean year in 2009 to win his second Group One King's Stand Stakes at Royal Ascot in 2010 – a success Barry had told everybody in advance was on the cards – he produced a variant, telling me: 'Some years you get more apples from the tree than others.'

If there is a secret to his success, then patience is certainly part of it. And if there was one key mentor after the early years skipping school for the horse lore to be picked up around Fred Rimell's Kinnersley yard, it was probably George Colling, the Newmarket trainer to whom Barry's apprenticeship was transferred. He told John Rickman in 1979: 'I go by the horses. They'll tell you when they are ready. That was George Colling's way. I haven't been one to have early two-year-olds. Mine always seem to want three or four runs before they come to themselves. I do not try them at home. They do nice progressive work. If you started trying horses on these stiff Lambourn gallops you'd soon be in the workhouse.'

Barry says of Colling, a kindly man of the old school who died at only 55 in 1959 after a long illness: 'He was always methodical and an absolute gentleman to work for. He was completely dedicated to his job. He worked his horses up progressively. He did not hurry them and was extremely patient. I probably learned a lot from him and I know I try to do as I think he would when I'm faced with certain situations.'

If Barry has a motto it is this: 'I never ask my horses much at home. The secret is to get them to peak fitness without really testing them.' He says: 'If you make a horse happy it will generally do well. They must like work and if they are used to doing a good day's work, like a human, they will be quite happy.' He sums up the essential task this way: 'You've got to take horses as they are. You've got to put down the foundations before you can start laying bricks.'

John Hills, formerly his father's assistant, says: 'He allows a horse time to progress. I never saw him trying to force horses. He has a great record for training two-year-olds but he doesn't force them – it looks as though it is happening naturally. He has the ability to spot if they are thriving and taking what he is giving them. He sees before most people when he needs to back off. He's got an instinct. You can't always see it and sometimes it's a bit confusing but he allows them to blossom.'

John argues that Barry is both a traditionalist and an innovator. 'It was an experience to work with him. I came back full of bright ideas from Australia and for someone who doesn't tolerate things he tolerated me quite a lot. He brought in before I even went to America these ice machines and ice Jacuzzis to keep the horses' legs right. He used American polo bandages before anybody else. He used to send some horses to Florida, which was a new concept.'

Barry is 'a proper stockman', says John Francome. 'He knows everything about the countryside, he can tell you all about the animals and the trees and what to plant where.' Part of Barry's joy in the countryside, of course, has been his love first of hunting and then, when he decided he had too much at stake to continue with that risky pursuit, of shooting with friends like Bobby McAlpine.

Nicky Henderson says: 'At Manton he was finding the hunting in Leicestershire a bit far to go and I said to him that he ought to take up shooting. He retorted: "If I'd wanted to take up shooting I'd have done it twenty years ago." About six months later he appeared with the guns, the dog, the vehicle, the cartridges, kitted right out. That's become his great winter pastime.'

Jimmy Lindley also recalls that, when the decision came to switch pursuits, in no time at all Barry was fixed up with the best-balanced guns, impeccable shooting attire and two perfectly trained labradors at foot. Beauty, the first, travelled over from Ireland on the same plane as Sir Harry Lewis after his victory in the 1987 Irish Derby. Lindley says: 'You'd think he'd had them all his life. Whatever he does he's got to have the whole shooting match and do it properly.' Fellow trainer and hunting enthusiast Peter Walwyn says: 'Barry is a beautiful shot and he was a very good rider too.'

As for the training, says Steve Cauthen, 'He is a traditionalist at heart but a great thinker. He was always looking for ways of doing things better – new open-air barns, walking machines. He was looking for ways of getting lads to travel the horses better.' And Barry acknowledges no trainer can afford to stick in the past. 'I have done well to keep numbers up. I have had to go out and get owners. I can't run a hotel on empty bedrooms.'

He was always looking for an edge, always willing to travel. In 1995, for example, he planned to set up a satellite yard near Dusseldorf in Germany to cream off some of the Continental prize-money. He said: 'The plan is to have runners not only in Germany but also in France and Italy. The world is getting smaller and it makes sense to spread your wings. One box costs us only £4.50 a day plus £13 each time we gallop on the grass, so it represents excellent value.' A scouting mission confirmed that he could catch a 7.30am plane out of Heathrow and be back in Lambourn by 2.30pm. John Ciechanowski agreed to supervise the experiment but the scheme was scuppered in the end by the obstructionism of German trainers and by local bureaucracy.

Son Michael, who has ridden more of Barry's winners than anybody, says that, while he goes down regularly to Lambourn to ride out every Wednesday and Saturday until the Newmarket Craven meeting in mid-April, his father does not want him around so much after that. 'Because those gallops are quite stiff and they go away from home, once they've been up there about ten to fifteen times the horses start to think, "Oh, I don't really have to work too hard to go up here," and they start pulling up.

'He has the most fantastic eye that can see all that. Because I'm a jockey, I go by feel and he knows that. He knows I'm going to be getting the wrong vibes. So after the Craven meeting I go down only if I'm riding for two days at Newbury or Salisbury or Bath, when I'll stay the night and ride work. But it will be phased out. I could go a month or six weeks without going down. But then I'll go into the paddock and I'll know from the way he talks to me or from his body language exactly what he thinks of a horse. He is such a good judge.

'He loves his two-year-olds now. He loves training two-year-olds more than anything. I think it's the unknown thing about them. He's looking for that one horse, that Mill Reef or Nijinsky, those freaks. He's been looking for one of those since he started training and he's never really had one.'

The first thing Barry teaches those two-year-olds was made clear when he took over the juveniles at Manton. 'I am just tackling things at half-speed at the moment and teaching them their jobs and discipline. Manners really. You have to teach them manners early. If you can't teach them how to do their job properly at home, what chance has a jockey got on a racecourse with his knees tucked up under his chin?'

Kevin Mooney, who started with Barry and kept a link with him while he rode nearly 400 winners as a jockey with Fulke Walwyn, has been an assistant trainer with Barry for nearly twenty years. He says the boss could train winners on the side of a mountain. 'It comes from the heart. He has a feel for a horse, a great eye for a horse. He's very determined. With some of the horses you think, "He won't do anything with that one," but he does.' In November or December of the previous year he will say, "I will win such and such a maiden with this horse," and he does. He's got patience. It was very difficult at first at South Bank. By August the horses were over the top. What he's done here is fantastic. It is all his own vision.'

Travelling head lad Geoff Snook says: 'He has such a good eye. He said Ghanaati would win the Guineas when all she had done was run twice on the all-weather and had never set foot on a turf track. The boss was adamant she wouldn't be far away.'

His travelling colleague Ian 'Scan' Willder, who had worked with the perfectionist Michael Dickinson at Manton before Barry took over and then asked him to come back to Lambourn, says: 'He always wants to know about the horses in every detail, how they've watered, everything. When new stabling was built at Redcar, for example, he came and had a look and complained there wasn't enough ventilation. He's a little man, but a big hat fits him. When you listen in the parade ring he is always working things out.'

It starts earlier than that with Barry. Jack Ramsden says: 'Barry is a wonderful judge of a yearling. I would back him in front of anyone to go and buy one. He'd have a look at a pedigree but he wouldn't allow it to dominate his mind. The training and everything else is done on instinct. It's an absolutely natural thing, like being able to go into a sales ring and pick a couple out and end up with the right ones. Everything is done on instinct. You've either got it or you haven't. He's got it in bucketfuls.'

There are, of course, other instinctive trainers with a good eye for a horse. What has helped to make Barry so successful is that he is also a businessman who keeps a sharp eye on the books as well. Some trainers seem to do their economics on the back of a racecard. The Faringdon Place operation is carefully costed with figures readily available charting the detail of profits and losses on training, on bloodstock dealing, on commissions and winning percentages. But in the end it is that instinct which is crucial. Barry absorbed racing though his pores, growing up amid the rattle of stable buckets and the swish of brooms alongside a father who also had the knack, although Bill Hills's poor health sadly meant he was never allowed to make the best of his talents.

Says Michael Hills of his own father: 'He obviously had a natural gift to start with, but as the years have gone by he's definitely got better at it. He can look at a horse and something inside tells him when it needs to be got on with. He just knows whether horses need time or a bit of a wake-up call.

'He doesn't overwork his horses. They do good, solid work, they're fit horses, but he doesn't feed them overly either, so they don't get too heavy. He has something natural inside him that tells him what they need and what they don't.'

Barry's long-time rider and friend Ernie Johnson insists: 'Barry is totally instinctive. He's got an eye for the smallest detail. He doesn't miss anything, whether it's the way the horse is turned out, tacked up, the way you're turned out. Everything is taken in.'

And Snowy Outen, the yard's long-time head lad, argues that Barry is always thinking ahead. 'He's got two brains, one for thinking now and one for planning. He would pinpoint one and see it with another few kilos in six months' time. If he says he is getting one ready for August, then it will be ready in August. He would ask you, "How is it working?" but he makes all the decisions. You won't move him. He sticks to a routine. When he asks how a particular horse is eating, you know that he has something not far away in mind.'

There is an essential inner certainty about what Barry Hills does. There was no conceit, no air of bragadoccio when he told me one day, matter of factly: 'I've always had the confidence that if things went bad I could produce a winner in a fortnight some way or another, which would keep me going.'

Of course Barry has had his leaner times too. His horses have often had a flat period at one stage of the season, which he used to blame at least partly on local farmers growing rape and the pollen getting in his horses' lungs. But he has always rolled with life's punches unless he sees the setbacks as his or somebody else's fault. 'I sleep well, but I might wake up at five in the morning. If you start to think of the horses in the dark all your problems are big ones.'

He has, of course, had particular success with fillies. Does he do anything different with them? 'I like to see the fillies be a bit tough. I like them to have a bit of fight about them.' So Maids Causeway, the 2005 Coronation Stakes winner, was his type then? 'Oh yes. She'd chase you out of the box. She was tough as they come. I like to see them have a bit of fight. You've got to kid them, but if there's something about them they can stand up to it. That usually means they've got a bit of ability. In the end it's all about the survival of the fittest. That's how it should be and that's the name of the game.'

Son and assistant Charlie says his father handles the fillies differently to the colts. 'He's a lot easier on them. He probably gives them a longer time between races and waits for them to bloom. He waits for their coats to come in, he waits for them to tell him they're ready.'

An astute eye at the sales is a vital ingredient, too, and Barry has had some famous bargains in his time, securing the Arc winner Rheingold, for example, for 3,000 guineas. One Steve Cauthen remembers was Desirable, winner of the Cheveley Park Stakes in 1983. 'Barry has a great eye for a horse and bought her for ten grand. He got new people into her. She was their first horse. Barry and Penny were partners in her. She became a Group One winner and was later a great producer, so it was a very good deal for them.' Duboff was secured for only 9,000 guineas, Our Mirage for 6,000.

Back in 1979 Barry said he bought ninety per cent of the horses himself. 'What I look for is a good walker, an active horse, not too heavy-topped. I never look at the catalogue. I go to the sales with the catalogue unopened. I acknowledge that pedigrees are important, but what I do is go round the yearlings in their boxes, just Pat Hogan (a private bloodstock agent) and myself. We see as many as we can. Then we start sorting them out. I go back and have another look at a horse that appealed to me. Then, and only then, do I look at the pedigree. What it boils down to is that I value the horse according to the pedigree after I have seen it.'

In recent years his partner in buying has been agent Adrian Nicoll. Barry told Julian Muscat in June 2008: 'I've always believed that money doesn't buy success in the yearling market. We never spend more than £150,000. If somebody came to me and said he'd like me to buy a yearling for 250,000 guineas I would say he should buy three for 75,000 guineas each.'

Nicoll says: 'We have to go for what we can afford. We've never really had the owners to spend more than £150,000. We don't have unlimited money to play with and we can't consider some of the fancy pedigrees.'

One of the first horses they bought together was the top-class sprinter Gallic League, winner of the Middle Park Stakes in 1987, and there have been plenty of good-value purchases since in the 30,000-60,000 guineas range, such as Swilly Ferry, winner of the £300,000 Weatherbys Insurance Two-Year-Old Stakes at Doncaster, Park Hill Stakes winner Alexander Three D and Lady Upstage, who won the Pretty Polly at the Curragh. Silk Blossom, who won the Lowther Stakes and the Goffs Million, was bought for 50,000 Euros.

Red Clubs, Ronald Arculli's tough and consistent winner of the Coventry Stakes, of a couple of Pattern races as a three-year-old and of the Group One Betfred Sprint Cup as a four-year-old, cost just £40,000 and Dark Angel, who was retired to stud after a two-year-old career that brought £187,692 for winning the St Leger Yearling Stakes at York and successes in the Middle Park and Mill Reef Stakes, was purchased for £61,000.

Barry suggests trainers can be inhibited by training expensive horses, as well as they might. 'If you gave £400,000 for a horse and it was not showing you very much you wouldn't be too keen to run it.'

Sheikh Hamdan Al Maktoum and Prince Khalid Abdullah do their own buying, or in the Prince's case mostly home breeding, but sometimes Barry and Nicoll will go to Angus Gold, for example, when he has bought a horse for Sheikh Hamdan and say that they had fancied it too and that Barry would like to train it.

Where the traditionalist shows in Barry is in his love of the rhythms of British racing. He likes the 'proper circuit' of racing starting with the Craven meeting, taking in Chester, York, Epsom, Royal Ascot, the Newmarket July meeting, Glorious Goodwood, the Ebor and St Leger meetings before returning to Newmarket. 'That's what I'm really interested in, not so much the other places. I like Sandown and going to Ireland and France if I have a horse good enough but the traditional English pattern of racing is what matters and I hope they don't muck it up.'

It is not just for the social side that he enjoys certain meetings. His success rate at Chester, seen as a quirky track by most, is phenomenal. He loves to lay out a horse to win the big handicaps there and has won more than 150 races on the Roodee. He won the Chester Cup there with Arapahos in 1980 and with Rainbow High in 1999 and 2001, saying on the first of those occasions: 'He's a neat, handy horse who has got better each time he has stepped up in trip.'

He won the race again with Daraahem in 2009. Gelded over the winter, 'which helped him a lot,' the horse nearly pulled Richard Hills's arms out in winning by a neck in a fifteen-runner field. 'It has been a long-term plan, as it is a race dear to my heart, and I knew this was a horse I could win it with.'

Barry, who hasn't missed the spring meeting there since 1971, sees the Chester experience as an educational one for his horses. 'They learn a lot going round there. They'll come back and they'll run better for you next time. There'll be more underneath you. It's a good track.' It is, he insists, a galloping track with long, sweeping bends. 'Short runners don't win there, they've got to get the trip.'

Others complain about Goodwood's switchback but again Barry likes the Sussex track. 'The form at Goodwood normally stands out as consistent because a lot of horses have to overcome a lot of things in order to win. They have to get out of trouble. It is more difficult nowadays because the winning post is quite a way shorter than where it was years ago. It used to be one of the best tracks to come from behind on. You had all the time in the world but now you haven't got as much time and everybody wants to be in the same place. That's why you get all this trouble. But it's a lovely course. You normally find that horses who can win their maidens there go on and do something.'

Barry is a fierce critic of race planners. He resigned some years ago from the National Trainers' Federation because he felt the trainers' 'trade union' wasn't doing enough to fight for higher-quality racing.

'There is too much racing, especially bad racing, and it all seems to have been put on because the bookmakers wanted it. They wanted Sunday racing and racing in the evenings so that they could open their shops. A great deal needs to be changed if we are to encourage owners to buy more horses. The handicapping system needs sorting out so that better horses have more opportunities to race because some are being forced to run at meetings where they have no chance of winning.

"It's all very well dropping a horse like Royal Applause a few pounds when the handicappers know he is never going to run in a handicap. But there are plenty of other horses caught in between handicaps and Group races with nowhere to go, or who simply have a mark that is too high for them to win off. Meanwhile, there are horses further down the scale who can run in almost any race on the all-weather. I thought all-weather racing was to keep us going during those months when it was not possible to be sure of racing on turf. Now it's virtually all year round. The public wants to see good horses, not moderate and poor ones, but no-one in authority appears to be listening.'

In 1998 he complained: 'With maiden races worth only £3,000 and some handicaps at £40,000 or £50,000, what is a trainer going to do? The answer is that he's going to get them handicapped. The present set-up is a cheat's charter. You don't have to be a magician to work that one out.'

Far too much money, he complains, is being spent on bureaucracy when it should be going into prize-money. Why spend so much on integrity and why, for example, are two starters required?

He also argues that too much racing is bringing down the standard of jockeyship. When Tony Culhane was banned for twenty-one days for dropping his hands on one of Barry's horses, the trainer blamed it partly on the race programme: 'During the whole of my career, the standard of riding has never been worse than it is now. They're not bad jockeys but they don't have time to reflect on their last ride. They are going out to ride in the next race not even knowing what trip it's over. There is simply too much racing.'

CAREER HIGHLIGHTS

1952   Barry Hills's first ride as an apprentice

1959   Becomes travelling head lad to John Oxley.

1968   Wins £60,000 on the Lincoln Handicap.

1969   On 18 April La Dolce Vita, ridden by Ernie Johnson, becomes the first of 17 winners in Barry's debut year at South Bank, Lambourn.

1970   First big handicap winner: Hickleton takes the Grand Metropolitan.

1973   Rheingold wins the Prix de l'Arc de Triomphe.

1974   Dibidale wins the Irish Oaks.

1975   Nagwa wins 13 two-year-old races – a record.

1978   Enstone Spark wins the 1,000 Guineas.

1979   Tap On Wood wins the 2,000 Guineas – Steve Cauthen's first English Classic.

1985   Tremulous becomes Barry's 1,000th winner in Britain at Haydock, 8 August.

1987   Moves to Manton. Sir Harry Lewis wins the Irish Derby.

1990   Barry's best year numerically with 113 victories.

1991   Moves back to Lambourn and builds Faringdon Place.

1992   Nomadic Way a Cheltenham Festival winner in the Stayers' Hurdle.

1992   Barry becomes only the fourth trainer (along with Henry Cecil, Dick Hern and Sir Michael Stoute) to win 100 Group races.

1993   Nicer wins the Irish 1,000 Guineas.

1994   Moonax wins the St Leger. Bolas wins the Irish 1,000 Guineas

1995   Further Flight wins his fifth successive Jockey Club Cup.

1996   Son Michael rides Shaamit to Derby victory for William Haggas.

1999	Summer Bounty at Lingfield becomes Barry's 2,000th Flat winner in Britain.
2003	Pablo becomes Barry's first Lincoln winner as a trainer.
2004	Haafhd wins the 2,000 Guineas, ridden by son Richard.
2005	La Cucaracha wins the Nunthorpe Stakes.
2009	Chapter And Verse becomes Barry's 3,000th winner.
2009	Redwood is Barry's 300th winner at Newmarket.
2009	Ghanaati wins the 1,000 Guineas.
2009	Chester Cup victor Daraahem is Barry's 150th winner at the Roodee.
2009	Ghanaati's Coronation Stakes victory helps Barry become Ascot champion trainer
2010	Redwood becomes Barry's 50th winner at Glorious Goodwood.

MAIN JOCKEYS

Ernie Johnson 1969-72, Willie Carson 1974-75, Steve Cauthen 1979-1984, Brent Thomson 1985-86, Cash Asmussen 1987, Michael Hills 1988-2010.

YARDS

1969-1986 South Bank, Lambourn, 1987-1990 Manton, Wiltshire, 1991- 94 South Bank, Lambourn, 1994-present Faringdon Place, Lambourn.

Ten Colts to Remember

How do you pick out horses to remember from the career of a man who has trained the winners of eleven Classics and almost fifty Group One races? Probably no two people in the racing world would agree on any list of the best ten colts Barry Hills has handled among his 3,000-plus winners. The successes vary from Rheingold's triumph in the Prix de l'Arc de Triomphe to Haafhd's victory in the 2,000 Guineas. He has succeeded with stayers like Gildoran, winner of a brace of Ascot Gold Cups, and sprinters like Handsome Sailor, Gallic League, Royal Applause and, more recently, Equiano. There was even success over hurdles at the Cheltenham Festival with Nomadic Way.

Rheingold, Further Flight and Moonax have, for different reasons, earned their own chapter in this book. But here are memories of ten equine competitors at the highest level who have helped significantly in building the reputation of a man who has an uncanny eye in the sale ring and a rare instinct on the gallops for spotting and nurturing the talents in his team.

TAP ON WOOD
2,000 Guineas winner 1979

Barry Hills has a formidable record at Newmarket. In April 2009 he trained his 300th winner at 'Headquarters', more than many long-established Newmarket trainers have managed. His first big success at the track came in 1979 when he was responsible for giving Steve Cauthen his first British Classic winner, taking the 2,000 Guineas with Tap On Wood, owned by Barry's old friend Tony Shead.

Barry's handling of Tap On Wood, who was by Sallust out of Cat O'Mountaine, was not conventional, but it was highly profitable for his owner. Derby-winning trainer Atty Persse once declared that 'horses which attract the trainer's eye as likely to win a Classic should not be run often as two-year-olds. Generally I am satisfied if they appear in five or six races.' But Tap On Wood ran thirteen times at two, winning on seven occasions.

Not only had his trainer gauged the toughness of the horse, he had a shrewd eye for where the money lay. No other English trainer sent a horse across to the Curragh in September 1978 for the Group Two National Stakes at the Curragh, but Barry seized the opportunity with Tap On Wood, having noted that the prize-money was second only to the Gimcrack among two-year-old Group races. Timeform called Tap On Wood's success in Ireland 'another example of how his trainer, who also handled Nagwa and Mofida, can keep a two-year-old in top form while racing it very hard'. (Nagwa's feats are described elsewhere. Mofida won five of her fifteen races in 1976 and took three top handicaps among her three wins from 12 runs in 1977).

For the 2,000 Guineas in 1979, Tony Shead had backed Tap On Wood at 100-1 and when Abbeydale, whom Tap On Wood had beaten earlier in the season, was second in the 1,000 Guineas the previous day he went in to mop up the 66-1 still available, shrinking the odds to 40-1. The owner says: 'Robert Sangster never liked being left out of a gamble and his plunge on course on the day shortened the price to 20-1.'

The Hills owners were helped in securing good prices because the unbeaten Kris, trained by Henry Cecil, owned by Lord Howard de Walden and ridden by Joe Mercer, was a hot favourite and there was a strong supporting cast. Tap On Wood appeared to have place hopes at best.

Cauthen had been careful not to give Tap On Wood too hard a race in the boggy conditions at Salisbury on the American rider's first day riding in Britain and it was Ernie Johnson, previously Barry's stable jockey, who then won a Classic trial on Tap On Wood. When Cauthen was given the Guineas ride, Johnson was angry at being jocked off and temporarily split with Barry over the decision, but in the race the American showed all his quality.

Kris broke well under Joe Mercer and lay up with the pace. In Shead's distinctive stripes, Tap On Wood was slower into his stride and had to be nudged to keep a prominent position on the outside. They went a decent, fast pace but then Mercer let out another notch at the Dip and looked to be sailing for home. Cauthen followed the move, however, and eased Tap On Wood up to Kris's quarters. He was pushing and probing to find what he could get from his mount in response. Slowly the gap closed and, although the crowd were shouting for Kris, Tap On Wood edged his head in front as they met the rising ground. Kris fought back but Tap On Wood ran on stoutly to win by half a length. The Kentucky Derby was being run the same day and the Press room there was said to have been in a ferment of excitement over Cauthen's Newmarket success.

Shead, with a huge return from the ante-post bets to enjoy on top of the prize-money, declared: 'I owe it all to Steve. He doesn't get flustered and he doesn't fluster a horse. He was magnificent. He had it all to do but waited for it to come right.'

Cauthen, who recalls that Penny Hills rode Tap On Wood in most of his work, says: 'It was great for me, probably the moment when the British public decided to accept me into their hearts. Barry gave me instructions to get him settled so that when we came to the Bushes he would be in a position to make one run. It went that way. I got him settled, we were in mid-division and I always had my eye on Kris. When we got to the Bushes and Kris made his move I had my sights set on running him down. I had him covered and then it was just a matter of continuing to the wire. It was a fantastic win for me.'

How confident had the trainer been? 'He knew he had a horse. He was quietly confident he was going to be in the frame. I'm sure Barry had a few bucks on him.'

Tap On Wood ran next in the Derby, along with Shead's Cracaval and Two Of Diamonds, who had each won Classic trials, but none of them finished in the frame. Barry's horses were then struck by a bronchial virus but Tap On Wood recovered to win a Group Two race at Doncaster in the autumn. After that he was retired to stand as a stallion in Ireland, having been syndicated for a seven-figure sum. Not bad for a colt who had cost Shead just 12,000 guineas at Goffs Yearling Sales.

The horse's name, incidentally, resulted from Shead's regular stays on business at the Carlyle Hotel in New York. In the evenings he used to listen to singer/pianist Bobby Short in the hotel nightclub. The tune 'Tap on Wood', written by Cole Porter for the 1936 film Born to Dance, was in Short's repertoire and was one of his favourites.

HAAFHD
2,000 Guineas winner 2004

At the time Barry called the victory of Sheikh Hamdan Al Maktoum's Haafhd in the 2,000 Guineas his sweetest moment in racing after Rheingold's Arc victory more than thirty years earlier. There must have been a few winners competing for that accolade, but this was a key triumph, marking the end of a ten-year gap in the Classics for the veteran trainer.

Racing is a precarious business. A sniffle or a stone bruise at the wrong moment can wreck months of planning. A jockey's split-second decision in a race to go for the wrong gap can turn potential triumph into disaster in the blinking of an eye. But with Haafhd everything went right.

As a two-year-old Haafhd had won a decent Newmarket maiden and then was a runaway winner of the Washington Singer Stakes at Newbury. He was only third when odds-on for the Champagne Stakes at Doncaster and again was third in the Dewhurst, back at Newmarket. It was when he won his first race as a three-year-old that his true potential showed. He won the Craven Stakes over a mile at

Newmarket, coming home five lengths clear of Three Valleys, and Barry knew what he was training. He said: 'I was expecting him to win today. Lack of pace was his undoing in the Dewhurst and he just wasn't right in the Champagne Stakes. But he showed today what a good horse he is – as good as any I have had over this trip. He has a lovely temperament and will get further.

'Haafhd would be a better-class colt than Tap On Wood and, while it is difficult to compare horses from different generations, he'd be the best miler I've had. He has such a high cruising speed, although I believe there's every chance he'd get a mile and a quarter. His dam, Al Bahathri, just about got a mile and a quarter.'

After the Craven, Richard Hills, who rode the colt in every outing, said: 'I didn't pinch it. If you look at the sectional times they'll show I gradually stepped it up from three out. I wanted to pick it up gradually as I wanted the horse to learn something. We didn't go slow and then quicken.'

Richard, Sheikh Hamdan's retained rider and like his father a particularly good judge of a developing horse, had realised from the first time he sat on Haafhd at three what the future could hold. It was, he explains, a smooth operation from start to finish.

'He was a good two-year-old. I came back from Dubai to ride in the Winter Derby and, after I landed at 6am, I went straight to the yard and rode him in half work. I just sat on him for an easy piece of work and I couldn't believe how well he had done physically. I went to Lingfield, rode in the race, and flew back to Dubai that night. I rang Sheikh Hamdan and said I thought the horse had done well. He asked if he had grown and I said, "No." At that he said, "Oh!" but I replied, "It's a good thing for me, sir, because he has strengthened rather than grown." When horses grow too much in the winter it tends to sap their strength.

'We came back and my first port of call was to ride work. We took him to Lingfield and he had a spin with six or seven horses just to wake him up because he was a bit of a character. He simply flew round. I rang Hamdan and I said, "Sir, this horse really has improved." So we went to the Craven and he won on the bridle by five lengths.

'Prior to the Guineas I rode him in work. (Brother) Michael was there too on a decent horse. The gallops in Lambourn are stiff and we had a good lead horse and I sat last on Haafhd and Michael kicked. I sat on Haafhd and then I gave him a dig and he just picked him up in three strides. I got to the top of the gallops and I had to take a turn otherwise I would have hit the trees. Michael said, "I've never seen a horse work so well. There is no way you were entitled to pick me up." And Michael knows those gallops better than anyone.

'The whole build-up was perfect. Each work morning I was ringing the boss and saying, "This is the best chance I've had of winning the Guineas for years." Nothing went wrong. Dad was quoted as saying he was the best miler he'd ever had. That's a lot of pressure when it comes from somebody who's been training as long as Dad has. So it was a relief for all of us when he won the Guineas. It was a great day. It was tremendous.'

The other element that Richard and everybody in the Faringdon Place yard enjoyed was that Haafhd was led up on his great day by the man who looked after him in the yard, former head lad Snowy Outen, the man who refuses to retire. Pictures of Haafhd dominate Snowy's front room, alongside a signed portrait of Steve Cauthen. The then 79-year-old, who had begun as an apprentice in 1938, said: 'This has to be the best day of my life and with horses like this in the yard I'll be around a bit longer. They won't be getting rid of me just yet.'

Barry said: 'They just don't make stablemen like Snowy any more. He started with me as my head lad and has been around ever since. He's so reliable. Snowy is supposed to be retired. He hasn't ridden for nine years but you can't keep him away and after all these years this is the first Classic winner he's led up.'

Richard confirms: 'There was lots of Hills family history involved.

Haafhd was out of Al Bahathri, who had been trained by Tom Jones. So that involved Tom Jones, where I had first started. With Haafhd being home-bred and Dad involved too, it was the perfect scenario.'

In the Guineas the little chestnut had to take on Aidan O'Brien's One Cool Cat, the 15-8 favourite. The Guineas run-up is notorious for its mixture of hype and hope and O'Brien had contributed to the word games by insisting he had 'never come across a horse with such a blast of speed'.

The fourteen runners, the smallest Guineas field for a decade, split into three groups. Richard says: 'I've never ridden in a race like it in my life. It was strange. The stalls opened and everybody scattered. One Cool Cat ran straight up the far rail. Frankie Dettori guided Snow Ridge towards the centre.'

Knowing that Haafhd would run straight and true, Richard tore up his own game plan. He held his line and took the shortest way home. After tracking Golden Sahara down the centre to the two-furlong pole, he let out the reins and asked Haafhd to go and win his race. The 11-2 second favourite never looked like being caught.

Andrew Longmore of the Sunday Times wrote: 'Richard Hills, often overlooked as a big-race jockey but rarely found wanting under pressure, talked more of his relief at getting the job done than the joy of upholding Hills family honour. "I know it was a surprise when my father said Haafhd was the best miler he had trained but 30 years of experience went into that claim." '

At Royal Ascot, often not the best time of year for Barry's horses, Haafhd was a disappointing fourth in the St James's Palace Stakes. He ran below par at Goodwood too. But in October he came storming back to his best. On ground described as 'soft, heavy in places', after continuous rain for nearly 48 hours, he won the Emirates Airline Champion Stakes at Newmarket.

Belief in Haafhd and the three-year-old crop had been evaporating, but then Azamour won the Irish Champion and Bago took the Arc.

Back at Newmarket, Haafhd, at 12-1, fended off Chorist and Azamour and two other Group One winners in Doyen and Refuse To Bend. When first joining Chorist entering the Dip, Haafhd hesitated but then he stretched for Richard, who had kept him handy without fighting the leaders. The pair went on for a two-and-a-half-length victory. Barry said: 'From halfway he wasn't going to be beat.' Richard added: 'How can you better winning a Classic and a Champion Stakes for your father?'

Barry greeted the victory by outlining possible plans for Haafhd's four-year-old season. But then came a blow for him, for Richard and for Snowy Outen. Within a week Sheikh Hamdan decided to retire Haafhd, who had won five of his nine races, to his Shadwell Stud. It was understandable but frustrating for the yard.

Sheikh Hamdan's racing manager, Angus Gold, told At The Races at the time: 'I think he was torn between keeping him in training and retiring him, but Sheikh Hamdan is a big owner-breeder and felt the horse was more important to him at stud. He had the speed to win over six furlongs and then we saw him win over a mile and a quarter. In between he defeated a high-class field in a Guineas run in a very fast time.

'What gave Sheikh Hamdan such immense pleasure with this horse is that he is a product of a stallion, Alhaarth, he bred himself and raced, who was a champion two-year-old out of Al Bahathri, who was the first really good filly he ever owned, so obviously he's close to Sheikh Hamdan's heart.'

Gold agrees now it was disappointing not to see Haafhd run as a four-year-old but he says: 'Sheikh Hamdan is mad about his breeding and he was terrified of something happening to the horse as a four-year-old. He was so important to us at the time as a potential stallion he felt he couldn't take the risk of keeping him in training.'

Barry told the *Racing Post*: 'Obviously it is disappointing as he was a very sound horse and he had a great future. But you can understand the decision as Sheikh Hamdan has a lot of broodmares and Haafhd is a wonderful size for a stallion.

'It is very hard to compare horses but he is one of the great ones I have had. He wasn't the greatest work horse at home but he saved himself for the course. He has a wonderful temperament and from the day he came here he was never any trouble.'

Gold says: 'In my 24 years in this job I reckon Haafhd was the second best horse we ever had, after Nashwan. He was very special.'

SIR HARRY LEWIS
Irish Derby winner 1987

In 1987 the Irish Derby was the most valuable event in the Anglo-Irish racing calendar. In the whole of Europe only the Prix de l'Arc de Triomphe carried a bigger prize and the success of Sir Harry Lewis in the race was a crucial signal to the world that Barry had put Manton back on the Classic map.

Sir Harry Lewis, by Alleged out of Sue Babe, a Mr Prospector mare, was seen out only once as a two-year-old. Owned by New York breeder Howard Kaskel, he reappeared in April 1987 to win a Haydock maiden in workmanlike style and then went on to take the Dee Stakes, one of the recognised Derby trials, at Barry's favoured Chester track.

At Epsom in the Derby it was Reference Point's year, the hot favourite dominating the race ahead of Most Welcome and Bellotto, with Sir Harry Lewis fourth and Entitled fifth. John Reid rode Sir Harry Lewis that day, a ride he picked up on a plane back from Italy, where he had partnered Lady Bentley, Lester Piggott's only Group One winner as a trainer. 'Barry grunted recognition and asked: "Got a ride in the Derby?" I said I hadn't and he replied, "Better ride Sir Harry Lewis then." That was it.'

Reid kept the ride for the Irish Derby three weeks later. It was a strange day, a test as much of the horses' temperament as it was of their racing ability. The runners were on their way to the post when it was decided to evacuate the grandstands following a bomb threat, leading one Irish commentator to utter the memorably unfortunate comment: 'I hope this doesn't turn out to be another hoax.'

For fifty minutes the contestants were kept circling at the start until the all-clear was given. When the race finally began on rain-softened turf Sir Harry Lewis forged ahead two furlongs out in the hands of Reid and held on gamely from Naheez, ridden with characteristic persistence by Ray Cochrane, to win by three-quarters of a length. 'The moment I picked him up it was all over,' said Reid. Confirming the Epsom Derby form, Entitled was third. The favourite Sadjiyd never showed.

Sir Harry Lewis, travelling head lad Geoff Snook recalls, used to have a football in his box to play with. 'He was a bit of a character to ride. When they came along from the village to the gallops he would stand and rear and wouldn't want to do his work. But once he jumped off he worked well, and after his first race the habit disappeared.'

After his exploits at the Curragh, Sir Harry Lewis ran three more times that season without winning, his best effort coming when he was third in the Rothman's International Championship at Woodbine. His year concluded with an unplaced run in the Breeders' Cup Turf at Hollywood Park. Later he raced in the US for trainer D. Wayne Lukas and, after spells at stud in Kentucky and New York, he returned to Britain, where he has proved to be a successful sire of jumpers.

GILDORAN
Ascot Gold Cup winner 1984 and 1985
Gildoran, by Barry's Arc winner Rheingold out of the unlucky Durtal, was one of the best stayers he has trained and is a member of the illustrious band to have won the Ascot Gold Cup, the top prize for distance horses and the highlight of the Royal Ascot festival, on more than one occasion.

In 1984 Robert Sangster's horse won the Sagaro Stakes and was sixth under a big weight in the Chester Cup before going on to score a notable double in the Ascot race and the Goodwood Cup. At Ascot, with Steve Cauthen riding, he was a 10-1 chance. He looked weary but rallied well to beat Ore and Condell and was clearly still developing. At Goodwood, Gildoran turned the race into a procession, simply galloping the others into the ground and winning by eight lengths and twelve lengths from Ore and Karadar.

In 1985, having been second in the Sagaro Stakes at Ascot and fourth in the Henry II at Sandown on soft going, rather than the firm or good ground he preferred, Gildoran faced eleven rivals in the Ascot Gold Cup. With the former New Zealand and Australian champion Brent Thomson riding a well-judged race, Gildoran led all the way through the two and a half miles and held on stoutly to win from Longboat and Destroyer. Longboat went on to win the race in 1986.

A relentless galloper, Gildoran was a tough horse to pass once he had found his rhythm. As Timeform's commentator put it after his second Ascot Gold Cup, 'No horse could better deserve the epithet "battler".'

After finishing third in the 1985 Goodwood Cup, Gildoran was retired to Australia.

DISTANT MUSIC
Dewhurst Stakes winner 1999

The frustrating thing about training is that horses liberally endowed with natural ability do not always win the string of prizes you expect. Perhaps the obvious example of a 'nearly horse' for Barry was Distant Music. I remember when working on a book about Lambourn in 1999 how even a man of Barry's iron control could not keep the excitement out of his voice when talking about him.

The brilliant unbeaten two-year-old, by Distant View out of Musicanti, the well-bred but underperforming daughter of Nijinsky, was duly installed as the winter favourite for the 2,000 Guineas after winning the Dewhurst, often a strong pointer to the next year's big races. But Distant Music never won the Guineas or any other Classic. Indeed, for all his natural brilliance, he never won another Group One.

Certainly the hopes were high. That Christmas Barry sent his jockey son Michael a book about Nijinsky as a Christmas present and he wrote in it, referring to Distant Music, 'This is Nijinsky.' And it wasn't just Barry who was excited by his potential. Son Michael said of the horse: 'He was brilliant in the morning and he was brilliant at the races. He cruised and he had this an amazing turn of foot. He did things on the gallops that not many have done.'

Distant Music emerged as a top prospect in the Group Two Champagne Stakes at Doncaster in September 1999. His only previous racecourse appearance had been a smooth victory on the same course in a maiden. In the Champagne Stakes he beat Aidan O'Brien's Rossini with not one but two devastating bursts of acceleration. He came from last to first a furlong out to repeat the stable's victory with Auction House in the same race the year before.

Rider Michael Hills revealed: 'At home he can kill a gallop in one stride. He is so quick. I switched him off at the back because I didn't want him to get into a battle early on. I wanted to know what was on the other end and I got a nice surprise.'

Barry said: 'I was very impressed. If anything he got there a bit too soon but he has a very good turn of foot.' But then he revealed that the stable's new star had the previous day had a 'seedy toe', a corn on his near fore, and was slightly lame. The foot had been poulticed and they had only taken the decision to run at six o'clock that morning. Charlie Hills, Barry's son and assistant, reckons it is one of the highlights of his career so far that they even got Distant Music to the race in which his bursts of speed stamped him as a potential star. 'He had a poisoned foot and we had to tub it all night and managed to drive him up in the morning.' Bob Street recalls that the horse was driven to Doncaster with his foot in an ice bucket. It was hardly the perfect preparation for any athlete.

Distant Music was to be plagued by his feet all through his career, and they do tend to be a rather important part of a horse's equipment in winning races. When he suffered a shock defeat on his first outing at three in the Greenham Stakes (that year transferred from Newbury to Newmarket) he was found to be lame afterwards.

But at two the colt built on his Champagne victory by winning the Dewhurst, in the process rattling up Barry's hundredth winner of the season, surprisingly a feat he had managed only once before. After Distant Music had sprinted to victory from O'Brien's Brahms, even Barry, for whom disciplined restraint is as much a habit as a meticulous morning shave, declared: 'This horse has got me really excited of late. He is probably the best I've trained and is certainly the best two-year-old. At home all the work riders are complaining that his lead horses aren't good enough.'

One of those work riders, Oliver Brennan, a former Dick Hern employee, said Distant Music was the best he had sat on since Brigadier Gerard, while the experienced former stable jockey Ernie Johnson, not one to mistake a goose for a swan, insisted: 'I've not sat on a horse that has impressed me so much. I can't put it into words. It's like with a genius – he just has that little bit extra.' Assistant trainer Kevin Mooney declared: 'Watching him canter on the all-weather you wouldn't necessarily pick him out from the other forty-one, but come back and see him when we work them on grass and he'll snatch your breath away.'

So why didn't Distant Music, unbeaten at two, deliver what was expected of him at three? His comparative lack of results seems to be down to two things – to the fact that he never really developed much after his two-year-old days and to his susceptibility to corns.

Early in March of Distant Music's Classic season, Barry told the

Sun's Claude Duval: 'He's not grown much and you have to say he is not the most perfectly formed colt. And he's never had the best feet.' But then he added: 'He does have an engine ... he has a touch of brilliance, shades of Nijinsky or Sir Ivor.'

Sometimes horses with precocious ability have a quirk of temperament that results in them failing to show their best on race days. But you could not say that of Distant Music. Mooney called him 'as placid as a park hack' and Michael Hills said: 'He's got a good outlook on life, he's not flustered by many things, doesn't pull and is a straightforward ride.'

Question marks first arose when Distant Music was pipped by Barathea Guest in the Greenham on his reappearance. That was excused by his lameness afterwards. Then in the 2,000 Guineas he finished only eighth behind King's Best, who he had slammed as a two-year-old. Michael came back and said the usual acceleration simply wasn't there. After the race, in which he lost eighteen kilos, Distant Music did not eat up and had a subnormal temperature.

Given a long rest, he bounced back in September, winning the Group Three Park Stakes by a neck from Valentino after seeing off Cape Town, Swallow Flight and Barathea Guest. Barry declared: 'It's been a long old year, you could certainly say it's been character-building, but I've never lost faith in this horse. I knew he could still do it. He will come on for that.'

Distant Music finished his British career that year by running a decent third to Kalanisi and Montjeu in the Champion Stakes. But he made no real showing when sent to America for the Breeders' Cup Mile and his sole victory at four was the Group Two International Stakes at the Curragh over nine furlongs.

All in all, it was a respectable career. Most owners, told at the start that their colt would rattle up victories in the Group One Dewhurst Stakes and three other Pattern races would settle happily for that. But it was not the results board of the superhorse he had promised to be.

DISTANT RELATIVE
Top-notch miler

By Habitat out of Royal Sister II, Distant Relative was a high-class miler whose acceleration made him truly exciting to watch. Regular rider Michael Hills said once of Wafic Said's colt: 'Riding Distant Relative is like opening a bottle of champagne. You have to shake him up to make him fizz but, once you do, he explodes.' He often looked good in the paddock and just as often depressed those who had backed him by moving poorly to post. (Barry said that at home he sometimes worked like a car with no tyres). But it was the way he came back that mattered.

As a two-year-old, in 1988, Distant Relative won a Newbury maiden despite finishing lame. He reappeared the following April in a Newmarket handicap but thereafter contested only Group races over seven furlongs and a mile.

Distant Relative was third in the Irish 2,000 Guineas and third in the Jersey Stakes at Ascot before winning the Group Two International Stakes at Phoenix Park in July. In August he won the Group Three Hungerford Stakes at Newbury, despite having to be niggled from two furlongs out, and he followed up that month by winning the Group Two Celebration Mile at Goodwood from his regular rival Great Commotion.

Kept busy, he then finished third in the Queen Elizabeth II Stakes at Ascot before concluding his season with victory in the Challenge Stakes at Newmarket in October, his third Group Two of the season.

But, although Michael Hills had won four Group races that year on a colt who had tough competition among the milers of the day from the likes of Zilzal and Polish Precedent, Distant Relative's three defeats aided those who were pressing Barry to drop him as stable jockey. In 1990, when Distant Relative came with his familiar late surge to win a brace of Group Ones, the Sussex Stakes and the Prix du Moulin in France, it was with other jockeys on board. .

In the Sussex Stakes you would not have given much for his chances as Willie Carson had to scrub him along on leaving the stalls and he was soon behind the field. But at the business end of the race he moved from six lengths off the pace to two lengths up within a couple of furlongs and was driven out to win the £133,000 prize by half a length.

After running a close third at Deauville, he won the Prix du Moulin at Longchamp in the hands of Pat Eddery, passing Linamix in the shadow of the post to add another £96,000 to his winnings. In his final race before injury finished his career, the admirably consistent Distant Relative was second to Markofdistinction in the Queen Elizabeth II Stakes after a long tussle down the straight with the pair eight lengths clear of the field.

SURE BLADE
Queen Elizabeth II Stakes winner 1986

Many of those who have worked closely with Barry Hills, including his son John and Steve Cauthen, regard his handling of Sure Blade, a son of Kris out of the mare Double Lock, as one of his most significant training successes.

In a well-planned campaign as a two-year-old, in 1985, Sure Blade, owned by Sheikh Mohammed, won his first three starts, including the Coventry Stakes at Royal Ascot and the Champagne Stakes at Doncaster. He also ran a good race in defeat in the Dewhurst.

He was first seen out at the Newmarket meeting in May where, somewhat to the surprise of his jockey Brent Thomson, who had been told little about the colt, he proved good enough to beat the much-fancied Michael Stoute colt Green Desert. From there he progressed to win the Coventry, running on to beat Moorgate Man by one and a half lengths. In the Champagne Stakes at Doncaster, Sure Blade started the hot favourite. Thomson was able to dictate terms from the start and said goodbye to the rest of the field with two furlongs left. Again favourite in the Dewhurst, Sure Blade tracked the leaders but was a little outpaced and had to be switched for a run at the Bushes. He had every chance one furlong out but was challenged and beaten by Huntingdale and Bakharoff.

The following year, Sure Blade started off with victory in the Thirsk Classic Trial and then was fifth in the 2,000 Guineas. He next came out for the St James's Palace Stakes at Ascot (then a Group Two but since upgraded to Group One) and once again beat the highly talented Green Desert. With Thomson aboard, he challenged after the turn and won going away. But then things went wrong for Sure Blade and he had to go on the easy list.

John Hills, then his father's assistant, says: 'Sure Blade lost his action after Ascot and had to be turned out in mid-summer. In racing terms there really wasn't a lot of time to get him ready again.'

Thomson says: 'Barry did an incredible job because the horse was off with a sore back and he didn't race for three months. We worked him at Newbury and I got a bollocking because we messed things up. But I told him the horse was spot on. He was as good as he could get him.'

Spot on he was. Timeform called it 'one of the training feats of the season' when Sure Blade came out at the end of September and took the Queen Elizabeth II Stakes, beating the tough old campaigner Teleprompter (who had won the race in 1984 and been second in 1985) and Efisio in a pulsating finish. Thomson reckoned it was one of the best rides of his career.

After finishing down the field in that year's Champion Stakes, Sure Blade was retired.

HANDSOME SAILOR
Prix de l'Abbaye winner 1988

Over the years Barry has had plenty of fast horses, winning the Nunthorpe Stakes with La Cucaracha, the King's Stand Stakes with

Equiano and the Haydock Sprint Cup with Royal Applause and Red Clubs. One of his most intriguing sprinters, though, was Handsome Sailor, who cost only 3,000 guineas as a yearling. He started his career running seventh of nine in a seller for Ron Thompson, who then went on to win three races with him, after which he was bought out of the Doncaster two-year-olds in training sales by Robert Sangster as a lead horse for the Michael Dickinson youngsters at Manton.

Handsome Sailor, a big, lengthy colt by Some Hand out of Found At Sea, was slow to come to hand as a three-year-old but raced four times for Dickinson, providing two of the four victories that represented the trainer's Manton total, before splitting a pastern.

Inherited by Barry on his move to Manton, Handsome Sailor won the Group Three Duke of York Stakes in May 1987 and the Group Three Prix de Ris-Orangis at Evry in July, on that occasion giving Sydney champion Ron Quinton his first winner in Europe.

The next year, with Michael Hills in the saddle on each occasion, Handsome Sailor won four big sprints worth a total of more than £180,000. In May he took the Duke of York again and the Temple Stakes at Sandown over five furlongs. In August he collected the £57,000 first prize in the William Hill Sprint Championship back at his favourite York track and then in October he secured the £70,000 first prize in the Prix de l'Abbaye at Longchamp. He was involved on that occasion in a ding-dong battle with Cadeaux Genereux, fighting back bravely after being passed, and was awarded the race on his rival's disqualification for interference with another horse. .

Interestingly, when I asked Barry which was the fastest horse he had ever trained, he had no hesitation in naming Gallic League, whose career overlapped that of Handsome Sailor. 'He certainly had more ability, though he wasn't probably the toughest at the end of the day. He was tricky in the stalls and was rather delicate as a two-year-old but he certainly had the ability. He'd be the fastest.'

As a two-year-old in 1987, despite giving his jockey some testing times in the starting stalls, Gallic League won the Flying Childers at Doncaster and the Middle Park Stakes at Newmarket, partnered by Steve Cauthen. Timeform's Racehorses of 1987 commented: 'Look no further than Gallic League for the champion sprinter of 1988.' But many three-year-old sprinters find it hard the first year tackling their elders and Gallic League, who was first tried over seven furlongs, proved no exception. He was down the field, for example, behind Handsome Sailor in the William Hill Sprint Championship.

He did, however, come back in 1989 to win the Group Three Ballyogan Stakes at Leopardstown in June and run a close third behind Indian Ridge in the King's Stand Stakes at Royal Ascot.

ROYAL APPLAUSE
Champion two-year-old

Royal Applause certainly stamped his authority on the two-year-old scene in 1995. Ridden on all four starts by Walter Swinburn, he followed his maiden victory at Newbury by winning the Coventry Stakes at Ascot, the Gimcrack at York and the Middle Park Stakes at Newmarket, becoming the first horse to achieve that treble since Crocket in 1962.

After the opening Group Three success at Ascot from twelve previous winners, Swinburn declared: 'He was always going well. When I gave him the office inside the two he really couldn't have been more impressive.'

The team struck again with Royal Applause in the Gimcrack, although he had a struggle to beat Tumbleweed Ridge. Of that success, Swinburn said: 'He was edgy and I think the large crowd and the heat upset him.' He ran seven pounds below his Royal Ascot form.

In September, Royal Applause won the Middle Park by four lengths. This time Swinburn's verdict was: 'I had the easiest of rides, just having to sit and steer. If he stays he has to win a Classic.'

The Middle Park performance had many rating Royal Applause as a potential threat to Alhaarth for the following year's 2,000 Guineas. Barry had originally doubted if Royal Applause would stay the extra two furlongs but he then mused: 'Alhaarth may just be more of a mile-and-a-half horse. He could be coming up for air against our fellow over a shorter trip.'

Sadly for Swinburn's hopes and Barry's Classics record, Royal Applause didn't stay and won only one race in 1996, having run tenth in the 2,000 Guineas. But in 1997 it was a different story. Back at the sprinting game, he won the Duke of York, the Cork and Orrery at Ascot (from a field of 23) and then the Group One Haydock Park Sprint Cup, beating Danetime and Tomba with more authority than the length-and-a-quarter margin suggested.

Royal Applause, who had been backed from 4-1 in the morning to 15-8 favourite, was swiftly out of the stalls with Michael Hills and immediately established his authority. Barry said: 'He has such a high cruising speed. His great asset is being able to burn them off in the middle of the race.' It was, said the Sporting Life, 'a display of controlled power', and the hope of inheriting some of that power has since made Royal Applause a popular sire.

RED CLUBS

Haydock Sprint Cup winner 2007

As a two-year-old Red Clubs had been Barry's third winner of the Coventry Stakes in 2005, the year Royal Ascot was run at York (he had won it in 1985 with Sure Blade and in 1995 with Royal Applause). Barry called him 'a nice bonny horse, not very big but with a wonderful temperament. You could put him at the bottom of your bed if you wanted to.'

On 8 September 2007, ten years after Royal Applause's victory in the race, Red Clubs won the Group One Sprint Cup at Haydock from Freddie Head's Marchand D'Or and Balthazaar's Gift. Red Clubs, owned by former Hong Kong Jockey Club chairman Ronnie Arculli, had won twice at Group Two level and one Group Three. Regular rider Michael Hills declared: 'He's a real star who doesn't do a lot at home of a morning but who saves himself for the racecourse in the afternoon.' Barry said: 'He deserved a Group One. He's a very game horse and a consistent one who has been campaigning at the top level for three seasons.'

Another top sprinter who will probably be equally long remembered in the Hills yard, though perhaps with a little less affection, is Cadeaux Cher.

Asked after Cadeaux Cher's victory in the Great St Wilfrid Handicap at Ripon in 1998 if he had backed him, Barry responded that he would never back him if he lived to be 100. Did he change his mind after the horse followed up with victory at 20-1 in the Portland Handicap at Doncaster? 'I wouldn't back him if I lived to 110.' Before Cadeaux Cher ran in the Ayr Gold Cup, where he was well beaten, Barry said he wouldn't back him if he lived to 120.

Why such disparagement? Because, until he put those victories together, the talented Cadeaux Cher had won just once in seventeen outings. Nick Browne, who runs tutorial colleges and who owned half the colt, had then had horses with Barry for fifteen years. Tweaking his trainer's nose, he explained: 'When a horse fails to do what Barry wants he gets fed up. When they disappoint continually on course, as Cadeaux Cher he did in the first half of the season, he'll say, "Oh God, it's obviously not trying." On one occasion he rang me and said, "You're not going to keep that horse, are you?" and even the win at Ripon failed to convince him. However, it was a changed story after the Portland. I think the first thing he said to me was, "We must take him out of that sale." '

The man who helped to find the key to Cadeaux Cher was jockey Ray Cochrane. In the 1998 season he won four out of five on the colt, who liked to thread through a field in a late charge. Browne said: 'Ray found the answer. He relaxes him right out the back, edges him a bit nearer and then in the final two furlongs asks him to go.'

Browne says Barry told him one morning, after Cadeaux Cher had won his maiden, that he was one of his favourite horses in the yard. 'Then, as Cadeaux began to disappoint, the tune changed a bit. He went from being "mediocre" to being "a cripple" and a few things worse than that.

'When Barry's horses were out of form earlier in the year he was in full Mr Grumpy mode, cursing everyone. Cadeaux Cher came in for his share – "He's got no discipline and just doesn't behave himself." The final straw came after he won his first small race that season. The handicapper raised him from 64 to 79. Barry went absolutely splenetic and wrote a seething letter to the handicapper. Before the official could reply Cadeaux Cher had won the Great St Wilfrid off 83.'

Horses can embarrass even the best of trainers ...

Barry's Finest Fillies

Getting the best out of high-quality fillies often requires virtuoso performances from a trainer, and Barry Hills undoubtedly has the knack. Quite apart from his multiple victories with fillies like Duboff, Nagwa and Mofida, he has won two 1,000 Guineas, two Irish Oaks, an Irish 1,000 Guineas and the Champion Stakes with Cormorant Wood, owned by his friend Bobby McAlpine, the longtime chairman of Chester racecourse.

Barry already knew Classic success with a filly before he was a trainer himself. As travelling head lad to John Oxley he escorted Homeward Bound to Epsom the year she won the Oaks. Dibidale, of course, won the Irish Oaks in 1974 and it was a filly too who gave Barry his first English Classic success, ending his long run of bad luck in the home Classics.

ENSTONE SPARK

1,000 Guineas winner 1978

Former stable jockey Ernie Johnson, the man who was aboard Rheingold in his Derby year, says: 'I've never heard Barry say this, but I think one of his best pieces of training was when he won the Guineas in 1978 with Enstone Spark.'

As a two-year-old Dick Bonnycastle's bay filly by Sparkler out of Laxmi (by the 2,000 Guineas winner Palestine) had won four of her nine races, including York's Lowther Strakes at 33-1, when trained by Richard Hannon. After the Canadian publisher bought her for 28,000 guineas, she was moved from Hannon to the Hills yard in the winter because her owner wanted to have all his seventeen horses together. Her new yard knew little about her, although they soon discovered that, like many of the female gender, she had her little ways. She had to have somebody behind her, for instance, to persuade her to go out onto the gallops. But the real problem was a wider one.

Johnson says: 'We had been running horses from the start of the season and it was a difficult, bad spring. It was cold, it was fluctuating. Some of them won, some of them didn't. Normally in three or four days a horse will put back what it has taken out of itself in running, but whether they won or lost the horses weren't putting back what they'd used up in a race as quickly as they should have done.

'Enstone Spark was going to run in a Guineas trial, but as each trial came Barry decided not to run her because of the weather, because of the way the other horses were not putting it back, not doing so well. I think that really won him the Guineas. She went to the Guineas without a run. Had she had a run, she probably wouldn't have won. The other horses, the ante-post favourites, the fancied horses, were running in trials and were either getting beat or running in poor style. She wasn't out of the top drawer but she was a hundred per cent on the day and she ended up winning a Classic.'

At 35-1, Enstone Spark was the longest-priced winner of the 1,000 Guineas since Ferry in 1918. Some said she looked out of place in the parade. But the race was a different story. Johnson, who had nearly been killed in a bad fall at Newmarket the previous August that necessitated five operations on a shattered left leg, kept her on the wide outside and was cool enough to drop her out after three furlongs. He then came with a storming run to challenge the leaders in the latter stages of the race.

Enstone Spark may have been in two minds – one report said her tail was spinning like a rotor blade – but her jockey was not. The pair swept past the favourite, Cherry Hinton, and, staying wide of her rivals, Enstone Spark had the power up the hill to hold off the stand-side challenge of Fair Salinia by a length. Seraphima was a further two and a half lengths away in third. Despite her price, Barry told reporters: 'She didn't surprise me because she has been going so well at home.'

This time at least, the luck was with her trainer, who gave Enstone Spark a couple of gallops over a mile and a quarter, longer than the Guineas distance, to make absolutely sure she was fit. 'It's a better way of getting them fit than doing a lot of short distances fast.' Dick Bonnycastle had planned to send her to race in California before joining his stud at Calgary, Alberta, but there had been an outbreak of equine metritis, which had led to a temporary ban on the export of horses that winter.

The Guineas was the summit of Enstone Spark's career. Her trainer says she might have won the Coronation Stakes at Royal Ascot, but she suffered a knock on the turn into the straight. All four legs were off the ground and the bump turned her over. After that she seemed to lose her taste for racing.

CORMORANT WOOD

Champion Stakes winner 1983

One of the most consistent fillies Barry trained was Cormorant Wood, bred and owned by Bobby McAlpine. By Home Guard out of Quarry Wood, she won four Group races, with her most impressive victory coming in the Group One Champion Stakes in 1983. Her rider, Steve Cauthen, said it was a case of 'Barry working the miracle with a horse who two weeks before wouldn't have won a seller.'

Cormorant Wood won as a two-year-old, in a maiden at Leicester. At three she ran second in the Oaks trial at Lingfield. Her owner believes she lost because she did not stay but it was partly put down to the bog-heavy ground. She was sixth in the Oaks and her owner remains convinced she should have been fourth, a position that carries prize-money and would have enhanced her stud prospects. She did not, he believes, 'because Lester Piggott dropped his hands in the last fifty yards'. When McAlpine put this to Piggott, he just threw back his head and laughed. 'I had never heard Lester laugh before.'

After another defeat over a mile and a half, in the Princess of Wales's

Stakes at Newmarket, Cormorant Wood was dropped back to ten furlongs and won the Virginia Stakes at Newcastle by three lengths, although McAlpine reckons she was lucky to keep the race. Barry and Cauthen flew up at a time when the American jockey, struggling with his weight, was apt to enjoy a glass or three of champagne. He enjoyed himself on the flight and, although he won the race, he could have lost it in the weighing room. To prevent fiddling, jockeys are allowed to lose only so much from their exertions during the race when weighing in and can be disqualified if they are over the margin. McAlpine says: 'Steve was so dehydrated that he lost more than five pounds in the race and would have been too light weighing in. But Willie Carson saw what was happening and put a finger on the scales.' Willie told the owner afterwards: 'You owe me a very large drink.'

Cormorant Wood won again at the trip in the Group Two Sun Chariot Stakes at Newmarket. But the big one was the 18-1 victory in the Champion Stakes on the same track a fortnight later.

With typical modesty, Cauthen describes the race like this: 'It was one of Barry's best training jobs. It had been a dry year and it was hard getting her going. He had worked her on the all-weather. Before the Champion, Barry said to me, "Ride her like a non-trier. Drop her out the back. Wait and wait. Keep her out of the wind as long as you can." It was a terribly windy day. I was biding my time watching who was going to go and things broke my way. I tracked a few of the right horses and I nailed Tolomeo at the end. Newmarket is a great place for finishes up that hill.'

Others were less restrained about a phenomenal ride. Brough Scott wrote at the time that Cauthen's role in the victory was 'as near to a masterpiece as you will get in race-riding'.

McAlpine says: 'She came from last to first in two furlongs. I have never known a windier day. I couldn't believe how he had threaded his way through without impeding another horse. Cauthen told me that he had, in fact, touched Tolomeo "and had to square with his jockey".'

Cauthen was famous for timing his late finishes but he probably never arrived later on the scene than on this occasion. He kept the filly covered up until the last furlong in a gale force and squeezed through the smallest of gaps between Tolomeo and Flame Of Tara. Last into the Dip, they just got up on the line.

The next season Cormorant Wood was not at her best early on. She was favourite for the Queen Anne Stakes at Ascot but finished only third and then she was sixth in the Eclipse. But she saved her best for what was to prove her final run in the Benson and Hedges at York. Settled in the rear by Cauthen, Cormorant Wood followed the Eclipse winner Sadler's Wells through as he and Raft took the lead with three furlongs left. Clearly going the best at the distance, she burst clear and left the others with no chance of catching her. Sadly, in her moment of victory she injured a tendon and never raced again.

GHANAATI
1,000 Guineas winner 2009

Thirty-one years after his 1,000 Guineas success with Enstone Spark, Barry Hills won the race once more with a comparatively long-priced filly who had not had a conventional preparation. Hamdan Al Maktoum's Ghanaati, ridden like all the Hamdan horses by Barry's son Richard and starting at 20-1, was racing on turf for the very first time when she forged clear of her rivals Cuis Ghaire and Super Sleuth to win by one and a half lengths.

Given the fact that her trainer had started the season with a strike-rate of twenty-five per cent and was lying second in the trainers' table, it might have seemed a generous price. But that year's first fillies' Classic boasted a strong field, headed by the brilliant ante-post favourite Rainbow View, who was unbeaten in her four races for John Gosden, and Serious Attitude, trained by Rae Guest, who was also unbeaten.

Perhaps not surprisingly, when Ghanaati, Serious Attitude and Rainbow View were given separate gallops on the Newmarket track before racing on the first day of the Craven meeting, the attention focussed on the two Newmarket fillies, but sensible punters would have noted Ghanaati's introduction to the track as a signal of determination from a trainer who does not do anything without a serious purpose.

Adding to the mix in the 1,000 Guineas of 2009 were the Godolphin filly Devotee, winner of the UAE Oaks in Dubai, and Lahaleeb, winner of the Rockfel and Fred Darling Stakes. Against such proven form Ghanaati's winnings list amounted to just one maiden as a two-year-old on the tight all-weather track at Kempton Park after she had finished third there in her only previous race.

Many tearing up their betting stubs after the 1,000 Guineas were, however, kicking themselves for not noting the obvious hints that Barry's filly might spring a surprise. By Giant's Causeway out of Sarayir, she came from the Nashwan family. Timeform's annual Racehorses of 2008 had noted that she was bound to improve.

Others had been rather more in the picture. 'Barry told me in January or February that he wanted to run Ghanaati in the Guineas first time out, without a previous run,' says Angus Gold, Sheikh Hamdan's racing manager. 'Sheikh Hamdan never wants to have horses running in Classics just for the sake of it. He wants to go there with a chance, so I was thinking, "Is she going to be good enough?" '

The Hamdan team had not seen the filly in action and Gold called Barry from the sales in Australia in April. 'I asked him if he was sure he still wanted to go to the Guineas. I was trying a little bit to talk him out of it, to steer him away. He simply said: "Yup," and with all the talk at the time of John Gosden's filly I didn't know how to word my next question, so I said: "I suppose she could be a good third or fourth." There was a slight pause and Barry replied: "Or she could win it."

'That's what sets him apart as a good trainer. Obviously he had seen something at home in a filly who had only won a maiden to feel she could go and win a Guineas. And he was gloriously right. He kept quieter and quieter about her all week before the Guineas, which is normally a good sign. I kept well out of it and they did a great job with her.'

The happy rider, who was completing a Guineas double for his father, having won the 2,000 on Haafhd in 2004, said: 'Dad went though a tough period last year, which he is over now. He's stuck his head down and got on with it, and things have gone in a good direction this year. It makes me very proud to win a Classic for him.' His father's reaction? 'He just said, "I told you so." I think he had a bit of 33-1 the other week.' Barry himself said afterwards: 'I have always thought she was a very good filly. She is pretty special and everything she has done she has done very easily. I have been singing her praises all winter and I was hoping for a very big run.'

In the race Richard had the handsome Ghanaati up with the leaders from the start. Two furlongs out they took up the running and she was clear with a furlong to go. In second place, Cuis Ghaire, from Jim Bolger's yard in Ireland, never looked like catching her. Not a bad performance from a filly who had not raced for six months and who had never before competed on turf. Rainbow View found the ground too firm and Serious Attitude didn't stay. But this was a worthy winner from a classy field.

That, however, was only the start. Ghanaati's next victory, in the Coronation Stakes at Royal Ascot, was one of special significance for the whole Hills family. Barry had been in a London hospital for five weeks, desperately ill with blood poisoning. He only came out that day. The latter stages of the filly's preparation had been brilliantly supervised by assistant trainer Charlie and she was ridden, of course, by Richard, who delivered her faultlessly to score a resounding success in what is traditionally the championship of the three-year-old female milers.

Striding to the front on the bridle two furlongs out, Ghanaati, the 2-1 favourite, quickly went clear to win in record time from Reggane, with the previous year's champion two-year-old filly Rainbow View in third and the Irish 1,000 Guineas winner Again only seventh. It was a performance that stamped her as the top three-year-old filly over a mile in Europe, with the Poule d'Essai des Pouliches winner Elusive Wave well beaten in fourth and the Irish Guineas second Lahaleeb fifth.

The family emotions were obvious after the race, with Richard revealing: 'We nearly lost my Dad, but thank God we didn't,' and Charlie confirming that it had been 'touch and go'. The Hills family bonds are tight as steel rope and Richard declared: 'This victory means more to me than any race I've won. I've worn my heart on my sleeve today. I'm very proud and pleased for my father. Dad helped me this morning and told me to keep her safe and that she would do the rest. I could hear his voice the whole way round.'

In one post-race interview, Richard was asked when he knew he had a good one in Ghanaati. 'When Dad told me,' he replied. That says it all, Hills-style.

Ghanaati had only two more runs. In the Sussex Stakes at Goodwood, taking on the colts, she finished third to Rip Van Winkle, who recorded the best performance in the race for thirty years, and Paco Boy. She returned home sore behind after that race and on her final appearance, when she had gone in her coat, she finished only second to the French filly Sahpresa.

Recalling Ghanaati's Guineas preparation, Timeform's Racehorses of 2009 noted it was an example of how far all-weather racing had come since its inception at Lingfield on 30 October 1989. All-weather racing is not the only thing to have stood the test of time: both Richard and Michael Hills rode winners on the twelve-race card that opening day.

NICER
Irish 1,000 Guineas winner 1993

Barry's third Irish Classic winner was a particularly sweet one for the trainer. Not only had his horses suffered a spell of poor form but the grey, owned by Mrs Catherine Corbett, was ridden by his son Michael, who was winning his first major European Classic. The emotions that Barry has often been at such pains to suppress on the racecourse were evident when he declared: 'This is the biggest thrill I have had since Rheingold won the Arc for me back in 1973. To win a Classic with your son riding is unbelievable.'

It was a courageous performance by Nicer. When Michael wanted to start making a move he found his way blocked by a wall of horses. Twice he had to go for the narrowest of gaps but she did not flinch. Michael said: 'Things got very tight at one stage but Nicer was travelling so strongly that she was able to slip through.' The jockey was also fortunate in that Darryll Holland had originally been down to ride Nicer but lost his opportunity through a suspension for a whip offence.

The family success was little thanks, it seems, to Michael's twin brother Richard, who was riding Ajfan that day. Michael revealed: 'At one crucial point I shouted to him to give me an inch. He promptly moved in on me by two inches.' Says his twin: 'I did. I thought I had a good chance that day as well. He was going well and he called for a bit of room and I wasn't going to give it. He didn't expect me to give it either.'

In the end it did not matter. Nicer, an 8-1 shot, took up the running over a furlong out and stayed on strongly to beat Goodnight Kiss and Lester Piggott's mount Danse Royale. She had missed the English 1,000 Guineas but that, for once, was down to good luck rather than training genius. After her two-year-old career Barry and her owner had not thought the filly was that good and, as her first run in her three-year-old season, the Masaka Stakes at Kempton, was after the forfeit stage for the English Guineas, connections had not felt justified in paying the £900 to keep her in at Newmarket. Going to the Curragh fresh, she beat the fillies who had finished third, fourth and fifth in the English Classic.

Nicer was owned by Chrysalis Records boss Chris Wright and Catherine Corbett, who has a passion for greys (among her others were Negligent, Desirable and Kim Bailey's jumper Nathan Blake.)

The victory also casts light on the affection that stable hands develop for the animals in their care. Bob Grace, who 'did' Nicer, announced that he would like the epitaph on his tombstone to read: 'Here lies the lad who looked after Nicer.'

BOLAS
Irish Oaks winner 1994

Barry's second Irish Oaks winner, Bolas, bred and owned by Prince Khalid Abdullah, scored in the hands of Pat Eddery. The filly, by Unfuwain out of Three Stars, would never have run in the race but for her trainer's belief in the potential of a filly who had disappointed as a two-year-old. It was also touch and go whether the champion jockey would be able to partner her.

After her victory at the Curragh the trainer revealed that Khalid Abdullah had put her in the sales the previous December. 'Luckily the Prince changed his mind. I knew she was good as she had shown me plenty at home. If he hadn't withdrawn her I would have found somebody to buy her. The filly has long been the apple of my eye.'

Bolas had won the the Cheshire Oaks and the Ribblesdale Stakes at Ascot. Barry said: 'She was like a child at Chester, spending the whole race looking at a TV camera instead of concentrating on her job. But she won and she did it again in good style at Ascot.' Not surprisingly, she was the 5-2 favourite at the Curragh, a ride any jockey would fancy. But Eddery revealed that when Glatisant ejected him from the stalls at Newmarket on the Wednesday before the big race he thought he had broken a bone and lost the chance of the Classic ride. 'On Wednesday evening I was in serious trouble. I thought I had broken my ankle. But luckily it was only badly bruised.'

It isn't only jump jockeys, however, who can work through pain barriers. 'I walked on it all Thursday to get it better, but I still had to ride on Friday to prove I was ready for Bolas.' Eddery was glad he had done so, and he chose bold tactics. 'I knew Bolas would get every yard, so I decided to go off in front. My only worry was the soft ground but as most of her family went in it I felt I was safe enough. I hardly saw another horse in the whole race. I did see a head coming up turning for home but it was only afterwards I learned it was Hawajiss (with Walter Swinburn aboard). My filly picked up again and kept galloping.'

The victorious trainer said: 'Bolas had to do it the hard way but she can gallop. It wasn't my plan to make the running but I am not going to tell the champion jockey what to do. I train them – he rides them.'

Also in the frame was son John's Wind In The Hair, who had finished second to Balanchine in the English Oaks. John said: 'She was going well enough until the straight where the going is softest and then she lost her action.'

Bolas's later efforts were less successful. She ran poorly in the Yorkshire Oaks and was retired after finishing last of fourteen in the Breeders' Cup Turf at Churchill Downs.

HULA ANGEL
Irish 1,000 Guineas winner 1999

A second Irish 1,000 Guineas winner for both Barry and Michael Hills, Hula Angel was owned by Australian Jim Fleming, the chairman of the Sydney Turf Club, who had a strategy of buying young horses in Europe and shipping a few to stud in Australia.

Hula Angel, by Woodman out of Jode, had first shown real promise by winning the seven-furlong Rockfel Stakes at Newmarket as a two-year-old the previous October. She had grown well and flourished through the winter but there was little money for her in the Irish race, largely because she had finished only sixth behind Wince in the English 1,000 Guineas.

In the Irish 1,000, nobody was prepared to set a true gallop and the favourite Wince, who was to finish only fifth, was one of those caught out by a sudden injection of pace as the tempo quickened, with Hula Angel one of the first to go on. When his filly Golden Silca came to challenge it looked for a moment as if former international footballer turned trainer Mick Channon was going to capture his first Classic. But with Michael Hills giving it everything he had got Hula Angel held on bravely in a driving photo-finish.

After her success Barry reckoned that the ground had been on the fast side for Hula Angel over the Rowley Mile at Newmarket and that she had been better suited by the good going in Ireland.

Hula Angel's subsequent career was a disappointment. She beat only one home in the Coronation Stakes at Ascot and in the Falmouth Stakes at Newmarket and was then retired to stud. But she had had her day of glory.

MAIDS CAUSEWAY
Coronation Stakes winner 2005

Although Maids Causeway never won a Classic she is worthy of inclusion in a list of Barry's top fillies for the courage she always showed in running. That quality was first shown as a two-year-old when she became another of Barry's good fillies to win the Group Two Rockfel Stakes. The gutsy filly, who inherited all the battling qualities of her sire Giant's Causeway, did so by fighting back after being headed inside the final furlong by Penkenna Princess. Seb Sanders, who rode the runner-up, told his filly's 'gutted' trainer Ralph Beckett, a one-time Hills assistant, 'I thought I'd won a head, I can't believe it.'

Earlier that season, Maids Causeway had won the Group Three Sweet Solera Stakes at Newmarket in August and finished third in the May Hill at Doncaster and runner-up in the Ascot Fillies' Mile. On the back of those performances she started as 5-1 favourite for the 1,000 Guineas in 2005 but could only finish second to Virginia Waters, who was brought from last to first by Kieran Fallon to make it a Guineas double for Aidan O'Brien and Coolmore, who had won the 2,000 the day before with Footstepsinthesand. Maids Causeway had beaten off the rest but Fallon's swoop never really gave her the chance to get into the kind of scrap she would have relished. Michael Hills said: 'I thought in the Dip I'd got it, but then the winner came with that good turn of foot.'

It was a different story in June, however, in the Coronation Stakes (the Ascot race run that year at York). The Group One contest usually brings together the best of the three-year-old fillies and it looked as though Maids Causeway would be bridesmaid again as she faltered in the final furlong and was passed by John Gosden's Karen's Caper. But with the pair locked together through the final furlong Maids Causeway fought back to win by a short head.

It later transpired that Maids Causeway had been even more courageous than it appeared.

Firstly she had lost a shoe. Michael Hills said: 'I felt it go just before the line. She faltered and I stopped riding for a split second, but when I shook her she just went again. On this firm ground it is like an athlete pulling off a plimsoll. She is one of the bravest fillies I've ever ridden. She was losing out in the battle but still put in one late surge when I asked her. She is unreal.'

But Maids Causeway had coped with more than just a lost shoe. The filly finished lame and Michael quickly jumped off her, fearing she had broken a leg. In fact, as well as her foot injury from losing the shoe, she had pulled a muscle off her hip and sustained a hairline fracture of the joint, making her determination to battle on even more praiseworthy.

American owner Martin Schwartz, a futures trader who had bought Maids Causeway to race in the US but had been so impressed that he kept her in the Hills yard, declared: 'I've had my share of thrills in life but this is top of the mountain, up there with seeing my children born.' Mrs Schwartz's views on the comparison were not recorded.

Maids Causeway, said Michael, 'gets her head down and just wants to win. She just keeps digging in for you. Once she gets upsides with another horse in her sight she does everything to keep her head in front.' In a typically concise summary, Barry declared: 'She is tough, she tries hard and I'd like a few more like her.'

It looked like he was getting the chance. The happy owner announced: 'Coming over here is such a thrill. I have got about £400,000 in the bank. I will leave it in jolly old England and let Mr Hills spend it as he sees fit.'

*

There are more fillies that some would feel were wrongly excluded from top billing, such as Spinning Queen, who beat three Group One winners to take the Sun Chariot Stakes by nine lengths in 2006 from the classy Soviet Song and the well-travelled Alexander Goldrun.

Others would no doubt make a case for La Cucaracha. The 7-1 winner of the Group One Nunthorpe Stakes, in August 2005, gave owner Guy Reed his first Group One success. (Barry also gave Reed his first Lincoln Handicap, with Pablo in 2003). Just a month before the Nunthorpe, La Cucaracha had picked up £50,000 in her first handicap, giving weight and a beating to fourteen rivals, having earlier in the season won a Group Three.

But with Barry's list of victories you have to stop somewhere …

INDEX